A SHORT ETYMOLOGY
OF LATVIAN

A SHORT GRAMMAR OF LATVIAN

TERJE MATHIASSEN

SLAVICA PUBLISHERS, INC.

Slavica publishes a wide variety of scholarly books and textbooks on the languages, peoples, literatures, cultures, history, etc. of the former USSR and Eastern Europe. For a complete catalog of books and journals from Slavica, with prices and ordering information, write to:

> Slavica Publishers, Inc.
> PO Box 14388
> Columbus OH 43214

ISBN: 0-89357-270-5.

Copyright © 1996 by Terje Mathiassen. All rights reserved. This book was published in 1997.

All statements of fact or opinion are those of the authors and do not necessarily agree with those of the publisher, which takes no responsibility for them.

Printed in the United States of America.

CONTENTS

	Page
Foreword	17
Chapter 0: Introduction	19
Chapter 1: Phonology	22
I Consonants	22
Phonetic realization	23
Orthographic representation	24
Consonant alternations	24
Clusters	26
1. Assimilation	26
A. Voicing	26
B. Devoicing	26
C. Other assimilations	26
2. Dissimilation	27
II Vowels	27
Short Vowels	28
Orthographic representation	28
Long Vowels	28
Orthographic representation	29
Notes on pronunciation of long and short vowels	29
Excursus: Distribution of close vs. open *e/ē*	29
Compensatory vowel lengthening	32
Diphthongs	33
Vocalization	35
Vowel alternations (ablaut)	35
Word final position	35
1. Consonants	35
2. Vowels	35
III Suprasegmentals	36
1. Stress	36
2. Quantity	37
A. Vowels	37
B. Consonants	38

3. Tone	39
Chapter 2: The noun	40
Grammatical categories	40
1. Gender	40
2. Number	41
3. Case	41
Declensional types	42
First declension	43
Comments on the paradigm	44
The form of the vocative	44
Second declension	44
Consonant alternations	45
The form of the vocative	45
Irregularities in the 2nd declension	45
Third declension	45
Fourth declension	46
The form of the vocative	46
Fifth declension	47
The form of the vocative	48
Sixth declension	48
Vacillations between declensions	48
Summing up of the endings	49
Reflexive nouns	49
Indeclinable nouns	50
Singular and plural nouns	51
Word formation of nouns	52
1. Suffixal derivatives	52
A. Persons	52
B. Abstracts	53
C. Collective nouns	54
D. Instrument	54
E. Location (place)	54
F. Diminutives and hypocorisms	54
2. Prefixal derivatives	55
3. Non-prefixal compositions	55
Chapter 3: The adjective	57
General characteristics	57
The short (indefinite) form	57
The long (definite) form	58
Degrees of comparison	59
1. The comparative	59

2. The superlative	60
Syntax of the adjectives	60
1. The short (indefinite) form	60
Equivalents of English *than*	60
Equivalents of English *too*	61
Equivalents of English *much, considerably* + the comparative	61
2. The long (definite) form	61
Substantivization	62
Word formation	63
1. Suffixal derivatives	63
2. Prefixal derivatives	64
3. Non-prefixal compound adjectives	64
Reduplication	64
Chapter 4: The pronoun	65
1. Personal pronouns	65
2. Possessive pronouns	66
A. Non-reflexives	66
B. Reflexives	67
3. Reciprocal pronouns	67
4. Demonstrative pronouns	68
5. The anaphoric pronoun of the 3rd Person	68
6. Interrogative and relative pronouns	69
Interrogative function	69
Relative function	70
7. Indefinite pronouns	70
8. Negative pronouns	72
9. Other pronouns	73
Chapter 5: Numerals	74
1. Cardinal numbers	75
A. Declension	75
a) Declinable	75
b) Indeclinable	76
B. Syntax	76
2. Ordinal numbers	78
A. Declension	78
B. Syntax	79
3. Fractions	79
A. Non-decimal fractions	79
B. Decimal fractions	80

Chapter 6: The verb	81
Grammatical categories	81
Finite and non-finite forms	82
Verb stems	82
Morphophonemic rules	83
The finite verb	83
Introduction	83
Principal forms	83
Conjugational types	84
Predictability of conjugational type on the basis of the infinitive	84
The formation of the tenses of the indicative active	85
Formation of the simple tenses	85
Formation of the present and the preterite	85
The first (short) conjugation	86
Subclasses 1-6	87
The irregular verbs *būt*, *dot* and *iet*	103
The second (long) conjugation	104
The third (mixed) conjugation	105
Conjugations I-III: The ending of the 2. p. sg.	107
Formation of the future tense	109
1. Vocalic stems	109
2. Consonantal stems	110
A. Stems ending in labials and velars	110
B. Sibilant stems	110
Examples of reflexive paradigms	112
Formation of the compound tenses	112
The present perfect	112
The past perfect	113
The future perfect	113
Aspect and tense	115
Introduction	115
I Aspect	115
Perfectivization	117
Imperfectivization	118
Aktionsarten	118
II Tense	118

Simple tenses	119
1. The present tense	119
2. The past tense	120
3. The future tense	120
Modal uses of the simple future	120
Compound tenses	120
1. The present perfect	121
2. The past perfect	121
3. The future perfect	122
Modal uses of the perfect future	122
Limitations	122
Mood	123
1. The indicative	123
2. The imperative	123
3. The subjunctive	125
A. Formation	125
B. Some major functions	126
a) The subjunctive in main clauses	126
b) The subjunctive both in the main and the subordinate clauses	127
c) The subjunctive in subordinate Clauses	127
4. The debitive	129
A. Formation	129
B. Syntax	130
C. Alternative constructions	131
5. The relative mood	131
A. Formation	131
B. Use	132
Voice	135
Definitions	135
Morphology of the active voice	135
Use of the active voice	135
Morphology of the passive voice	136
1. Expression of the passive voice in Latvian	136
A. The indicative	136

Sample of a passive paradigm in the indicative mood	137
B. Other moods than the indicative	137
Examples of paradigms of the subjunctive and relative passive	138
2. Expression of the passive voice in English	139
Motivations for choosing passive constructions. General considerations	139
1. Functional sentence perspective (FSP)	139
2. Agent deletion	140
The equivalents of English passives in Latvian	140
Constructions with an agent	140
Constructions without an agent	141
Verb in the 3rd person active without an explicitly expressed subject	141
Constructions of the type 'it is/was confirmed that [...]'	141
Reflexive passives	141
Formal passives with intransitive verbs	142
Reflexive and non-reflexive verbs	143
The Non-finite forms of the verb	145
I The infinitive	145
Formal characteristics	145
A. Active	145
B. Passive	145
Syntax	145
II Gerunds and participles	146
1. The gerunds	147
Formation	147
A. Indeclinable gerunds	147
B. Partly declinable gerunds	148
a) the *dam*-gerund	148
b) the *us/uš*-gerund	149
Syntax and semantics of the gerunds	149

A. Indeclinable gerunds	150
B. Partly declinable gerunds	151
2. The participles	152
Formation	152
A. Active participles	152
a) The present participle	152
b) The past participle	153
B. Passive participles	155
a) The present participle	155
b) The past participle	155
Syntax	156
A. Active participles	156
a) Attributive function	156
b) Appositive function	156
B. Passive participles	157
a) Attributive function	157
b) Appositive function	157
Concluding remarks on participles	157
Participles in the function of other word classes	158
III The verbal noun	158
The Verb: Word formation	159
Suffixation	159
Prefixation. Verb prefixes	159
Chapter 7: The adverb	162
Degrees of comparison	162
Syntax and semantics	163
The negation	164
Chapter 8: Case	165
Introduction	165
The genitive	166
I Adnominal function	166
1. Non-partitive genitive	166
A. The governing word is a noun	166
a) The possessive genitive	166
b) The subjective and c) the objective genitive	166
d) The descriptive genitive	167

e) *genitivus definitivus*
(explicativus) 167
f) The genitive of material 168
g) The genitive of purpose 168
h) The genitive of reinforcement (Emphasis) 168
   B. The governing word is an adjective 168
   C. The agentive 168
 2. Partitive genitive 169
   A. The governing word is a noun 169
   B. The governing word is an adjective 169
   C. The governing word is a numeral 170
   D. The governing word is a quantifier other than a numeral 170
II Adverbal function 170
 1. Non-partitive 170
   A. Genitive-governing verbs 170
   B. Negative constructions 171
 2. Partitive 172
III Adverbial function 172
   The genitive in exclamations 173
The accusative 173
 I Adverbal accusative 173
 II Adverbial accusative 174
   The accusative in exclamations 175
   A contrastive view of the genitive and accusative 175
The instrumental 176
The dative 176
 I Adnominal dative 176
  1. The governing word is a noun 176
  2. The governing word is an adjective 176
  3. The dative of age 177
 II Adverbal dative 177
  1. Dative + nominative 177
  2. Dative + accusative 177
  3. Dative as the only object 177
    A. Verba commodi 177
    B. Verba incommodi 178
  4. Dative + *ir/bija/būs* etc. as equivalents to *have*-constructions in English 178

5. Dative in impersonal constructions	179
A. Verbal	179
B. Nominal	179
6. Dative in the debitive construction	179
7. Dative with the infinitive passive	179
8. Dative + infinitive constructions	179
Dative with gerunds (The absolute dative)	179
III Adverbial function	180
The locative	180
The nominative	181
The vocative	182
Chapter 9: Prepositions	183
Preposition vs. prefix	183
Preposition vs. adverb. Semi-prepositions	183
Preposition vs. noun	184
Preposition vs. postposition	184
Case government	184
Subsequent disposition	185
1. Prepositions of place	186
A. Accusative governing prepositions	186
B. Genitive governing prepositions	187
C. Dative governing prepositions	188
D. Prepositions governing more than one case	188
2. Prepositions of time	188
A. Accusative governing	188
B. Dative governing	188
C. Genitive governing	188
3. Prepositions designating the instrument	189
4. Prepositions of purpose	189
5. Prepositions of comparison	189
6. Prepositions of cause	189
7. Prepositions of other meanings	189
Chapter 10: Time expressions	191
1. The 24 hours cycle	191
2. Hours	191
3. The days of the week	192
4. The months	192
5. The seasons of the year	192

6. The year	192
7. The century	192
8. Dates	192
9. Undetermined time expressions	193
10. How long? How often?	193
11. For how long?	193
12. Before/after	193
13. From-to (till)	193
14. During	193
15. In (after)	193
16. Towards	193
17. Ago	193
Chapter 11: Conjunctions	194
1. Coordinate	194
A. Copulative	194
B. Adversative	194
C. Disjunctive	194
2. Subordinate	194
A. Explicative	195
B. Adverbial	195
a) Conjunctions of time	195
b) Conjunctions of purpose	195
c) Conjunctions of result	195
d) Conjunctions of reason	195
e) Conditional	195
f) Concessive	195
g) Comparative	195
Chapter 12: The sentence	196
Definition	196
The members of the sentence	196
The principal members	197
The subject	197
Omission of subject pronoun	197
The only principal member	197
The predicate	198
Omission of copulative verb	198
The syntactic relationship between subject and predicate	199
The dependent members	199
The object	199
The adverbial	200

Difficulties in distinguishing objects from adverbials	201
The attribute	201
The apposition	202
Classification of the sentence	202
Subsequent disposition	203
The simple sentence	203
Two-part sentences	205
One-part sentences	205
Verbal one-part sentences	206
Infinitive sentences	207
Nominal one-part sentences	207
The compound sentence	208
Coordination	208
Subordination	209
1. Explicative clauses	209
A. Non-interrogative	210
B. Interrogative	210
2. Determinative clauses	210
3. Adverbial Clauses	211
A. Clauses of time	211
B. Clauses of purpose	212
C. Clauses of result	212
D. Clauses of reason	212
E. Clauses of condition	213
F. Clauses of concession	213
G. Clauses of comparison	213
Equivalents of English *than* and *the – the*	213
H. Clauses of manner	214
Final remarks	214
Asyndetism	214
Chapter 13: Agreement	**215**
1. Special cases of agreement in gender	216
A. Common gender nouns in *-a* and *-e*	216
B. Personal pronouns of the 1st and 2nd person	217
C. Indeclinable nouns	217
D. Abbreviations	217
E. Noun combinations	217
F. Interjections	217
2. Special cases of agreement in number	218
A. Plural nouns	218

B. Collective nouns	218
C. Indeclinable nouns	218
D. Abbreviations	218
E. Two (or more) coordinate nouns qualified by one and the same adjective	218
F. The polite form of the 2nd p. pl. pronoun	218
G. The interrogative pronoun *kas*?	219
H. Group subjects	219
3. Special cases of agreement in person	219
4. Special cases of agreement in case	219
Constructions with *kā* 'as' and similar	220
Chapter 14: Word order	221
Introductory remarks	221
I The Position of the members of the sentence	223
1. Declarative sentences	223
A. Non-extended sentences	223
B. Extended sentences	224
a) Adverbial extensions	224
b) Object extensions	224
One object	224
Two objects	224
2. Interrogative sentences	225
II The position of the members of the noun phrase	226
Non-participle attributes	226
Participle attributes	227
Reference literature	228
Indexes	231

FOREWORD

The idea behind this grammar is the same as that behind its "twin", *A Short Grammar of Lithuanian* (Slavica 1996).

The present volume has been written primarily for students of Latvian as a foreign language at university level, but it can also be used by others. It fulfills (and goes slightly beyond) the grammar requirements for the BA-degree in the UK and the USA, or the Foundation level (a one-year unit of study following an introductory course) in Scandinavia. It can also be used for foreign students studying Latvian in Latvia. Thus, the grammar presented here includes the fundamentals of phonology, morphology (with some short passages on word formation), and syntax in Latvian. Syntax is concentrated in the last chapters of the book, i. e. 8-10 (Case), 12 (The Sentence), 13 (Agreement) and 14 (Word Order). The syntax of adjectives, numerals and participles has, for practical reasons, for practical reasons has been incorporated and dealt with in the corresponding chapters: 3, 4 and 5.

This book is primarily a synchronic, prescriptive (normative), not a descriptive grammar. Notes on certain diachronic items as well as supplementary information are given in small type.

Where appropriate, short Latvian-English, Latvian-Scandinavian comparisons and similar remarks are provided.

The examples used to illustrate grammatical rules have been taken mainly from dictionaries and newspapers, or have been made up by the author and checked with informants.

Stress and intonation are given only for single words, not for sentences or word groups.

To facilitate lucidity and readability, the book is supplied with a relatively comprehensive table of contents at the beginning of the volume, as well as an index at the end, where a list of reference literature is also given. There should be no need for a table of abbreviations and symbols used, since they are either explained in the text or are likely to be immediately understandable. Thus, for example, C stands for 'consonant', V for 'vowel' and R for 'resonant'. For designating length in phonetic transcription, two points after the vowel/consonant are used and for semi-length one point (somewhat raised above the line).

This grammar has been used in manuscript form by my students of Latvian at the University of Oslo. I am grateful to them for their positive criticism. I am equally indebted to Jānis Štālbergs for having read the manuscript critically and for his corrections as well as good suggestions. Thanks also to Carolina D. Ramos for having checked my English carefully, to Knut Skrindo for technical assistance as well as to The Norwegian Academy of Sciences and Letters for its support and to Slavica Publishers for printing the manuscript.

Oslo, in December 1996

Terje Mathiassen

Chapter 0

INTRODUCTION

Latvian and Lithuanian (along with the extinct Old Prussian) to the Baltic language group which constitutes a branch of its own of the Indo-European (IE) family of languages. To IE also belong the Slavic languages – among them Russian, Byelorussian and Polish – as well as the Germanic languages, whose main members are English, German, Dutch and the Nordic languages. Thus, there is a remote link between English and Latvian. Within the Indo-European framework the Baltic languages are more closely related to the Slavic branch than to any other IE linguistic subdivision. The alleged similarities between Baltic and Slavic should, however, not be exaggerated. At any rate, there is obviously no mutual understanding between – let us say – a Russian and a Latvian when they speak their mother tongues, whereas a Russian and a Pole will (to a certain extent) be able to communicate.

During the Middle Ages, history, culture and religion separated Latvia from Lithuania because the latter entered the Polish sphere of influence, while the former experienced an impact above all from German language language and culture. Thus, the Teutonic and other orders invaded the territory corresponding to present-day Latvia and later on Germans (consisting of gentry, tradesmen and clergy) settled there. In terms of language, Latvian was also influenced by the now almost extinct Livonian, which along with Estonian, Finnish and some minor languages (Karelian, Vepsian, Votic) constitutes the Balto-Finnic branch of the Finno-Ugric language family.

In the vocabulary of Latvian several layers can be distinguished. First, there is a basic IE vocabulary – for instance, the word for 'heart', *sirds*, which has cognates in other IE languages. The same is true for the words for 'mother', 'sun', 'moon', 'day' etc: **māte, saule, mēness, diena**. Then, there is the Balto-Slavic stratum, containing words known exclusively within these two groups of IE; for instance, Latvian **galva**, Lithuanian *galva*, Russian *golova*, Polish *głowa,* meaning 'head' in all of thelanguages quoted. Another example is the word for 'hand, arm': Latvian **roka**, Lithuanian *ranka*, Russian *ruka* and Polish *ręka* (all from earlier *ranka*). A third layer may be discerned of words limited to the group of Baltic languages alone, e. g. Latvian **kāja** and Lithuanian *koja*, both meaning 'foot, leg'. If we continue with the body, the word for 'hair' may serve as an example of where the Baltic languages are split from another: the Latvians say **mati**, the Lithuanians *plaukai*. This scheme of several layers should not be oversimplified and regarded as an automatic indicator in terms of chronology, but should be looked upon as a purely guiding and schematic principle. Finally, both Latvian and its sister language, Lithuanian, have through the centuries adopted a great number of borrowings and international words from different sources and languages, most frequently from or through (Old and Modern) Russian (e. g. **grāmata** *book*, **džinsi** *jeans*) and (Low) German (e. g. **brokastis** *breakfast*, **slims** *ill*, **un** *and*), but a Finno-Ugric (Livonian) impact (e. g. **māja** *house*, the interrogative particle **vai**) is also strongly felt. Today the impact of English on the vocabulary is (of course) considerable.

Latvian is spoken by roughly 1.5 million people in Latvia proper which means about 55% of the population (the bulk of the remaining inhabitants are Russian speaking). In addition, there are approximately two hundred thousand ethnic Latvians living abroad – above all in Germany, Great Britain and Sweden and overseas in America and Australia.

The Latvian language map can be split into a number of subdialects. The main division, however, is that between High Latvian (or Latgalian, in the east where we find such cities as Daugavpils and Rēzekne), and Low Latvian. Low Latvian is divided between the Central dialect (encompassing such centers as Riga and Jelgava) and the so-called Tamian dialect (found on both sides of the outer parts of the Riga Bay, as well as the area around the city of Ventspils). Although the standardization process took a relatively long time, the Modern Standard language came into use during the second half of the 19th century, on the basis of the Central dialect (Latv. *vidus dialekts*). Several factors favored this dialect to become the foundation of the Standard language; i. e., presence of important economic, commercial and cultural centers within the region where this dialect is spoken, as well as a lesser degree of influence from neighbouring foreign languages (Slavic and Finno-Ugric) than in High Latvian and the Tamian dialects.

The use of the Latvian language was hampered by German supremacy over the centuries. In this century, its use was limited during the Soviet regime (1945-1991), but today it has regained the dominant role it had achieved during the first period of independence (1920-1940). A manifestation of this is the Latvian Language Law of 1989 (with subsequent Amendments), according to which Latvian is given the status of the official State Language of Latvia.

The oldest texts in Latvian are religious in content, and date back to the era of the Reformation; i. e., the sixteenth century (to be exact, the years of 1585, with the Catholic Catechism, and 1586, with the Lutheran Catechism).

The Latvian language has undergone many secondary developments, in contrast to Lithuanian, which has preserved many archaic features.

Chapter 1

PHONOLOGY

I Consonants

There are 26 consonant phonemes in Standard Latvian. As can be seen in the table below, the binary *unvoiced : voiced* opposition constitutes 9 pairs (i. e. /p/ vs. /b/, /t/ vs. /d/ etc.). Another, less comprehensive opposition is that between *non-palatalized : palatalized* which encompasses 4 pairs, e. g. /t/ vs. /t̪/, /n/ vs. /n̪/.

	labial	dental	alveolar	palatal	velar
plosives	p b	t d t̪ d̪			k g
fricatives	f v	s z	ʃ ʒ	j	x
affricates		t͡s d͡z	t͡ʃ d͡ʒ		
nasals	m	n n̪			
vibrants		r			
laterals			l l̪		

Note: The above table takes into consideration only the so-called *upper articulator* (i. e. the upper lips, the upper teeth and the palate), neglecting the *lower*. However, in the comments on the pronunciation of the different consonants which follow the lower articulator is also referred to where appropriate, especially the tongue and its different zones, i. e. the *apex* (adj. *apical*) 'tip of the tongue', the *corona* (adj. *coronal*) 'tongue blade' and the *dorsum* (adj. *dorsal*) 'back of the tongue'.

It should also be emphasized that the table is based on phonemic principles and further that palatalization is looked upon as an additional articulation which allows us to place palatalized phonemes in the same zones (dentals etc.) as their unpalatalized counterparts. It is vital to say this in order to prevent students from making false conclusions regarding the *pronunciation* of Latvian consonants. For guidelines on pronunciation the next paragraph should be consulted.

Phonetic Realization

Comments on pronunciation of the separate sounds will be limited to those which may cause the greatest difficulties to the student. In addition certain allophones will be commented upon.

First of all it should be stated that the Latvian unvoiced plosives *p, t, k* are *unaspirated.*

[n] has an allophone [ŋ] which is encountered before [k] and [g], e. g. [baŋka] (written **banka**, cf. below) 'bank', [buŋgas] (written **bungas**) 'drum'.

[t̪] and [d̪] (which are encountered mainly in borrowings) differ in their pronunciation from [t] and [d] in that they are *palatalized,* which means that they are pronounced with the (middle part of the) *tongue raised in the direction of the zone of the hard palate, i. e. to the j/i-position.* The [j] and the consonant in question are pronounced simultaneously in such a way that the [j] is "absorbed" in the process and therefore not heard. Two more sounds, i.e. [ņ] and [ļ] are palatatalized.

Palatalization is regarded as an *additional* articulation superimposed on the corresponding non-palatalized consonant, which is regarded as basic and the point of departure for the palatalized variant, for example, [ņ] vs. [n]. [j] is unique in that it is not palatalized, but an original palatal.

[v] is regarded as a fricative, not an approximant, in Latvian. It differs from [f] only with respect to the feature [+ voiced].

[z] is the voiced counterpart of [s] and is pronounced like the English -s- in *please* whereas the [ʒ] is similar to the sound heard in *vision* or to the *j* in French *jour.* Of the affricates, [t͡s] is pronounced like *ts* in *hats,* [dz] like *dz* in *buds,* [t͡ʃ] like *ch* in *church* and [d͡ʒ] like *g(e)* in the English pronunciation of *George.*

The sound [x] is pronounced approximately like the *ach*-Laut of German. It has a soft (i. e. palatalized) variant [xj] which may still be heard before or after front vowels, e. g. [texjnika] and [arxjeoloks], in emigré milieus, but not usually in Latvia proper.

[r] has an apico-dental (or apico-alveolar) articulation which is pronounced with 2-3 vibrations. It used to have a palatalized counterpart [ŗ] which, however, is not spoken any more in the Standard language and has practically no support in the dialects.

Latvian [l] is difficult to pronounce correctly. It is an apico-alveolar and is realized as such also in the position before front vowels, e.g. in **liels** *big.* To a student familiar with Russian it may remind of the hard (i. e. non-palatalized) Russian *l,* but upon closer examination it is clearly distinct from it. The student should practice the Latvian *l* carefully in language laboratory exercises. As is seen in the above table, [l] has a palatalized counterpart which is close to the Russian palatalized [l].

Orthographic Representation

Except for the following deviations the consonants of Latvian are represented in the orthography in the same way as illustrated in the phonemic chart above:

The affricates /t͡s/, /d͡z/, /t͡ʃ/ and /d͡ʒ/ are written *c, dz, č* and *dž* respectively.

The fricative /x/ is expressed through *h*. Until the orthographic reform of 1957 the digraph *ch* was also used (it is still partly preserved in emigré press). Discussions on the orthographic representation(s) of [x] are frequently observed. Many Latvians react against such notations as, for example, *Bahs* against the earlier, traditional *Bachs* for the name of the famous composer.

The sounds [t̡] and [d̡] are written *ķ* and *ğ* respectively. To some readers our phonetic classification of them on a par with the dentals *t* and *d* (cf. the above table) may seem somewhat odd and radical. Nevertheless, this conception is in conformity with the phonetic reality behind them. One may in this connection remind about the Latvian way of treating the Gorbachovian word *glasnost'* which the Latvians wrote *glasnosķ*. Examples of *ğ* are **kuğis** ship and **ğēnijs** *genius*.

Until 1946 (and still in parts of the emigré press) one could find the grapheme *ŗ* to denote a palatal *r*. Thus, one would, for example, write *kaŗa* – and not as now – *kara* in the genitive sg. of the word for 'war' *karš*. A trace of the former palatalization in this word form is the nominative marker *-š*, and not *-s* as, for example, in **gars**, gen. **gara** *spirit*.

Consonant Alternations

In the inflectional morphology the following alternations are encountered:

p	→	pj
b	→	bj
f	→	fj
v	→	vj
m	→	mj
t	→	š
s	→	š
d	→	ž
z	→	ž
c	→	č

dz	→	dž
n	→	ņ
l	→	ļ
(r	→	ŗ - only in older writing and emigré press, cf. preceding paragraph)

Note: The letters š, ž, č, ļ, ņ (and ŗ) along with the digraphs dž, pj, bj, fj, vj and mj represent historically and morphophonemically palatalized phonemes. All other consonants may be labeled unpalatalized.

In addition, the velars *k* and *g* alternate with *c* and *dz* respectively, but not within the nominal declension.

Also certain consonant clusters (i. e. *s-/z*-clusters) can undergo alternations. Thus, *sl* alternates with *šļ*, *sn* with *šņ*, *zl* with *žļ*, *zn* with *žļ*. The geminate *ll* alternates with *ļļ*.

The consonants *j* and *h* never alternate. The same holds true for *ķ* and *ğ* (except for certain cases in derivational morphology).

Examples with consonant alternations:
skapis, gen. **skapja** *locker*, **gulbis**, gen. **gulbja** *swan*, **kareivis**, **kareivja** *soldier*, **kurmis**, gen. **kurmja** *mole*, **menēsis**, gen. **menēša** *month*, **latvietis**, gen. **latvieša** *Latvian*, **nazis**, gen. **naža** *knife*, **briedis**, gen. **brieža** *deer*, **lācis**, gen. **lāča** *bear*, **pusaudzis**, gen. **pusaudža** *backfish*, **Jānis**, gen. **Jāņa** *John*, **brālis**, gen. **braļa** *brother*, **troksnis**, gen. **trokšņa** *noise*, **rullis**, gen. **ruļļa** *roll, coil*. (Alternations of the same kind are also encountered in other inflectional classes and parts of speech; this type was chosen only for the sake of simplicity.) Observe the absence of alternation in **kuģis**, gen. **kuģa** *ship*.

The historical basis for these alternations was clusters consisting of consonant + *j* (as opposed to the consonant in question not followed by *j*) which were originally assimilated to palatalized consonants (see p. 23 above), except in the case of labials, where the clusters were preserved. Consonants like *š* and *ž* have given up their palatalization and are palatalized only in a historical sense of the term (but the former palatalization has left a trace in morphology, whence the term 'morphological palatalization'). The clusters **kj* and **gj* yielded *c* and *dz* respectively. The consonants *c* and *dz* may also derive from *k* and *g* before front vowels, as illustrated in the above examples. It should, however, be emphasized that not every *-i* triggers the change from *k > c* or *g > dz*, cf. pp. 31 and 44.

Clusters

1. Assimilation

A basic rule of consonant clusters in Latvian is that the (second or) last consonant in a sequence determines the character of the preceding one(s) (so-called *regressive assimilation,* although *progressive assimilations* do also occur, cf. p. 27). This is the case both with the *s-/z-* clusters mentioned in the preceding passage (in a historical perspective) and with clusters such as *sd* rendering *zd* or *zt* yielding *st.* The latter are illustrations of voicing and devoicing respectively, which consist of the following:

In the case of *voicing,* unvoiced consonants adopt the feature [+voiced] from an immediately following voiced consonant. *Devoicing* implements *mutatis mutandis* the same principle: a voiced consonant adopts the feature [-voiced] from an immediately following unvoiced consonant.

Examples:
a) *Voicing:*
apdraudēt [ˈabdraudɛːt] *endanger,* **atbilde** [ˈadbildɛ] *answer,* **nākdams** [ˈnaːgdams] *coming,* **pusdiena** [ˈpuzdiena] *noon; dinner,* **trešdiena** [ˈtreʒdiena] *Wednesday,* **piecdesmit** [ˈpied͡zdɛsmit] *fifty.*

b) *Devoicing:*
labs [laps] *good,* **gads** [gat͡s] *year,* **derīgs** [ˈdɛriːks] *suitable,* **mazs** [mas·] *little,* **izteikt** [ˈisteikt] *express,* **mežs** [mɛʃ·] *forest* (for the realization of *žs* as [ʃ·], see p. 27; the symbol · designates semilength, p. 38).

Note: Though phonetically voiced, the resonants *r, l, m, n* have no assimilating effect on neigbouring unvoiced consonants (nor are they themselves affected by other consonants). The same holds true for *j* and *v.* Examples: **slepen**s [slɛpːɛns], not *[zlɛpːɛns] *secret,* **svaigs** [svaiks], not *[zvaiks] *fresh.*

In rapid speech voicing/devoicing can also occur across word boundaries in certain cases.

Observe further that – unlike, for example, in German and Russian – *voiced consonants in word final position are not devoiced* in Latvian, e. g. **kad** [kad] *when,* **gandrīz** [ganˈdriːz] *almost.*

c) *Other Assimilations*
Assimilations with respect to place of articulation occur with the sibilants *s, z, š* and *ž* which undergo (partial or complete) assimilations

(word initially, i. e. on the boundary between prefix and root, and word finally, i. e, before the nom. *s*-marker) in the following environments:

sč > *šč* ׃ **puscetri** ['puʃtʃɛtri] *half past three* (about the clock)
zš > *šš* : **uzšķirt** ['uʃ·tjirt][1] *open*
zž > *žž* : **izžāvēt** ['iʒ·a:vɛ:t][1] *make dry*
šs > *šš* : **gaišs** [gaiʃ·][1] *light, bright*
žs > *šš*׃ **mežs** [mɛʃ·][1] *forest*

[1]for the (semi)long [ʃ] and [ʒ], see p. 38. A colon is used to symbolize length, a (raised) stop (point) for that of semi-length.

The first three are *regressive* assimilations in contrast to the last two which are *progressive*.

Note also assimilations of the type:
*ljs > **l's* > *[lʃ]* (in, for example, **ceļš** *way, road* vs. **ceļa**, cf. p. 42),
*rjs > **r's* > *[rʃ]* (in, for example, **karš** *war*, vs. gen. **kara**, cf. p. 42). The *r* subsequently lost its softening, see p. 24.

The last assimilation which should be mentioned is:

nk > *ŋk:* **banka** ['baŋka] *bank*
ng > *ŋg:* **bungas** ['buŋgas] *drum*

(which means that the dental *[n]* is replaced by its velar allophone *[ŋ]* before a velar stop).

The same kind of assimilation is known in English. In Nordic languages the same phenomenon is observed in the case of *nk*. For *ng* it should be added that in many cases [ŋ] is spoken alone, without the subsequent [g], in Nordic.

2. *Dissimilation*
A dissimilation **tt* and **dt* to *st* takes place in Baltic, e. g. **mest** *throw* < **met-ti* (with present and preterite stem *met-*) and **atrast** *find* < **at-rad-ti* (with present stem **ra-n-d* and preterite stem *rad-*).

II Vowels

Standard Latvian has a symmetrical system of 6 short vowel phonemes and 6 long.

Short Vowels

The short vowels can be shown diagrammatically in a triangular system:

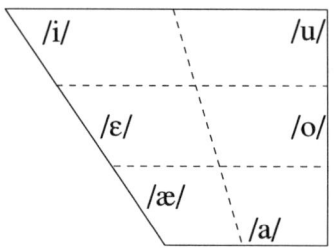

One of the above phonemes, namely /o/, is marginal and attested only in words of foreign origin (for example, see below).

Short vowels are found both in stressed and unstressed position.

Orthographic Representation

In Latvian orthography the vowels are spelled as in the above chart, except for /æ/ and /o/ which are written as *e* and *o* respectively. This means that /e/ and /æ/ are not distinguished in Latvian orthography.

> One reason for the orthographic non-distinction between the two *e*-sounds could be that originally they were likely to have constituted a situation of *complementary distribution* whereby the open variant occurred before a back vowel in the next syllable, the closed one before a front vowel or before pausa (#). There are, however, certain deviations (see p. 31) from this original assimilative system (which could be regarded as a kind of vowel harmony), which from the point of view of Modern Standard Latvian forces us to speak of them not as variants of one and the same phoneme, but as two separate phonemes.
>
> Over the centuries various attempts have been made to distinguish between the two *e*-sounds also in the orthography. From 1920 onward *e* has been written for both.

Examples of short vowels from the vocabulary of Latvian:

/i/: **pils** [pils] *castle*, /e/: **bet** [bɛt] *but*, /æ /: **ledus** ['lædus], /a/: **mati** ['mat:i][1] *hair*, /u/: **ute** ['ut:e][1] *louse*, /o/: **Oslo** *Oslo*.

[1]For the long consonants, see p. 38 below.

Long Vowels

The long vowels can be shown diagrammatically in a scheme parallel to that of the short vowels:

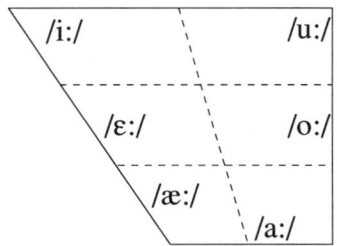

As with short vowels, long vowels are found both in stressed and unstressed position.

Orthographic Representation
The long vowels of Latvian are spelt in the following way: /i:/ as ī, /e:/ and /æ:/ as ē, /a:/ as ā, /o:/ as o (sic). A comparison with the short vowels reveals that they are written in the same way, except for the macron (¯) which indicates length. In the case of o, however, there is no macron to indicate when o is long; the short and the long /o/ are written in the same way. This inconvenience of written Latvian is to some extent justified by the fact that short and the long /o/ are marginal phonemes, restricted to borrowings.

Examples of long vowels in the vocabulary of Latvian:
/i:/: **trīs** [tri:s] *three*, /ɛ:/ **mēs** [mɛ:s] *we*, /æ:/: **lēni** ['læːni] *slowly*, /a:/: **māte** ['ma:te] *mother*, /ɔ:/: **Eiropa** ['eiro:pa] *Europe*, /u:/: **ūdens** ['u:dens] *water*.

Note on Pronunciation of Short and Long Vowels
We find it unecessary to make statements of the type: "vowel x is pronounced approximately as in the English word so and so" since we use (a variant of) the IPA system of transcription with which the readers of this grammar are expected to be familiar.

Excursus: Distribution of Closed vs. Open *e*/*ē*

As previously stated, see p. 28, the distribution between the closed ɛ/ɛː and open æ/æː sounds (both represented as *e*/*ē* in the orthography) is determined by assimilative processes, which implies a split into two (originally) positionally determined variants of one and the same phoneme. However, various secondary (morphophonological) developments have obscured this original situation, such that the distribution between the two sounds is no longer fully predictable. The result has been an evolution from allophones into different phonemes. In spite of the fact that the rules are rather complicated with numerous exceptions (and partially unstable norms), it appears practical (and possible) to give certain guidelines for conditions under which the orthographic *e/ē* are pronounced as [ɛ]/[ɛ:] and when as [æ]/[æ:]. The following survey can be presented:

Closed e/ē are spoken:
1 a) in all word-final syllables (without exception), for example, **upe, upes, upēm** (different inflectional forms of the noun **upe** *river)*; infinitives in *-ēt*, e. g. **gulēt** *lie.*

1 b) in some old *monosyllabics*:
Examples:
es *I*, **mēs** *we*, **te** *here*, **vēl** *still, yet*, **bet** *but*, **bez** *without*, **ne** *not*, **nē** *no*,

2 a) when the immediately following syllable contains one of the front ("palatal") vowels *i/ī, e/ē* or the diphthongs *ie/ei*.
Examples:
gulēsim *let's sleep/lie*, **pētīt** *investigate*, **drebēt** *tremble*, **sēdēt** *sit*, **esiet** *be!*, **ēdiet** *eat!*, **zemei** (dat. sg. of **zeme**) *earth*.

In polysyllabics such as **mellene** *blueberry* we can conclude, first, from 1 b) that the *-e* has a closed articulation, and second, that according to 2 a) the *e* of the internal syllable must be a closed *e*, and third, the articulation of this *e* in turn triggers the closed articulation of the *e* of the first syllable.

2 b) when followed by a (synchronically or diachronically) palatalized or palatal consonant (cf. p. 25), i. e. *ķ, ģ, ļ, ņ, š, ž, č, j*:

sēžam *we are sitting* (: **sēdēt** *sit*), **sešas** (fem. nom. of the numeral) *six*, **dzeja** *poetry*,

So far the pronunciation of closed *e/ē* has been predictable according to phonetically definable environments.

Definable on the basis of other criteria is the pronunciation of closed *e/ē* in:

3 a) the nouns of the sixth declension (p. 48), e. g. **debess** *heaven*,

3 b) the simple present of verbs of the Ist conjugation (p. 94) with infinitives in *-r-t*, e. g. **dzeru** ['dzɛru] (: **dzert** *drink*).

The historical explanation for this is that the *-r-* in the present stems of this type reflects an earlier soft (palatalized) *ŗ* (< **rj* which is now depalatalized, but has left a trace in the closed articulation of the *e/ē*). In pre-war Latvian texts (as well as in some present-day emigré publications) it was represented as *ŗ* in the orthography.

3 c) the simple past of verbs of the Ist conjugation, cf., for example, **nesu** [ˈnɛsu] ... **nesa** [ˈnɛsa] ... **nesāt** [ˈnɛsat] (: **nest** *carry*), **ņēmu** [ˈŋʲɛːmu] ...**ņēma** [ŋʲɛːma] ... **ņēmāt** [ˈŋʲɛːmat] (: **ņemt** *take*).

This state of affairs seems also to have a historical motivation: common East Baltic must have possessed both an *-ā* and an *-ē*-preterite (this state is still preserved in Lithuanian). In Latvian the two types seem to have fused into one, the *-ā*-type (cf. **nes-a** (< *-ā, see p. 35), **nes-ā-m, nes-ā-t, ņēm-a** (< *-ā, see p. 35), **ņēm-ā-m, ņēm-ā-t**), but the former *ē*-preterites have left a trace in the timbre of the stem vowel, namely a closed [ᴇ] in contrast with the open [æ] of the present tense of these verbs, e. g. **nesu** [ˈnæsu) ... **nes** [næs]... **nesat** [ˈnæsat], **ņemu** [ˈŋʲæmu]... **ņem** [ŋʲæm]... **ņemat** [ˈŋʲæmat].

3 d) words of foreign (i. e. non-Latvian) origin, irrespectively of the character of the vowel or consonant following it, e. g. **problēma** [ˈprɔblɛːma] *problem*.

Note: contrary to the above combinatory rules, *open e/ē* [æ/æː] are spoken before:
• the adverb marker *-i*: **reti** [ˈræt:i] *rarely*, **lēni** [ˈlæːni] *slowly*,
• the nominative pl. ending *-i* of 1st declension nouns (as well as adjectives in *-s*): **bērni** [ˈbæ·rni] *children*, **cilvēki** [ˈtsilvæːki] *men*.

From a diachronic perspective, the pronunciation of open [æ/æː] in *reti, lēni, bērni*, **cilvēki** (not **cilvēci*) is due to the fact that certain *i*-sounds in end-syllables of Latvian have their origin in the diphthong *-ai* (reconstructed on the basis of Lithuanian data).

The rules for pronouncing open [æ]/[æː] can be roughly determined by stating that when conditions for pronouncing closed *e/ē* are absent (and care is taken for exceptions mentioned in note to point 3 c) above), the open sounds are spoken.

In positive terms, however, the main occurrences of open *e*-sounds can be summarized as follows:
1. in all cases and both numbers of nouns of the first declination (cf. p. 43 f.), e. g. **ezers** [ˈæzærs] *lake* (when not overruled by 2b) on p. 30),
2. in all cases, both numbers and both genders of adjectives, e. g. **pelēks** [ˈpælæːks] *grey* (when not overruled by 2b) on p. 30),
3. in the 3rd p. of IIIrd conjugation verbs, e. g. **redz** [rædz͡] *see(s)*, cf. p. 105 ff. (This violates the principle set forth in point 1 b) above.),
4. in adverbs in *-i*
5. in (some) borrowings before the sound *r*, e. g. **nervs** [nær-] *nerve*. (This is contrary to rule 3 d) above.)

The rules for the distribution of closed and open *e/ē* in compounds are too complicated to be presented in short.

Compensatory Vowel Lengthening

In Latvian compensatory vowel lengthening occurs where an *n* has been lost in the position between a vowel and a consonant. The *n* has left a trace in the lengthening of the preceding vowel. The process can be described according to the following formula:

$$VnC > \bar{V}C \text{ or before } \#$$

where *V* can be *i*, *u*, *e* or *a* (and # means pausa).

It should be noticed that whereas the high vowels *i* and *u* yield *ī* and *ū* through simple lengthenings, in the case of *e* and *a* the result is *ie* and *o* [uo] respectively (cf. section on diphthongs p. 33). Since in terms of duration a diphthong counts as a long vowel (long monophthong), we prefer for the sake of simplification of the rule to speak of lengthening also in this case. Notee that it is not important to distinguish between open and closed *e* in this process, since the result in both cases is *ie* (which is pronounced as [ɪɒ]). We are then left with the (short) monophthong *o,* which occurs only in words of foreign origin and is not affected by the (historical) development in question.

Examples:

i > *ī*: **mīt** *to tread* (vs. **minu** *I tread*); *u* > *ū*: **jūtu** (< **junt-*, cf. Lith. **juntu**) *I feel* (vs. **jutu** *I felt*, Lith. **jutau** *I felt*); *en* > *ie*: **pieci** (vs. Lithuanian **penki**) *five*; *an* > *o* [uo]: **roka** ['ruoka] *hand, arm*.

Observe that the change operates only with the nasal *n*, and not with *m*. Cases such as, for instance, Latvian **zobs** [zuops] *tooth* vs. Lithuanian **žambas** and **top** [tuop] *becomes* vs. Lithuanian **tampa** can be explained by the assimilatory development of **n* > *m* before labials.

For instances with preserved *n* in the environment *VnC*, see the comment under (semi-)diphthongs (p. 35).

An example of loss of the sound *n* in word final position with subsequent lengthening would be the accusative singular of *o*-stems Baltic *a*-stems, cf. p. 42): **-om* > **-am* > **an* > *[uo]* in **darbu** (: **darbs** *work*). In the same case and number of *ā*-stems (p. 43) we cannot tell whether the vowel was shortened before the *-n* was dropped. The result would in any case be *[-uo]*, e. g. **roku** (< **rankān* < **rankām*).

Diphthongs

Diphthongs can be defined as a *sequence of two vowels which constitute one (long) syllable*. They represent one unitary phoneme.

1. Pure diphthongs:
Latvian has a system of 10 diphthongs, namely:
/ei/, /eu/, /ai/, /au/, /oi/, /ou/, /ui/, /iu/, /ie/, /uo/.

Examples:
teikt [tɛikt] *say*, **sev** [sɛu] *-self*, **laiks** [laiks] *time*, **tauta** [tauta] *people*, **boikots** [ˈbojkots] *boycott*, **džouls** [dʒouls] *joule*, **puika** [ˈpuika] *boy*, **pliukšķināt** [ˈpliukʃṯinaːt] *clap*, **liepa** [ˈliepa] *lime*, **ola** [ˈuola] *egg*.

The most common diphthongs in Latvian are the following five: /ei/, /ai/, /au/, /ie/(phonetically [ɪɒ]) and /uo/ (phonetically [uɒ]). These spellings also reflect their orthographic representation with the exception of /uo/ which is written *o*.

This means that the grapheme *o* can represent three different phonemes (and sounds) in Latvian, namely in addition to the diphthong /uo/ also the short and long monophthongs /o/, /oː/. As mentioned on pp. 28 and 29, the latter are restricted to borrowings. Certain borrowings (as, for example **roze**) have been assimilated to the mainstream corpus and are pronounced [uo].

The remaining five diphthongs, /oi/, /ou/, /eu/, /ui/ and /iu/, are more or less marginal. Thus, the first two are found in borrowings only. Further, /eu/ is restricted either to special environments in Latvian words whereby it is written *-ev-* (see under point Vocalization, p. 35) or to rare borrowings (e. g. **Seula** *Seoul*). In most borrowings it is replaced by *ei*, cf., for example, **Eiropa** *Europe*, **pseidonīms** *pseudonym*. As demonstrated in the above examples, the diphthongs /ui/ and /iu/ are encountered in autochthonic (indigenous) words, but are of rare occurrence.

It should not be necessary to say much about the pronunciation of diphthongs. Observe that the first component in [ei] is spoken semi-narrowly. It should further be noticed that sequences written *aj, ej, oj, uj* are spoken as diphthongs (i. e. with the second element realized as a semi-vowel): **klajš** (masc. sg. nom.) *open*, **dzejnieks** *poet*, **birojs** *office*, **šujmašīna** *sewing-machine*.

The relative duration of the components of a diphthong will vary dependent on the intonational pattern, cf. p. 39.

2. *Semi-dipthongs:*

Besides the "pure diphthongs" referred to under point 1) above, sequences of a vowel *(e, a, i or u)* + one of the resonants *r, l* (palatalized/unpalatalized) or *m* (+ C) are also customarily regarded as diphthongs in the Latvian (and Baltic) linguistic tradition. They can be labeled "semi-diphthongs" or "mixed diphthongs".

Examples:

dzert *drink*, **karsts** *hot*, **cirst** *cut*, **kurpe** *shoe*, **zelts** *gold*, **galva** *head*, **svilpe** *whistle*, **gulbis** *swan*, **vemt** *vomit*, **dzimt** *be born*, **jumts** *roof*.

The main argument for letting such sequences count as diphthongs is that they are intonational units in the same way as the pure diphthongs (and long monophthongs), cf. p. 39.

In certain cases we find a long (or semi-long) vowel before *r*, e. g. **vērt** *open*, **kārta** *layer*, thus presenting us with a (semi-)long diphthong. A long vowel before a resonant + C is also encountered in cases like masc. sg. nom. **rāms** *quiet, silent*, where a dipthong has arisen as a result of vowel syncope (< *rāmVs*, cf. fem. sg. nom. **rāma** (< *rāmā*), see section on Word final position, p. 35 f.). A (semi-)long pure diphthong is found in **tēvs** [te:us] *father* (<*tēvas*, cf. the gen. sg. **tēva** *(<*tēvā)*), (see also section on Vocalization, p. 35).

In the environment *vowel (e, a, i, u) + n + C* the diphthongal status is eliminated in most Latvian dialects according to the compensatory lengthening rule described on p. Where a diphthong is found in this distribution in the Standard language, we have a borrowing either from the Tamian dialect (cf. p. 20), e. g. **dzintars** *amber*, or from a foreign (i. e. non Latvian) source (cf., for example, **tinte** *ink* from German).

Sequences of the type CVRC[1] are labeled *tautosyllabic* (or real diphthongs), in contrast to *heterosyllabic*, quasi-diphthongal sequences CVRV. For example, **dzert** *to drink* vs. **dzeru** *I drink*, **aut** *to put on (shoes, boots etc.)* vs. **āvu** *I put on* (past tense); the form **āvu** also indicates via the consonantal *v* (instead of the semi-vowel *u*) that the diphthongal characteristic is absent.

[1] where C stands for Consonant, V for Vowel and R for Resonant.

Vocalization

This phenomena refers to the transformation of /j/ and /v/ to *[i]* and *[u]* respectively in the environment *j/v* preceded by a short vowel in the same syllable. The development results in diphthongs of different kinds.

Examples:
a) *j > i:* **klajš** [klaiʃ] *open*, **dzejnieks** [dzeinieks] *poet*, **šuj** *sews* (: **šūt**),
b) *v > u:* **tavs** [taus] *your(s)*, **tev** [tɛu] *for you* (dative), **tēvs** [tɛ·us] *father*, **Dievs** [dieus] *God*, **zivs** [zius] *fish*, **govs** [guous] *cow*.

In certain cases vacillation occurs, e. g. **gatavs** ['gat:aus] or ['gat:avs] *ready*.

VOWEL ALTERNATIONS (ABLAUT)

Vowel alternations known as *ablaut* are inherited from Indo-European. Some of the original *ablaut* pairs have been preserved in Baltic. In addition, certain secondary vowel alternations have developed.

Ablaut is observed above all in Latvian verbs in whose primary verbs (cf. p. 86 ff.) one will find alternations of the type *e : ē, i : ie, a : o* [uo], *i : ī , u : ū*.

Illustrations:
ņemt : ņemu : ņēmu *take*, **likt : lieku** (Lith. **lieku**, cf. p. 87) : **liku** *put*, **tikt : tieku** (Lith. **tenku**, cf. p. 87) : **tiku** *get*, **rakt : roku** (cf. p. 87) : **raku** *dig*, **krist : krītu** (cf. p. 87) : **kritu** *fall*, **just : jūtu** (cf. p. 87) : **jutu** *feel*.

WORD FINAL POSITION

1) Consonants:
As previously stated (p. 26 above), voiced end-consonants preserve the feature [+ voiced].

2) Vowels:
In Latvian, short vowels (except *-i* and *-u*) undergo syncope in end-syllables, while long ones are shortened in the same environment.

Examples:
nesa (3 p. preterite verb form: **nest** *carry*) < *[nɛsa:], cf. **nesām** ['nɛsa:m].

The following question then arises: why hasn't the -ā in the end-syllable -ām been shortened to *-am? The answer is that this -ām did not originally occupy end-syllable position. This *-ām reflects an earlier *-āmV (with subsequent syncope of this short vowel symbolized as V), cf. Lith. -Vme.

Parallel examples can be given from other word classes, e. g. nouns, for example, nom. sg. **meita** (< *meitā) vs. dat. pl. **meitām** (< *meitāmV).

III Suprasegmentals

We will deal here with the three prosodemes *stress, quantity* and *tone (pitch)*. Only quantity is reflected in the orthography.

1. Stress
(Uzsvars)

The basic rule for Latvian is *initial* stress (i. e stress on the first syllable): **dzīvotājs** ['iedzi:vuota:is] *inhabitant*, **republika** ['rɛpublika] *republic*. The same rule is also observed in most *compounds*, e. g. **nevaru** ['nɛvaru] (I) *cannot*, **piedzīvot** ['piedzi:vuot] *experience,* **jaunkundze** ['jaunkundzɛ] *miss*.

The most important exceptions to the general rule can be summarized as follows:

a) *negative pronouns* and *adverbs*: **nekas** [nɛ'kas] *nothing*, **nekāds** *none*, **neviens** [nɛ'viens] *nobody*, **nekad** [nɛ'kad] *never*, **nekur** [nɛ'kur] *nowhere*, **nemaz** [nɛmaz] *not at all*,

b) *superlatives* with the prefix **vis-** of adjectives and adverbs, e. g. **vislabākais** [vis'labakais] *the very best*, **vislabāk** [vis'laba:k] *in the very best way*, **vismaz** [vis'maz] *at least*,

c) in compounds with *jeb-*: **jebkāds** [jɛp'ka:ts] *whoever; whatever*, **jebkurš** [jɛp'kurʃ] *whoever; whatever*, **jebkad** [jɛp'kad] *whenever*, **jebkur** [jɛp'kur] *wherever*,

d) in some instances with *ik*-compounds: **ikkatrs** [ik'katrs] *everyone*, **ikviens** [ik'viens] *everyone*, **ikreiz** [ik'reiz] *every time,* but in **ikdiena** ['igdiena] *everyday*, **ikdienišķs** ['igdieniʃts] *everyday*- the stress is on the first syllable.

e) in certain compounds with *pus-*, e. g. **pusotra** [pus'uotra] *one and a half*, whereas for instance **puslaiks** *half-time* (in sports), **pussala** *peninsula* follow the mainstream tendency with the stress on the first syllable.

In addition, deviations from the general rule are found in a scattered number of cases, e. g. **gandrīz** [gan'dri:z] *almost*, **joprojām** [juo'pruoja:m] *still*, **labdien** 'lab'dien] *how do you do*, **labrīt** [lab'rīt] *good morning*, **nupat** [nu'pat] *just now*, **paretam** [pa'rætam] *rarely*, **patlaban** [pat'laban] *now*, **tāpat** [ta:'pat] *in the same way*, **tikpat** [tik'pat] *as much/many as*, **turklāt** [tur'kla:t] *in addition*, **turpat** [tur'pat] *just there; in the same place*, **turpretim** [tur'pretim] *on the other hand*, **varbūt** [var'bu:t] *perhaps*, **vienalga** [vien'alga] *all the same*.

In all of these exceptions the stress has been on the *second* syllable. There also exist, however, words with the stress on the *third syllable* from the beginning of the word: **nepavisam** [nɛpa'visam] *not at all; (in) no way*, **neparko** [nɛpar'kuo] *not for everything in the world*.

The last set of exceptions is found among international words (IWs) of the type **komunikē** [komuni'kɛ:], **ateljē** [atel'jɛ:], **esperanto** [ɛspɛr'anto]. The first two have end-stress whereas the latter has penultimate stress.

Because of the dominating principle of first-syllable-stress in Latvian, stress is practically phonologically irrelevant. Among the few *minimal pairs* which can be established are: **nekā** ['nɛka:] *than* vs. **nekā** [nɛ'ka:] (genitive of **nekas** [nɛ'kas] *nobody; nothing*), **pārlieku** ['pa:rlieku] *move* vs. **pārlieku** [pa:r'lieku] *too much*, **vienādi** ['viena:di] *alike* vs. **vienādi** [vien'a:di] *always*.

2. Quantity
(Kvantitāte)

A. *Vowels*

As evident from the exposition on p. 28 f. and above Latvian contrasts between short and long vowels.

The duration of the long vowels in Latvian is claimed to be twice that of the short ones.

Unlike stress, vowel quantity can have distinctive function in Latvian. Oppositions of this kind play a very important role. Thus, quantity can distinguish:

1) between *different lexemes*, e. g.

ja *if* : **jā** *yes*; **kara** (gen. sg. of **karš**) *war* : **kāra** (fem. sg.) *greedy, desirous of*; **sals** (3 p. fut. tense of **salt**) *freeze* : **sāls** *salt* (nom. sg.),

2) between *morphosyntactic words*:

a) with respect to oppositions in *tense*: **braucam** (1 p. pl. pres. tense of **braukt**) : **braucām** (1 p. pl. past tense of the same verb),

b) with respect to oppositions in *case*: **Rīga** (nom. sg.) : **Rīgā** (lok. sg.); **valstis** (nom. pl. of **valsts**) *state* : **valstīs** (loc. pl.),

c) with respect to oppositions of *indefiteness* vs. *definiteness*:

liela (fem. sg. nom. indef.) *big* : **lielā** (fem. sg. nom. def.), **lielas** (fem. pl. nom. indef.) : **lielās** (fem. pl. nom. def.).

Minimal pairs of these types (above all b) and c)) are very numerous in Latvian.

B. Consonants

Latvian has both short, semi-long and long consonants, but – unlike in the case of vowels – differences with respect to consonant quantity are said to be phonologically irrelevant, since they are only of phonetic character. However, some minimal pairs can be found, e. g. **nule** *just* ['nule] vs. **nulle** ['nul:e] *zero,* **gals** [gals] *end* vs. **galls** [gal:s] *Gal,* **mana** [mana] (fem. sg. nom. or m. sg. gen.) *my* vs. **manna** [man:a] *manna.*

Rules for the occurrence of *long* consonants in Latvian:

a) *unvoiced* plosives, fricatives or affricates (i. e. *p, t, k, ķ; s, š; c, č*) are pronounced as long or semi-long in the position between a stressed short vowel and an unstressed vowel (in word forms with three or more syllables always as semi-long).

Examples:

upe ['up:ɛ] *river,* **kaķis** ['katʲis] *cat,* **klusa** ['klus:a] (fem. sg. nom. of **kluss**) *silent; quiet,* **kluča** ['klutʃ:a] (gen. sg. of **klucis**) *block.*

Note: consonant length is in this case not reflected in the orthography in contrast to:

b) words like **balle** *ball, feast,* **dilemma** *dilemma* where *one long consonant* is pronounced, i. e. [l:] and [m:] respectively. Such gemination in orthography is not characteristic of Latvian, but is found in a number of borrowings (such as those just mentioned). In autochthonic (indigenuous) words they are encountered only very rarely (e. g. **mellene** ['mɛl:ɛnɛ] *blueberry*),

c) two consonants in word final position are pronounced as one semi-long consonant. This pertains also to cases where two consonants in this environment become identical as the result of an assimilation (p. 26): **ass** (masc. sg. nom.) *sharp,* **balss** (masc. sg. nom.) *voice,* **pareizs** ['parɛis·] *correct,* **mežs** [mɛʃ·] *forest.*

d) a long (or semi-long) consonant is also pronounced where there is a prefix ending in the same consonant as the initial consonant of the word root, for example **attīstība** ['at:i:sti:ba] *development,* **pārraidīt** ['pa:r:aidi:t] *broadcast.* The same holds true for instances like **atdot** ['ad:uot] *return, give back.* Observe further *compounds* of the type **pussala** ['pus:ala] *peninsula,* **lappuse** ['lap:usɛ] *page.*

In all other instances *short* consonants are spoken. It should be emphasized that quantity relations may differ from those found in most of the modern Germanic languages (English, German, Dutch, the Nordic languages), since Latvian can have short consonants between short vowels, as for example in **labi** [ˈlabi] *well*, **maza** [ˈmaza] (fem. sg. nom.) *small*.

3. Tone

Tone in Latvian consists of different intonational patterns realized in long syllables (i. e. long vowels, diphthongs and semi-diphtongs, cf. above).

Depending on the dialect three different tones or intonations are discernable, namely the **even tone** *(stieptā intonācija),* written in linguistic texts with the symbol ˜ , **the falling tone** *(krītošā intonācija),* written as ` , and the **broken tone** *(lauztā intonācija),* written as ^.

The even and the falling tones do not need much comment: in the former case the vowel/diphthong is pronounced on a level tone throughout, in the latter, the tone starts more intensely and falls off towards the end. The broken tone is segmented into two parts in a way which reminds one of a weakened Danish *stød (glottal catch).* In most areas in Latvia, however, only two intonational patterns are contrasted. Thus, in some parts of the country the falling and even intonations have fused while, in others the falling and the broken have done so. The latter pattern is the one found (among other places) in Riga, where an even and a falling intonation are distinguished.

In Contemporary Standard Latvian there are only very few *minimal pairs* with oppositions consisting in tone alone. For example: **zāle** [ˈzãːlɛ] *grass* vs. **zāle** [ˈzâːlɛ] *hall;* **loks** [luoks] *garlic* vs. **logs** [luôks] *window* vs. **loks** [lùoks] *bow.*

Tone may be said to be of much lesser importance than stress and quantity and can be more or less ignored by the student – the more so because of the variations in the system(s) mentioned above.

Chapter 2

THE NOUN
(Lietvārds)

Grammatical Categories

The grammatical categories of the Latvian noun are the same as those of the other nominal parts of speech (adjective, pronoun, numeral), namely *gender, number* and *case*. Some general remarks should be made about these categories:

1. Gender
(Dzimte)
There are only two genders, *masculine* and *feminine*, in Latvian. The masculine is the *unmarked* member of this binary opposition which is seen (among other things) in the fact that it is the masculine and not the feminine which has replaced the lost neuter in examples like **ir skaidrs, ka** *it is clear that* and others. To a certain extent, adverb forms ending in *-i* can be said to fill the gap after the loss of the neuter, in such constructions as **viņai ir auksti** *she feels* (lit. *is*) *cold,* vs. the unmarked masculine adjective form in **šodien ir auksts** *today it is cold,* cf. p. 207.

Nouns are said to have an *inherent* gender, expressed through agreement with modifiers (i. e. adjectives, participles, certain pronouns and numerals).

The rules for determination of gender in Latvian are simple, since there is a very high degree of harmony between *form* and *gender*. Thus, nouns ending in *-s/-š, -is* or *-us* (reflecting declensions 1-3, regarding which see below) are masculine, whereas the remainder, i. e. those ending in *-a, -e* or *-s* (i. e. declensions 4-6) are feminine. Exceptions are those very few nouns ending in *-a* which refer to male persons, where the gender is determined by the biological gender (sex), e.g. **puika** boy. Further, a few nouns ending in *-a* and *-e* can be of so-called *common gender* (Latvian *kopdzimte*), which means that they are of masculine gender if a male is referred to and feminine if a female is referred to, e.g. **nejēga** *idiot,* **bende** (usually masc.) *hangman*. First names and family names also comply with this rule.

Finally, it should be added that masculine nouns ending in -s/-š which denote occupations are regularly opposed to feminine nouns ending in -e (-a after -j), e.g. **direktors** *director* : **direktore** *woman director*, **skolotājs** *teacher* : **skolotāja** *woman teacher*. When sex is unmarked as, for example, in **mūsu fabrikā tagad jauns direktors** *at our factory there is now a new director (our factory now has a new director)* – the masculine form is used.

Observe finally oppositions such as **Kalniņš** *Mr. K.* : **Kalniņa** *Mrs./Miss K.*, **Lācis** *Mr. L.* : *Mrs./Miss L.* in Latvian *surnames*.

2. Number
(Skaitlis)

Latvian distinguishes between two grammatical numbers, *singular* and *plural*. A peculiarity of Latvian – along with Lithuanian – is the richness in plural nouns (so-called *pluralia tantum*, see p. 51 f. below).

3. Case
(Locījums)

Traditionally, grammars of Latvian have worked with a system of seven cases: the nominative, the genitive, the dative, the instrumental, the accusative, the locative and the vocative.

However, the status of the alleged instrumental (which is identical in form with the accusative in the singular, the dative in the plural) in modern Latvian can be questioned, since it occurs only with the preposition **ar** *with*. As will be seen in the chapter on prepositions, all prepositions in Latvian take the dative case in the plural. Thus, it seems legitimate to assert that in modern Latvian there is no instrumental, and that the preposition **ar** governs the accusative (as does, for example, **par** *about*). However, departing from distributional criteria, it is problematic to claim that a given preposition governs one case (variably the accusative, genitive or dative) in the singular and another (invariably the dative) in the plural. A solution to the dilemma would be to assume two systems; i. e. one involving an accusative$_1$, genitive$_1$, etc. for non-prepositional use, and another for prepositional use involving an accusative$_2$, genitive$_2$ etc., but this conclusion would pose an obstacle to making simple generalizations. In this grammar we will agree with Fennell (1975, pp. 41-48), Lötzsch (1978, pp. 667-671) and others, who have denied the existence of a separate instrumental case in Latvian, whence we arrive at a system consisting of six cases. For certain adverbialized residual traces of the Indo-European instrumental, see chapter 8: Case.

Of the remaining dependent (oblique) cases, it should be noted that the Latvian locative never occurs after a preposition. This is due to the fact that from a diachronic point of view, the locative in Latvian seems to originate in the old Indo-European locative, with superposition of an imbedded postpositional element with subsequent rearrangements. The vocative is, in virtue of its function as a case of address, somewhat apart, since (unlike the rest) it is not incorporated in the syntax of a sentence.

Declensional Types

The Latvian noun is usually grouped into 6 declensional classes, three masculine (1-3) and three feminine (4-6).

Thus, the Latvian noun inflection constitutes a symmetrical *gender-* determined system. The endings are vocalic in the nominative plural of the masculine declensions, consonantal in those of the feminine. In the nominative singular, the situation is almost the reverse, with consonantal endings in declensions 1-3, vocalic in 4 and 5.

In addition, the following generalizations should be mentioned:

All six declensions have the ending *-u* in the genitive plural. The dative(-instrumental) plural ends in *V(owel) + m,* the accusative and the locative plural in short *V + s* and long *V + s,* respectively. The vocative plural is always identical with the nominative plural.

Furthermore, in declensions 1-3 the plural case endings are the same. Declensions 4-6 have a different set of essentially identical plural endings; only the vocalic constituent varies.

Consonant alternations (according to the principles set forth on p. 24-25) are encountered in declensions 2, 5 and 6.

The *first declension* is characterized by *-s* or *-š* in the nominative singular and *-a* in the genitive, e.g. **vārds**, gen. **vārda** *word; name*, **ceļš**, **ceļa** *road, way*.

From an Indo-European point of view nouns of this class are labeled *o-* and *jo-*stems (Baltic/Latvian *a/ja-*stems). The *a-*type is attested in *vārds (< *vordas,* cf. p. 34 f.), that of *ja* in *ceļš* (reflecting **keljas* with palatalization of the *l* through the effect of the **j* and subsequent progressive palatalization of **s > š,* due to the *ļ*).

The *second declension* has the ending *-is* in the nominative singular: **brālis** *brother*.

From a historical perspective, nouns of this class form a subgroup of the 1st declension. They seem to reflect **-ijo-*(Baltic/Latvian *-ija-*)stems.

The *third declension* is characterized by *-us* in the nominative singular: **tirgus** *market*.

From a historical point of view *-us* nouns are referred to as *u-*stems. The plural forms are due to analogy from the **o-/jo* and **-ijo-*stems.

The *fourth declension* has -a in the nominative singular: **māsa** (hard variant) *sister,* **veļa**.(soft variant) *linen.*

Nouns of the fourth declension are, from a historical point of view, called *ā*- and *jā*-stems *(=* hard and soft variants respectively). As will be seen from the concrete paradigm presented on p. 46, this **ā* has in many instances been shortened according to the principles mentioned on p. 35 f. The long vowel in the locative sg. – here as with other stems – is the result of a special treatment. The *-u* in the accusative singular reflects **-ān < -ām*, cf. Phonology p. 32 and 35 f.

The *fifth declension* has the ending *-e* in the nominative singular: **egle** *fir.*

Nouns ending in *-e* are, in historical terms, referred to as *ē*-stems. Outside the Baltic subfamily they lack evident parallels. The principles for shortenings are the same as with *ā*-stems. In so far as they reflect **-ijā*-stems, *ē*-stems may, from a diachronic perspective, be said to form a subgroup of the **-ā*-stems (cf. 4th decl. above), thus parallelling **-o/jo-stems* (1st decl.) vs. **-ijo*-stems (2nd decl.).

The *sixth declension* is characterized by *-s,* both in the nominative and genitive singular: **zivs** *fish.*

From a diachronic point of view, the 6th declension represents a merger of *i*-stems and consonant stems. Positive evidence of the latter is observed in cases without a consonant shift in the gen. pl., cf. p. 48. Certain consonant stems have also merged with other stems.

First Declension

Example paradigms:
tēvs *father* (subset *a*) , **ceļš** *road, way* (subset *b*)

	SINGULAR		PLURAL	
N	tēvs	ceļš	tēvi	ceļi
G	tēva	ceļa	tēvu	ceļu
D	tēvam	ceļam	tēviem	ceļiem
A	tēvu	ceļu	tēvus	ceļus
L	tēvā	ceļā	tēvos	ceļos
V	tēv(s)	ceļš	tēvi	ceļi

Comments on the Paradigm

As mentioned on p. 42, this declension shows a split into two subsets, one ("hard" = subset *a*) with a nom. sg. ending in -*s*, the other ("soft" or palatalized (cf. p. 24 f.) = subset *b*) (often) ending in -*š*.

Nouns with a stem in -*j* have -*js* if they contain one of the suffixes -*ēj*- or -*(t)āj*-, e.g. **skolotājs** *teacher*. In other cases it seems difficult to give clearcut rules for the distribution between -*js* and -*jš*, cf., for example, **klājs** *deck* vs. **vējš** *wind*.

Observe the situation with stems ending in -*r*, as illustrated through the contrast **gars**, gen. **gara** *mind* : **karš**, gen. **kara** *war*. For an explanation, see pp. 24 and 42 above.

Notice further that *k* and *g* do not undergo a shift to *c and *dz before the the nom. pl. -*i* marker, e.g. **cilvēki** *men, persons*, **karogi** *flags, banners*.

e/*ē*-sounds have an open articulation if they occur in nouns of subset *a*, whereas they are spoken with a narrow *e*/*ē* in nouns belonging to subset *b*.

The Form of the Vocative

This form needs a special comment. As becomes apparent from the paradigm, it can either be identical with the nominative or end in -Ø (zero). The Ø-ending seems to be mandatory with the suffixes -*nieks*, -*(t)ājs* and -*ējs*, e.g. **skolnieks**, voc. **skolniek** *pupil*, **skolotājs**, voc. **skolotāj** *teacher*, **pircējs**, voc. **pircēj** *customer*.

For *reflexive nouns*, see p. 49 f..

Second Declension

Example paradigm:
brālis *brother*

	SINGULAR	PLURAL
N	brālis	brāļi
G	brāļa	brāļu
D	brālim	brāļiem
A	brāli	brāļus
L	brālī	brāļos
V	brāl(i)	brāļi

Consonant Alternations

As seen in the above paradigm, consonant alternations take place in all cases in the plural and in those cases which do not have the ending -i/-ī in the singular. Since a full table with concrete examples of the consonant shifts encountered with 2nd declensional nouns has been given on p. 24-25, there is no need to repeat this material here. The historical motivation for the shift has already been mentioned. It was also stated that words with $ķ/ģ$ before the -is in the nom. sg. retain the $ķ/ģ$ in all forms of the paradigm. There is no shift $*k > ķ, g > ģ$. The shift $r : ŗ$ is obsolete (cf. p. 25). It is encountered in older writings and can still be found in emigré publications.

The Form of the Vocative

As indicated in the **brālis**-paradigm, the vocative ends in -i or Ø (zero). The former alternative is the more frequent. With diminutives ending in -ītis it is practically an absolute rule: **brālītis**, voc. **brālīti**.

Irregularities in the 2nd Declension

1. The noun **viesis** (gen. **viesa**) *guest* does not have consonant alternation. The same applies to surnames ending in -*skis* (e.g. **Brunovskis**, gen. **Brunovska**), as well as to first names ending in -*tis* and -*dis*: **Atis** (gen. **Ata**), **Valdis** (gen. **Valda**). This rule, however, is not observed in compounds: **Visvaldis**, gen. **Visvalža**.

2. The noun **suns** *dog* follows the **brālis**-pattern except for the nom. sg., i. e. **suns, suņa, sunim, suni, sunī; suņi, suņu, suņiem, suņus, suņos**. The vocative is identical with the nominative.

3. The nouns **akmens** *stone*, **asmens** *blade*, **mēness** *moon*, **rudens** *autumn*, **sāls** *salt*, **ūdens** *water* and **zibens** *lightning* are declined like like *suns*, except that the genitive is identical with the nominative. The same applies to the vocative. The rest of the paradigm is identical to that of **brālis: akmens, akmens, akmeņam, akmeni, akmenī; akmeņi, akmeņu, akmeņiem, akmeņus, akmeņos**.

The reason for the above irregularities is that the nouns in question were originally consonant stems, cf. note to the sixth declension pp. 43 and 48. The same can be said about *viesis* (in point 1 above). This declension has become specialized to include feminines only.

Third Declension

This declension includes only a few nouns.
Example of paradigm:
tirgus *market*

	SINGULAR	PLURAL
N	tirgus	tirgi
G	tirgus	tirgu
D	tirgum	tirgiem
A	tirgu	tirgus
L	tirgū	tirgos
V	tirgu	tirgi

Other examples:
alus *beer*, **klepus** *cough*, **ledus** *ice*, **lietus** *rain*, **medus** *honey*, **vidus** *middle*, **Jēzus**, **Kristus**, **Mikus**.

Fourth Declension

Example paradigm:
māsa *sister*

	SINGULAR	PLURAL
N	māsa	māsas
G	māsas	māsu
D	māsai	māsām
A	māsu	māsas
L	māsā	māsās
V	mās(a)	māsas

There are no complications with respect to the declensional pattern of these feminine nouns, since hard and soft variants (p. 43), e.g. **māsa** and **veļa** ('linen'), are treated in exactly the same way. Care should, however, be taken for nouns designating males. They are of masculine gender (cf. p. 40) and have the ending *-am* (not *-*ai*) in the dative sg., e.g. **puika** : **puikam** *boy*, **Kabelka** : **Kabelkam** (family name).

The Form of the Vocative
There is a tendency towards dropping the *-a* in the vocative with *a*-nouns denoting persons (e.g. **Iev-Ø**, **mās-Ø**) as well as with nouns containing a suffix (**skolotāj-Ø**).

For *reflexive nouns*, cf. p. 49 f.

Fifth Declension

Example paradigm:
māte *mother*

	SINGULAR	PLURAL
N	māte	mātes
G	mātes	māšu
D	mātei	mātēm
A	māti	mātes
L	mātē	mātēs
V	māt(e)	mātes

Consonant alternations are restricted to the gen. pl. The shifts are those mentioned on p. 24-25. Other examples: **mašu: upe : upju** *river*, **zilbe : zilbju** *syllable*, **skrūve : skrūvju** *screw*, **bilete : bilešu** *ticket*, **priede : priežu** *pine(tree)*, **klase : klašu** *class*, **roze : rožu** *newspaper*, **egle : egļu** *fir(tree)*, **sēne : sēņu** *mushroom*, **skolniece : skolnieču** *pupil (female)*, **kundze : kundžu** *lady*, **sacīkstes : sacīkšu** (plural noun, cf. p. 51 f.) *contest*, **izloksne : izlokšņu** *dialect*, **zvaigzne : zvaigžņu** *star*.

There are a number of *exceptions* to this rule of consonant shift in the genitive plural, of which the following should be mentioned here: **mute : mutu** *mouth*, **pajumte : pajumtu** *shelter*, **kase : kasu** *booking-office; cashbox*, **pase : pasu** *passport*, **kaste : kastu** *box*. The consonants **ķ** and **ģ** remain unaltered, e.g. **puķe : puķu** *flower*, **ģeoloģe : ģeoloģu** *geologist (female)*. The same applies, according to the existing standard to *r* (**niere : nieru** *kidney*).

The motivation for using an unchanged consonant in words such as **mutu** and **pasu** is claimed to be the wish to avoid homonymy, cf. **mušu** (inflected form from **muša** *fly*), **pašu** (inflected form from **pats** *-self*). In other instances the reason for an unchanged consonant may be phonotactical; thus, for instance, *-st*-clusters are, as a rule, left unchanged.

As was also the case in the fourth declension, nouns designating males follow the biological sex, and are consequently masculine. They further parallel masculine *a*-nouns in requiring the ending *-em* instead of *-ei* in the dative sg., e.g. **bende : bendem** *hangman*, **Terje (Matiasens) : Terjem (Matiasenam)**.

THE NOUN

The Form of the Vocative
The guidelines for formation of the vocative are the same as with nouns of the fourth declension.

Sixth Declension

Example paradigm:
zivs *fish*

	SINGULAR	PLURAL
N	zivs	zivis
G	zivs	zivju
D	zivij	zivīm
A	zivi	zivis
L	zivī	zivīs
V	zivs	zivis

As in the case of *e*-nouns (5th declension), the nouns of this declension are also subject to the rule of consonant change in the genitive plural. In addition to the above **zivs : zivju, nakts : nakšu** *night*, **sirds : siržu** *heart*, **pils : piļu** *castle* should also be mentioned as illustrations.

There are, however, a good number of examples without a consonant shift in the genitive plural: **acs : acu** *eye*, **auss : ausu** *ear*, **balss : balsu** *voice*, **debess : debesu** *sky*, **uts : utu** *louse*, **valsts : valstu** *state*, **zoss : zosu** *goose*. The same holds true for the plural nouns (cf. p. 51 f.) **brokastis** *breakfast* and **Cēsis** (name of a town in Latvia), with genitive forms **brokastu** and **Cēsu** respectively.

The historical explanation for the presence vs. absence of consonant shift in the genitive plural of nouns of the sixth declension should be sought in the fact that *i*-stems and consonant stems have merged in this declension, cf. also note on p. 43. In the former a shift is expected, but not in the latter.

The *vocative* of this declension has the same form as the nominative.

Vacillations between Declensions
The following nouns have changed declensional type:
strīde *dispute, quarrel* from IV to I: **strīds**; **krogus** *pub, tavern* from III to I: **krogs**; **birze** *grove* from V to VI: **birzs**;

For the obsolete *pluralic feminine* nouns (with special endings) **dzirnus** *mill*, **pelus** *chuff* and **ragus** *sledge*, see under *Singular and Plural Nouns* below.

Summing up of the Endings
The following table shows the endings of the six declensions:

SINGULAR

Case/Decl.	Masculine			Feminine		
	I	II	III	IV	V	VI
N	-s, -š	-is, -s	-us	-a	-e	-s
G	-a	-(j)a, -s	-us	-as	-es	-s
D	-am	-im	-um	-ai	-ei	-ij
A	-u	-i	-u	-u	-i	-i
L	-ā	-ī	-ū	-ā	-ē	-ī
V	-Ø, -s, š	-Ø, -i	-u	-Ø, -a	-Ø, -e	-s

PLURAL

Case/Decl.	I	II	III	IV	V	VI
N	-i	-(j)i	-i	-as	-es	-is
G	-u	-(j)u	-u	-u	-(j)u	-(j)u
D	-iem	-(j)iem	-iem	-ām	-ēm	-īm
A	-us	-(j)us	-us	-as	-es	-is
L	-os	-(j)os	-i	-ās	-ēs	-īs
V	= N	= N	-= N	= N	= N	= N

Reflexive Nouns

A peculiarity of Latvian is its possession of reflexive nouns. They are all derived from verbs. The most frequent types have the ending *-šanās* and *-tājās* (both feminine). The latter has a corresponding masculine form in *-tājies*. Forms in *-umies* (masc.) are rare. Thus, reflexive nouns are restricted to the patterns of nouns of the 1st and (most frequently) 4th declensions. Their inflection is characterized by syncretism and defectiveness (in that dative and locative forms are lacking). Plural forms are possible, but rather rare.

Example of paradigms:
velējumies *desire (:* **vēlēties** *wish),* **piedalīšanās** *participation (:* **piedalīties** *participate).*

	4th declension (fem.)	1st declension (masc.)
SG		
N/V	dalīšanās	vēlējumies
G	dalīšanās	(missing)
D	(missing)	(missing)
A	dalīšanos	vēlējumos
L	(missing)	(missing)
PL		
N	dalīšanās	vēlējumies
G	dalīšanos	(missing)
D	(missing)	(missing)
A	dalīšanās	vēlējumos
L	(missing)	(missing)

Compared to the non-reflexive nouns of the 4th and 1st declensions, the endings of the reflexive nouns can be accounted for by implementation of the same strategy mentioned in connection with the long form adjective (p. 59).

Observe the difference between the minimal pairs non-reflexive **vēlēšanas** *elections* (: **vēlēt** *to elect*): reflexive **vēlēšanās** *desire* (: **vēlēties** *to wish*). An example of a reflexive noun is provided by the greeting formula **uz redzēšanos** (accusative) *good-bye* (: *redzēties lit. see one another, meet*).

Indeclinable Nouns

Words of this group are restricted to *nouns of foreign origin* with a morphological shape which makes it difficult to incorporate them in the mainstream (i. e. declinable) corpus of Latvian. Thus, nouns ending in -*u*/-*ū* and -*o* are not declined, e.g. **Tartu, Baku, Peru, ragū; auto, kino, radio, Hugo, Oslo**. The same is the case with nouns ending in the long vowels -*ī, ē* and *ā*: **Kirī** *Curie*, **pietā, Zolā; ateljē, foajē**. Nouns ending in -*i* are also undeclined: **Kapri, Deli**.

One might wonder why foreign words ending in -*i* have not been made declinable by joining the group of plural nouns (p. 51 f.). An analysis of *Kapr+i, Del+i* would, however, violate the very integrity of the foreign word. An exception is **Helsinki** which is treated like the plural noun **Talsi** (name of a city in Latvia), i. e. **Helsinkos** *in Helsinki*.

In a case like **birojs** *office* the integrity of the word has been preserved even though it has been made declinable. It has been adapted to Latvian inflection through stem expansion using *-j-*. A similar strategy is observed in **ale-j-a** *avenue*.

The *gender* of indeclinables ending in *-i, -u, -o* with *inanimate* reference is *masculine* (which according to p. 40 is the unmarked gender of Latvian). For deviations with so-called *associative* agreement, see chapter 13.

The gender is expressed through modifiers, e.g. **garšīgs ragū** *a tasty ragout*, cf. chapter 13.

The gender of *animate* indeclinables is determined by the biological gender (sex).

Singular and Plural Nouns
(Singularia and pluralia tantum)

By this term are meant nouns which possess either only 1) singular or 2) plural forms.

Group 1 (the *singularia tantum*) encompasses:

A. abstracts (like **mīlestība** *love*, **sirdsapziņa** *conscience*),

B collectives (e.g. **jaunatne** *youth*, **inteliģence** *intelligentsia*),

C. many designations of materials (**dzelzs** *iron*, **sudrabs** *silver*, **zelts** *gold*, **eļļa** *oil*, **darva** *tar*, **koks** *wood*, **mērce** *sauce*, **speķis** *fat*, **krējums** *cream*, **piens** *milk*, **sula** *juice*, **ievārījums/džems** *jam*),

D. names like **Latvija, Rīga** etc.

To group 2 (the *pluralia tantum*) belong:

A. designations of ceremonies, feasts and similar, like **svētki** *holiday*, **Ziemsvētki** *Christmas*, **Lieldienas** *Easter*, **kāzas** *wedding*, **bēres** *funeral*,

B. a good number of mass nouns like **alimenti** *alimony*, **milti** *flour*, **graudi** *corn, grain, cereal(s)*, **kvieši** *wheat*, **mieži** *barley*, **auzas** *oats*, **rudzi** *rye*, **rīsi** *rice*, **garšvielas** *spice*, **dilles** *dill*, **pētersīļi** *parsley*, **pipari** *pepper*, **pīšļi** *ashes* (pl. also in English), **putekļi** *dust*, **tauki** *grease*, **kvēpi/sodrēji** *soot*, **mēsli** *manure*, **ziepes** *soap*,

C. the directions of the compass: **dienvidi** *south*, **austrumi** *east*, **rietumi** *west*, **ziemeļi** *north*,

D. some geographical names like **Alpi** *The Alps*, **Atēnas** *Athens*, **Balkāni** *The Balkans*, **Himalaji** *The Himalayas*. Within Latvia itself there is a considerable amount of pluralic nouns designating cities, villages and suburbs, for example **Cēsis** (6th decl.), **Talsi, Broceni, Līvāni, Ķemeri, Baloži, Bulduri, Pumpuri, Jaunpļavas**.

E. a group of more or less heterogeneous nouns like **iesnas** *cold*, **bakas** *small-pox*, **masalas** *measles* (pl. also in English), **bikses** *trousers* (pl. also in English), **šorti** *shorts* (pl. also in English), **brokastis** (6th decl.) *breakfast*, **mēbeles** *furniture*, **vārti** *gate*, **durvis** (6th decl.) *door*, **ļaudis** (6th decl.) *people (= Leute)*, **meli** *lie*.

One is intrigued by the great number of plural nouns in Latvian, not least those referring to mass nouns (second group 2 B above). The reason for this development remains obscure. From a practical point of view, however, one should not take for granted that nouns within this semantic sphere are automatically pluralic. Regular nouns with both singular and plural forms are among others the designations of berries, fruits and vegetables.

Plural nouns in *-i* are declined in accordance with the masculine plural declension pattern, whereas those in *-as*, *-es* and *-is* follow the feminine declensions, i. e. the 4th, 5th and 6th respectively. Note that the three irregular feminine pluralic *u*-stem nouns **dzirnus**, **pelus** and **ragus** in contemporary Latvian (referred to on p. 48 above) have been replaced by the normalized **dzirnavas**, **pelavas** and **ragavas** respectively.

Word Formation of Nouns

Within word formation two main areas are distinguished: *derivation* and *composition*.

Suffixation is a derivational strategy (cf. I below), whereas *prefixation* is a compositional device (treated in II below). Some of the examples given in II are hybrids since a change in the suffix is also observed. In III non-prefixed compositions are discussed.

1. Suffixal Derivatives

A. Persons
a) deverbative:

-āj-s (masc.),**-āj-a** (fem.); **-tāj-s** (masc.), **-tāj-a** (fem.); **-ēj-s** (masc.), **-ēj-a** (fem.). With the help of these suffixes agentive nouns (*nomina agentis*) are derived from verbs. The derivational mechanism is regulated in such a way that **-tāj-** derives nouns from (the past stem of) verbs of conjugations II and III (see p. 104 f.), whereas **-ēj-** and its more rare variant **-āj-** derive nouns from (the past stem of) verbs of conjugation I. Examples: **lidotājs/-āja** *pilot* (: **lidot** (II) *fly*), **lasītājs/-āja** *reader* (: **lasīt** (III) *read*), **pircējs/-ēja** *customer* (: **pirk-u, pirkt** (I) *buy* – notice the automatic shift from *k* > *c* before the *-ē-* of the suffix), **dzērājs/-āja** *drunkard* (: **dzēr-u, dzert** (I) *drink*);

b) (mostly) denominal:
-niek-s/-iniek-s (masc.), **-niec-e/-iniec-e** (fem.). This suffix derives nouns designating occupation or origin from nouns; e.g., **dārznieks/dārzniece** *gardener* (: **dārzs** *garden*), **skolnieks/skolniece** *pupil* (: **skola** *school*), **vēsturnieks/vēsturniece** *historian* (: **vēsture** *history*), **zinātnieks/zinātniece** *scientist, scholar* (: **zinātne** *science*), **strādnieks/strādniece** *worker* (: **strādāt** *work*), **rīdzinieks/rīdziniece** *inhabitant of Riga* (: **Rīga** – observe the automatic shift of *g* > *dz* before the *-i-* of the suffix);

-iet-is (masc.), **-iet-e** (fem.). With the help of this suffix, nouns (most frequently designating nationality) are derived from nouns:
latvietis / **latviete** *Latvian* (: **Latvija** *Latvia*), **vācietis/vāciete** *German* (: **Vācija** *Germany*). Notice that the masculine counterpart of **-iete** in many cases is not **-ietis**, but **-is** or **-s**, for example, **amerikāniete** : **amerikānis** *American*, **angliete** : **anglis** (: **Anglija**) *English*, **igauniete** : **igaunis** (: **Igaunija**) *Estonian*, **norvēģiete** : **norvēģis** (: **Norvēģija**) *Norwegian*, **krieviete** : **krievs** (: **Krievija**) *Russian*, **somiete** : **soms** (: **Somija**) *Finland*, **zviedriete** : **zviedrs** (: **Zviedrija**) *Swede*.

B. Abstracts
-atn-e. This suffix derives nouns from adjectives: **jaunatne** *youth* (< **jauns** *young*);

-īb-a. With the help of this suffix nouns are derived from nouns and, more frequently, from adjectives and verbs. Examples: **tautība** *nationality* (: **tauta** *people*); **brīvība** *freedom* (: **brīvs** *free*), **slimība** *illness* (: **slims** *ill*), **veselība** *health* (: **vesels** *healthy*); **attīstība** *development* (: **attīstīt** *develop*), **cerība** *hope* (: **cerēt** *hope*), **palīdzība** *help* (: **palīdzēt** *help*);

-um-s. This suffix derives nouns from adjectives and verbs. For example: **aukstums** *cold(ness)* (: **auksts** *cold*) as well as **skaitstums** *beauty* (: **skaists** *beautiful*), **vecums** *age* (: **vecs** *old*), **jautājums** *question* (: **jautāt** *ask*), **notikums** *event* (: **notikt** *happen*), **teikums** *sentence* (: **teikt** *say*);

-šan-a, refl. **-šan-ās** (cf. also the verbal noun, p. 158). This suffix derives nouns from (the infinitive stem of) any verb, e.g. **krāšana** *collecting* (: **krā-t** *collect*), **lasīšana** *reading* (: **lasī-t** *read*), **piedalīšanās** *participation* (: **piedalī-ties** *participate*).

C. Collective Nouns

The suffix **-ība** can have collective meaning; for example, **labība** *crop* (: **labs** *good*), **biedrība** *association, Gesellschaft* (: **biedrs** *friend, comrade*).

D. Instrument

The following suffixes derive nouns from nouns and verbs:
-ulis/-ule: **zīmulis** *pencil* (: **zīmēt** *draw*), **klausule** *receiver* (telephone) (: **klausīties** *listen*);
-ējs: **(radio)uztvērējs** *(radio)receiver* (: **uztvert** *catch*);
-eklis: **grābeklis** *rake* (: **grābt** *rake*).

E. Location (Place)

a) deverbative:

-tava and **-tuve**: With the help of the former of these suffixes, nouns are derived from (the infinitive stem of) verbs of conjugations II and III (p. 104 f.), whereas the latter derives nouns from (the infinitive stem of) verbs of the Ist conjugation. Examples: **mazgātava** *laundry* (: **mazgāt** (II) *wash*), **frizētava** *hairdresser's saloon* (: **frizē-t** (II)), **lasītava** *reading room* (< **lasī-t** (III) *read*), **virtuve** *kitchen* (: (now obsolete) **vir-t** (I) *cook*);

b) (mostly) denominal:

The suffix **-nīca** derives nouns from (mostly) nouns and adjectives. For example: **-nīca**: **vārdnīca** *dictionary* (: **vārds** (noun) *noun*); **viesnīca** (noun) *hotel* (: **viesis** *guest*), **vasarnīca** *summer house* (: **vasara** (noun) *summer*); **slimnīca** *hospital* (: **slims** *ill*). Note **ēdnīca** *cafeteria* (: **ēst** (verb) *eat*).

F. Diminutives and Hypocorisms

Diminutives are abundantly present in Latvian. Here the suffixes **-iņ** and **-īt** should be mentioned first. With the help of the former, derivatives from declensions 1 and 4 are made, whereas the latter produces derivatives from declensions 2 and 5: **dēliņš** (: **dēls** I *son*), **māsiņa** (: **māsa** IV *sister*), **brālītis** (: **brālis** II *brother*), **upīte** (: **upe** V *river*). Another important suffix in this group is **-tiņ**, e.g. **akmentiņš** (: **akmens** *stone*), **gredzentiņš** (: **gredzens** *ring*).

Another diminutivizing suffix is **-ēns** (NB always pronounced with an open *-ē-*). Examples: **dēlēns** *sonny, little boy* (: **dēls** *boy*), **pelēns** *young/little mouse* (: **pele** *mouse*).

A sociolinguistically interesting feature of today's Latvian is the seemingly strong tendency among female speakers to use diminutives. Moreover, diminutives are characteristic of certain literary genres, above all folksongs and traditions based on them.

2. Prefixal Derivatives

As will become apparent from the subsequent material, a rich variety of prefix or prefix-like formations is encountered:

aiz-: **aizdegune** *nasopharynx*
ap-: **apkakle** *collar*
apakš-: **apakšzeme** *Hades; underground*
ār-: **ārzemes** *foreign countries*
at-: **atbalss** *echo*
bez-: **bezdarbība** *unemployment*
caur-: **caurskate** *radioscopy*
ie-: **ierosme** *initiative, impulse*
iekš-: **iekškabata** *inside pocket*
līdz-: **līdzjūtība** *compassion*
no-: **nodaļa** *department*
pa-: **pamāte** *stepmother*
pakaļ-: **pakaļdurvis** *backdoor*
pār-: **pārcilvēks** *superman*
pēc-: **pēctecis** *descendant, successor*
pie-: **piekraste** *coast*
pret-: **pretkalpojums** *service in return*
priekš-: **priekšvārds** *foreword, preface*
starp-: **starplaiks** *interval, break*
uz-: **uzplecis** *epaulette*
virs-: **virsraksts** *heading, title*
zem-: **zemapziņa** *subconsciousness*
ne-: **neuzmanība** *carelessness*

In some cases (with prefixes in the form of a preposition), the compound noun occurs in a petrified oblique case, e.g. **pirmskara** *prewar*, **pēcoperācijas** *postoperative* and is used in the function of an (undeclined) adjective (non-congruent attribute, cf. p. 201). Example: **pirmskara gados** *during prewar years*.

3. Non-Prefixal Compositions

Only a few examples need be given:
ziemassvētki (noun in the genitive case in the first component) *Christmas*, **lieldienas** (adjective without connecting or stem vowel in the first component) *Easter*, **pirmdiena** (ordinal number without connecting

or stem vowel in the first component) *Monday*, **ēdamistaba** (participle without connecting or stem vowel in the first component) *dining room*, **stāvlampa** (verb stem in the first component) *floor lamp*.

In translating, for example, *bookshop* into Latvian, one may be in doubt as to whether a suffixal formation **grāmatnīca**, the compound **grāmatveikals** (without connecting vowel) or a two word genitive combination **grāmatu veikals** would be preferable. The latter strategy is very frequent in Latvian, cf. **priežu mežs** *pine forest*, **sudraba karote** *silver spoon*, **kafijas tasīte** *coffee cup*, while German and the Nordic languages make much wider use of compounds (*Tannenwald, furuskog* etc.)

Chapter 3

THE ADJECTIVE

(Ipašības vārds)

General Characteristics
The Latvian adjective appears in two variants: the *short* (or indefinite) and the *long* (or definite) respectively.

Both forms are declined in *gender, number and case*. In addition, many adjectives (i. e. the qualitative ones) are inflected according to *degrees of comparison*, whereby the *comparative* and the *superlative* are distinguished from the *positive*.

Two *genders* are distinguished: *masculine* and *feminine*.

In the field of syntax the Latvian adjective distinguishes between three functions:
1. *attributive*,
2. *appositive*, and
3. *predicative*.

In functions 1) and 2) there is agreement (see chapter 13) between the noun and the adjective in gender, number and case whereas in 3) there is agreement with the subject with respect to gender and number (chapter 13). For the special case of the predicate adjective in debitive constructions, again chapter 13 should be consulted.

The Short (Indefinite) Form
The masculine form is declined like the first declension of nouns, the feminine like nouns of the fourth declension. As with the corresponding noun declensions two subtypes, *hard* (e.g. **liels**) and *soft* (e.g. **vājš** *weak*, **dziļš**, see pp. 44 and 46), are distinguished.

Example of paradigm:
liels (hard variant) *big*, **dziļš** (soft variant) *deep*.

THE ADJECTIVE

	M		F	
SG				
N	liels	dziļš	liela	dziļa
G	liela	dziļa	lielas	dziļas
D	lielam	dziļam	lielai	dziļai
A	lielu	dziļu	lielu	dziļu
L	lielā	dziļā	lielā	dziļā
PL				
N	lieli	dziļi	lielas	dziļas
G	lielu	dziļu	lielu	dziļu
D	lieliem	dziļiem	lielām	dziļām
A	lielus	dziļus	lielas	dziļas
L	lielos	dziļos	lielās	dziļās

Note: the short form adjective does not have vocative function.

The Long (Definite) Form
Example of paradigm:
lielais (hard variant) *big*, **dziļais** (soft variant) *deep*

	M		F	
SG				
N	lielais	dziļais	lielā	dziļā
G	lielā	dziļā	lielās	dziļās
D	lielajam	dziļajam	lielajai	dziļajai
A	lielo	dziļo	lielo	dziļo
L	lielajā	dziļajā	lielajā	dziļajā
V[1]	= N/A[1]	= N/A[1]	= N/A[1]	= N/A[1]
PL				
N	lielie	dziļie	lielās	dziļās
G	lielo	dziļo	lielo	dziļo
D	lielajiem	dziļajiem	lielajām	dziļajām
A	lielos	dziļos	lielās	dziļās
L	lielajos	dziļajos	lielajās	dziļajās
V = N				

[1] for the distribution between nominative and accusative forms, see p. 62, point 5 below.

The student will be able to derive correct long adjective forms from the corresponding short ones by applying one of the two following rules: 1) lengthening, 2) insertion of *-ai-* (before consonant), *-aj-* (before vowel). 1) consists of lengthening short vowels to a corresponding long monophthong (viz. *a* > *ā*) or to a diphthong (viz. *u* > *o, i* > *ie*). 2) is implemented in cases where the vowel is already long (monophthong or diphthong) or where there is no vowel at all (as in the masc. sg. nom.).

1) should be regarded only as a synchronic rule, which does not reflect diachronic data. From a diachronic point of view the process is rather the reverse: the short vowel and Ø-vowel endings of the short form adjectives (cf. p. 58 f.) are the result of shortenings and syncope. For a didactic and synchronic description, however, it is easier to move from the morphologically simpler forms represented by short form adjectives to the more complicated sets of endings found in the long form adjective paradigm. This approach to long form adjective inflection was introduced by T. G. Fennell (1980).

DEGREES OF COMPARISON

So far only forms of the positive degree have been given. In the following section the comparative and superlative degrees will be introduced.

1. The Comparative

The comparative is formed by adding the suffix **-āk-** to the positive stem. Both short (indefinite) and long (definite) forms are distinguished. The endings are the same as in the positive degree for all cases and both numbers and genders.

Examples of short form comparatives:

lab-s (masc.) → **lab-āk-s, lab-a** (fem.) → **lab-āk-a** *better,* **dziļ-š** (masc.) → **dziļ-āk-s, dziļ-a** (fem.) → **dziļ-āk-a** *deeper.*

Examples of long form comparatives:

lab-ais (masc.) → **lab-āk-ais, lab-ā** (fem.) → **lab-āk-ā, dziļ-ais** (masc.) → **dziļ-āk-ais, dziļ-ā** (fem.) → **dziļ-āk-ā**.

Note: for formal and/or semantic reasons comparative forms are not constructed from all types of adjectives. Thus, for example, many adjectives in **-isk-** do not form comparatives. However, when comparatives are found in Latvian, they are always of a synthetic type, e.g. **demokrātiskāka kustība** *a more democratic movement.* Analytic comparatives of the type *****vairāk demokrātiska kustība** are avoided.

2. The Superlative

The long form of the comparative can function also as a superlative.

Unambiguously superlative meaning is obtained by adding the prefix **vis-** *all* or the word **pats** (masc.)/**pati** (fem.) to (usually) the long form of the comparative:

vis-lab-āk-s/vis-lab-āk-ais (masc.), **vis-lab-āk-a/vis-lab-āk-ā** (fem.);

pats labākais/pati labākā *best, the (very) best.*

The stress is never on **vis-**, but will always rest on the the immediately following syllable: **vislabākais** [vis´laba:kais], cf. p. 36 above. For the declension of **pats/pati**, see p. 73.

SYNTAX OF THE ADJECTIVES

1. The Short (Indefinite) Form

As already mentioned, the Latvian adjective has the following three functions: (1) attributive, (2) appositive, and (3) predicative. This holds true for all degrees of comparison, i. e. the positive, the comparative, and the superlative.

Example of predicative function: **istaba ir maza** *the room is small.*

Note the use of the dative case in predicative function in general statements and when the logical subject is in the dative: **nav ir viegli būt mazam** (masc.)/**mazai** (fem.) *it is not easy (for anyone) to be small,* **Jānim nav viegli būt mazam** *it is not easy for John to be small,* **Ievai nav viegli būt mazai** *it is not easy for Eve to be small.*

In functions (1) and (2) the short (indefinite) form is used in the environments where the long (definite) form (see p. 61 f.) is not used. Thus, the short form is encountered in the *rhematic* function (p. 221), i. e. it designates something which is new or unknown in the situation or context ("new information"): **maza meitene** *a little girl* (note the indefinite article in English).

In function 3) the short form is used, e.g. **meitene ir maza** *the girl is small.*

Equivalents of English *than*

In Latvian both the preposition **par** + the accusative and the conjunction **nekā** (most frequently followed by the nominative) can correspond to English *than:* **viņa ir jaunāka par mani/nekā es** *she is younger than me.* In negative utterances **nekā** must be replaced by **kā**: **viņa nav/nebija jaunāka kā es** *she is/was not younger than me.*

In cases like **Latvijā cenas ir zemākas nekā Norvēģijā** *prices in Latvia are lower than in Norway* it is self-evident that only **nekā** *is* possible to the exclusion of the accusative governing preposition **par**.

The conjunction **nekā** is most frequently encountered in sentences of the type *x is -er than y* which explains its frequent affinity with the nominative. The etymological meaning of **nekā** is *not as/like*, cf. the above example **viņa ir jaunāka nekā es (esmu)** lit. *she is younger:(and) not as/like I (am)*. The etymology of this conjunction also explains the use of **kā** and not *****nekā** in negative utterances.

Equivalents of English *too*

For this purpose the adverb **pārāk** is used, e.g. **pārāk liels** *too big*. An alternative is to put the prefix **pār-** before the adjective (cf. p. 161): **pārliels** *too big*.

Equivalents of English *much, considerably* + the Comparative

Whereas the positive degree is strengthened by **ļoti** *very* (e.g. **ļoti interesanta filma** *a very interesting movie*), the comparative is strengthened by **daudz** *much* or the more bookish **ievērojami** *considerably*, cf., for example, **viņa ir daudz jaunāka nekā viņš** *she is much older than he* and **Eiropā dzīves līmenis ir ievērojami augstāks nekā Āfrikā** *in Europe the standard of living is considerably higher than in Africa*.

2. The Long (Definite) Form

The following guidelines should be given:
The long form of the adjective can be used only in the function of the attribute and the apposition, not in that of the predicative (except for the superlative, cf. p. 60 above).

Basically its function is *thematic*, i. e. it designates something which is known from the situation or context ("given information"): **Mazā meitene raudāja** *the little girl was crying* (note the definite article in English; in German, Dutch and the Nordic languages there is an additional lead in the form of the adjective *das kleine Mädchen, het kleine meisje, den lille piken* (Norwegian)).

In addition a set of formalized rules can be given. Thus, the use of the long (definite) form is obligatory:

1. after *demonstrative* pronouns: **šis jaunais direktors** *this young director*;

2. after *possessive* pronouns and possessors in the genitive case: **mana/viņu/tēva jaunā automašīna** *my/their/father's new car;*
3 a) after the pronoun **viss: visi jaunie pilsoņi** *all new citizens;*
3 b) after **abi/abas: abas mazās māsas** *both the little sisters;*
4. with *proper nouns*: **Pēteris Lielais** *Peter the Great,* **mazā Mārta** *little Martha;* **Melnā jūra** *the Black Sea.*
5. in *address* (vocative function): **Mīļie draugi** *dear friends.* Observe that in the singular the nominative form of the adjective is used if the noun is also in the nominative case (e.g. **mīļā māmiņa** *dear mother*); if the noun has a special vocative form, the adjective can either have the form of the nominative or the accusative, i. e. **mīļā māmiņ** or **mīļo māmin; mīļais tētiņ** or **mīļo tētiņ** *dear father*).
6. in the expression **vien- no [...]** *one of*: **viens no ievērojamākajiem** (comparative/superlative) **latviešu rakstniekiem ir Kārlis Skalbe** *Karlis Skalbe is one of the greatest Latvian writers.*
7. for the purpose of *substantivization* (see also below): **kurlmēmais** *deaf-and-dumb*, **Balto armija** *The White Army* (lit. "the army of the white").
8. in so-called *generic* use: **melnā birža** *the black market*, **baltais lācis** *white/polar bear*, **Sarkanais krusts** *The Red Cross.*

Note: Deviations from these rules can be found in fiction. In addition, it should be stated that the norm was less stable in older writings.

Observe finally that some few adjectives (e.g. **galvenais** *chief, main*; **pēdējais** *last*) are always long.

Substantivization

A certain amount of adjectives in Latvian can be substantivized (cf. also point 7 in the preceding paragraph). They are mostly in the *definite* (long) form.

Examples:

mazais *the little one (boy)*, **mazā** *the little one (girl)*, **sarkanādainie** *(the) Indians (redskins; lit. red skinny)*, **bagātie** *the rich (people)*; **brīvpratīgo armija** *an army of volunteers (voluntary)*; **kas jauns?** *anything new? what new(s)?;* **kurināmais** *fuel* (lit. sth. burnable), **dzeramais** *(something) potable/to drink.*

Notice the use of the (unmarked) masculine form (cf. p. 40) as a substitute for the (lost) neuter in the last three examples.

Although the last two examples quoted are *participles* (cf. p. 155) strictly speaking, nevertheless they have so much in common with adjectives that they can be included here.

Word Formation

For some general principles, see Nouns: Word Formation above.
1. Suffixal Derivatives
The most common suffixes are:

-īg-s/-a:
This suffix derives adjectives from nouns and other parts of speech, e.g. **spēcīgs/-īga** *vigorous* (: **spēks** *force, strength*) – notice the automatic shift of *k > c* before *-ī-*.

-isk-s/-a:
Adjectives with this suffix are derived from nouns, e.g. **mutisks** *oral* (: **mute** *mouth*), **zinātnisks** *scientific* (: **zinātne** *science*). It is frequently encountered with words of foreign origin: **demokrātisks** *democratic*, **elektrisks** *electric*, **ģeogrāfisks** *geographic*, **politisks** *political*. To some extent adjectives with this suffix can also be derived from other adjectives, cf. **lielisks** *remarkable, excellent* (: **liels** *big*).

-ain-s/-a:
This is a desubstantival suffix which designates a large amount/quantity of the substance indicated by the noun, e.g. **kalnains** *hilly, mountaneous* (: **kalns** *hill*), **miglains** *foggy* (: **migla** *fog*), **saulains** *sunny* (: **saule** *sun*), **putekļains** *dusty* (: **putekļi** *dust*).

-en-s/-a:
With this suffix adjectives are derived from nouns (of the 4th declension), cf. **varens** *mighty* (: **vara** *power*), **slavens** *famous* (: **slava** *fame, glory*). The *-e-* of the suffix has an open articulation (cf. rule 1 on p. 31 above).

-gan-s/a:
This is a deadjectival suffix with a modifying meaning, e.g. **zilgans** *bluish* (: **zils** *blue*).

-ād-s/-a:
This suffix derives adjectives from pronouns and numerals, e.g. **savāds** *strange* (: **savs** *my, his, her, its, our, your, their*), **vienāds** *identical* (: **viens** *one*).

-ēj-s/-a:
With this suffix adjectives can be derived from adverbs and nouns with reference (above all) to time and place: **tagadējs** *of today, nowadays* (: **tagad** *now*), **vidējs** *middle* (: **vidus** (noun) *middle*).

2. Prefixal Derivatives
Only some few examples should be given:
bez-: **bezjedzīgs** *meaningless*; **ne-**: **nemorāls** *immoral*; **pa-**: **pabāls** *somewhat pale*; **pār-**: **pārmērīgs** *too big*; **pret-**: **pretfašistisks** *antifascistic*, **starp-**: **starptautisks** *international*.

Note: Latvian may also use international prefixes such as, for example, **a-** (**amorāls**) and **anti-** (**antifašistisks**).

3. Non-Prefixal Compound Adjectives
As in the case of nouns, compounds are constructed without any connecting vowel between the components. Examples: **lietderīgs** *useful*, **garlaicīgs** *tiresome, boring*.

Reduplication
Latvian adjectives can be strengthened by reduplication, cf., for example, **gargars** *very long* (**gargara pasaka** *a very long fairy-tale*), **zilzils** *very blue*, **dziļdziļš** *very deep*.

Chapter 4

THE PRONOUN
(Vietniekvārds)

The pronoun is a heterogeneous word class. The following description will be based on more or less traditional classificatory criteria.

Many pronouns are characterized by a special pronominal inflection, whereas others follow the pattern of adjectives.

In terms of syntax a distinction is often made between adjectival and non-adjectival (substantival) pronouns. Whereas the former are subordinated to a head noun in gender, number and case (attributive function), the latter can be used "independently" like a noun. Certain pronouns can be used in both the adjectival and substantival function.

1. Personal Pronouns

Paradigms:

SINGULAR

	1st person	2nd person	3rd person	3rd person
N	es	tu	viņš	viņa
G	manis	tevis	viņa	viņas
D	man	tev	viņam	viņai
A	mani	tevi	viņu	viņu
L	manī	tevī	viņā	viņā

PLURAL

	1st person	2nd person	3rd person	3rd person
N	mēs	jūs	viņi	viņas
G	mūsu	jūsu	viņu	viņu
D	mums	jums	viņiem	viņām
A	mūs	jūs	viņus	viņas
L	mūsos	jūsos	viņos	viņās

In the polite function the forms **Jūs, Jūsu** etc. are written with a capital letter. The same is often the case with **Tu, Tevis** etc. in written correspondence.

The reflexive personal pronoun has the following forms:

N (lacking)
G sevis
D sev
A sevi
L sevī

The reflexive pronoun does not have a nominative form and is therefore incapable of being part of the subject syntagm. It always refers to the (nominative) subject.

Further, its use is not restricted to the 3rd person alone. It can refer to the 1st and 2nd persons as well, cf. the folowing example:
es redzu sevi spogulī *I am looking at/seing myself in the mirror.*

2. Possessive Pronouns

A. Non-Reflexives

The pronouns of this class might also be labeled personal, along with the preceding ones. It has, however, become customary to group them under a separate heading as *possessive* pronouns, according to their specialized function. The group encompasses **mans/-na** *my/mine*, **tavs/-va** *your(s)*, **savs/-va** *one's own* (declined as short form adjectives, cf. p. 57-58) and **viņa** *his*, **viņas** *her(s)*, **mūsu** *our(s)*, **jūsu** *your(s)*, and **viņu** *their(s)*, which are all undeclined regardless of the gender, number and case of the word to which they refer.

The latter five are merely the genitive case of the corresponding personal pronouns (see point 1 above). The others (**mans, tavs, savs**) are declined like the short form of the adjective (type masc. **labs**, fem. **laba**).

Examples using possessive pronouns:

mans/mūsu brālis; mani/mūsu brāļi; mana/mūsu māsa; manas /mūsu māsas / mana/mūsu grāmata; manas/mūsu grāmatas *my / our brother / brothers / sister / sisters / book / books;* **par tavām grāmatām** *about your books;* **šī grāmata ir jūsu** *this book is yours,* **šeit ir viņas brālis** *here is her brother.*

B. Reflexives

The reflexive possessive refers to the subject of the sentence regardless of the person and number expressed by the subject, i. e. **es paņēmu savu grāmatu, tu paņēmi savu grāmatu, viņš/viņa paņēma savu grāmatu, mēs paņēmām savas grāmatas, jūs paņēmāt savas grāmatas, viņi/viņas paņēma savas grāmatas** *I took my book, you took your book, he took his book, she took her book, we took our books, you took your books, they took their books*.

The **sav**-form, like its non-possessive counterpart - **sevis, sevi** etc. (p. 66), can never be part of the subject syntagm. Thus, a sentence such as **sava grāmata ir te* is impossible. Only when the meaning is that of *one's own*, is **sav-s/-a** encountered in the function of a subject, e. g. **katram ir sava grāmata** *each one has his/her/their own book*.

3. Reciprocal Pronouns

Latvian has two reciprocal pronouns, **viens/viena otr-** and **cits/cita cit-**, both meaning *each other, one another*. There is, however, a difference in use in that **viens/viena otr-** is applied with reference to two (or pairs) whereas **cits/cita cit-** refers to more than two.

The first element (**viens/viena; cits/cita**) is always in the nominative case and singular in number, whereas the case of the second (**otr-, cit-**) is determined by its syntactic position[1]. Both elements are inflected according to gender.

Examples:

Viņi mīl cits citu[1] *they love each other* (**viņi** either points to a group of males or a mixed group consisting of males and females – to designate a group of females alone, the form **viņas** must be used); **Aina un Pēteris mīl viens otru** *Aina and Peter love one another*; **viņi sēdēja viens blakus otram** (i. e. **viņi sēdēja: viens blakus otram**) *they were sitting next to each other*; **Aina un Anda sēdēja viena blakus otrai** *Aina and Anda were sitting next to one another*. If one says **mēs patīkam viens otram** *we like each other*, **mēs** (*we*) can imply more than two, but in that case it seems that one is referring to pairs of two and two.

---

[1] the construction can probably be understood in the light of historical syntax through a bifurcation into two sentences **Viņi mīl* and **Viens* (nominative subject) **(mīl) otru** *They love. One (loves) the other*. The two sentences were then combined into one unit: **Viņi mīl viens otru** with deletion (omission) of the second **mīl**.

4. Demonstrative Pronouns

The demonstrative pronouns are the following:
šis/šī *this*
tas/tā *that*
šāds/šāda *such (as this)*
tāds/tāda *such (as that)*

šis/šī and **tas/tā** have the following inflection:

	Masculine				Feminine			
	S G		P L		S G		P L	
N	šis	tas	šie	tie	šī	tā	šīs /šās	tās
G	šī /šā	tā	šo	to	šīs	tās	šo	to
D	šim	tam	šiem	tiem	šai	tai	šīm	tām
A	šo	to	šos	tos	šo	to	šīs /šās	tās
L	šajā	tajā	šajos	tajos	šajā	tajā	šajās	tajās
	šai	tai	šais	tais	šai	tai	šais	tais
	šinī	tanī	šinīs	tanīs	šinī	tanī	šinīs	tanīs

šāds/šāda and **tāds/tāda** are declined in the same way as the short form of the adjective (type **labs/laba**).

5. The Anaphoric Pronoun of the 3rd Person

This pronoun is identical in form and inflection with the demonstrative pronoun **tas/tā** in section 4 and corresponds to English "it" (sg.), "they" (pl.). In grammars of Latvian this function is usually not found under a separate heading. The anaphoric pronoun refers to and agrees in gender and number with a noun (common noun or proper name) mentioned in the preceding sentence:

Rīga ir Latvijas galvaspilsēta. Tajā ir apmēram viens miljons iedzīvotāju
Riga is the capital of Latvia. It has (lit. in it (there) is/are) *about one million inhabitants.*

Govs ir labs dzīvnieks. Tā mums dod pienu
The cow is a good animal. It gives us milk.

As illustrated by the two examples just quoted, the **tas/tā** pronoun in anaphoric function is used with reference to non-persons (things and animals). If a person is referred to, the personal pronoun (**viņš/viņa**) is usually applied, e. g.

Pagalmā spēlējās daži bērni. Viņi bija latvieši

In the yard there were some children playing. They were Latvians.

The **tas/tā** anaphoric pronoun can also refer to animate beings, but primarily in an *introductory* function:
Istabā ienāca meitene. Tā bija Jāņa māsa
A girl entered the room. It was John's sister.

If **viņa** is used instead of **tā** in the last sentence quoted, the translation would be as follows: *She was John's sister.* As is seen from this example the personal pronoun (**viņa**) also has an anaphoric function.

6. Interrogative and Relative Pronouns

The following pronouns – all of them characterized by an initial *k-* – can have either an interrogative or a relative function:

kas *who, what*
kurš/kura *who, which*
kāds/kāda *what (kind of)*
The last is more or less restricted to the interrogative function

kas is declined like the *masc. sg.* of **tas** (see above). Note, however, that **kas** is not used in the locative. In that case it is replaced by the local adverb **kur?** *where?* or the locative of **kurš** (i. e. **kurā**).

kurš/kura and **kāds/kāda** are inflected in the same way as short form adjectives (type **labs/laba**).

Interrogative Function
Kas (nom.) **tas ir?** *Who/what is that?*
Ko (acc.) **tu lasi?** *What are you reading?*
Ar ko (acc.) **jūs esat runājis?** *With whom did you speak?*
Kam (dat.) **jūs devāt rozes?** *To whom did you give the roses?*

Kurš/kura is often accompanied by the preposition **no** to designate *who in a certain group*, e. g.
Kurš no brāļiem atnāks? *Who of the brothers will come?*
Kura no māsām atnāks? *Who of the sisters will come?*

Kāds/kāda is used attributively (cf. pp. 60 and 201 f.):
Kāds šodien laiks? *What kind of weather is there today?*
Kādu grāmatu tu lasi? *What kind of book do you read?*

Notice the locution **kas par** + accusative: *what kind of* (German *was für ein*): **kas (tas ir) par dzīvnieku?** *what kind of animal (is that)?*

Relative Function
The relative pronoun agrees with its correlate in gender and number, whereas case is determined by its function (subject, object etc.) in the subordinate clause, e. g. **te ir grāmata** (fem. sg. nom.), **kuru/ko** (fem. sg. acc. = object) **tu man devi** *here is the book (which) you gave me*. Unlike in English (and some other languages, among them the Nordic languages), the relative pronoun can never be omitted in Latvian.

The genitive of **kas** is used only after prepositions, e. g. **to cilvēku, pie kā mēs bijām vakar, sauc Valdmanis** *the person with whom we were yesterday, is called Valdmanis.*

In the non-prepositional function of *whose?* the genitive of **kurš** is used, i. e. **kura** for the masc. sg., **kuras** for the f. sg. and **kuru** for the plural (both genders): **te ir puika, kura tēvs [...]** *here is the boy whose father [...]*, **te ir meitene, kuras tēvs [...]** *here is the girl whose father [...]*, **te ir bērni, kuru tēvs [...]** *here are the children whose father [...].*

Irrespective of the fact that **kas** is formally singular, it can be used with reference to nouns in plural form as well, e. g.

studenti, kas (or **kuri**) **piedalījās ekskursijā [...]** *the students who participated in the excursion [...]*

Kas can be regarded as the main (and unmarked) relative pronoun. It should be replaced by **kurš/kura** only when the gender and number reference will be unclear.

7. Indefinite Pronouns

The most important indefinite pronouns in Latvian are:

kāds/kāda *somebody, anybody; some, any*
kas *something, anything*

For inflection, see preceding point (6).

kaut kāds/kāda *somebody*
kaut kas *something*
kaut kurš/kura *some*

jebkāds/jebkāda [jɛp′ka:d-] *anybody*
jebkas [jɛp′kas] *anything*

dažs (labs) / daža (laba) *some*

More rarely used are:
diezin kāds/kāda *anybody* (lit. *god knows who* (< **dievs zin**))
diez(in) kas *anything* (lit. *god knows what*)
nez(in) kāds/kāda *anybody*
nez(in) kas *anything*

The elements **kaut, jeb-, diez(in)** and **ne(zin)** are not inflected. The elements **kāds/kāda, kurš/kura** and **dažs/daža** are declined as short form adjectives (type **labs/laba**). **Kas** is declined like the masc. sg. of **tas** (cf. paragraph 5 above).
Examples:
Dzirdu kādu runājam *I hear somebody coming*
Atnāca kāds cilvēks/kādi cilvēki *There came a man/some men*
Viņš paņēma kādu grāmatu *He took a/some book (or other)*
Ja kas, (tad) zvanī *If there is something, (then) give me a call*
Ja kas kaut notiek *If something happens*
Iedod man kaut ko padzerties! *Give me something to drink!*
Iedod man kaut ko dzerāmu! *Give me something to drink!*
Viņš palika bez jebkādiem līdzekļiem *He remained without any means (at all)*
Viņš palika bez jebkā *He remained without anything (at all)*
Dažu vakaru tēvs atgriezās vēlu *Some (one) evening father came back lat*
Pagalmā spēlējās daži bērni *In the yard there were some children playing*
Aizbraukt uz dažām dienām *Go away (leave) for some days*
Man ir dažas fotogrāfijas *I have some photos*
Dažs labs to domā *Some think that (that way)*

These examples illustrate which of the indefinite pronouns can be used independently and/or attributively. They also demonstrate the distribution between animate and inanimate reference.

The pronoun **kāds** in attributive function (pp. 57 and 60) can have a meaning close to that of an indefinite article in Germanic and Romance languages.

It may often be difficult to choose between **kāds** and **dažs**. They are not (always) interchangeable. Thus, it is impossible to replace **daži** by **kādi**, **dažām** by **kādām** or **dažas** by **kādas** in the last examples given above. **Kāds** seems to have preserved something of the quality-meaning (cf. **tāds**), whereas **dažs** is more neutral.

Moreover, the **daž**-pronoun can have a pejorative or ironic shade of meaning as, for example, in **daži no mums vakar nebija skolā** *some of us were not at school yesterday.*

Note: For rendering English 'not any', Nordic (Norwegian) 'ikke noe(n)' in Latvian a *negative* pronoun (see next point), not an indefinite one must be used.

8. Negative Pronouns

The negative pronouns in Latvian include the following:

neviens / neviena [nɛ'vien-] *nobody*
nekas [nɛ'kas] *nothing*

Observe that **nekas** cannot mean *nobody*, only *nothing*!

nekāds / nekāda [nɛ'ka:d-] *no(ne)*

neviens / neviena are declined as the masc. and fem. sg. short forms of the adjective (type **labs / laba**).
nekas is declined as the masc. sg. of **tas** (cf. paragraph 4 above)
nekāds / nekāda is – beside in gender – also declined in number (both singular and plural forms). Its declension is that of the short form adjectives (**labs / laba**).

Illustrations of use:
neviens nebija pie mums *nobody has been with us*
šādu pārtiku nevienā / nekādā veikalā šeit nav *such products are not to be found in any shop here*
viņš nekad ne par vienu nerunā *he never talks about anybody*
mums gandrīz nekā nav *we have almost nothing*

The examples show that 1) negative pronouns require an additional negation with the verb (so-called "double negation"), 2) negation + an indefinite pronoun in English (and the Nordic languages) must be rendered by a negative pronoun + negation in Latvian, 3) **neviens** can be used both in substantival (i. e. independently without accompanying noun) and adjectival (attributive) function, 4) **neviens** is split by prepositions (with the group written in three words).
Observe constructions of the type **viņam nav ar ko runāt** *he has nobody to talk with.*

9. Other Pronouns

abi/abas *both*
cits/cita *another*
otrs/otra *(the) other*
katrs/katra *each, every*
ikviens [ik'viens] *everybody*
viss/visa *all, (the) whole; everything*
viens/viena *no one of*
pats/pati *-self/-selves*
tas pats / ta pati *the (very) same*

These pronouns are declined as short form adjectives with the exception of **pats/pati** which is declined as follows:

	Masculine		Feminine	
	SG	PL	SG	PL
N	pats	paši	pati	pašas
G	paša	pašu	pašas	pašu
D	pašam	pašiem	pašai	pašām
A	pašu	pašus	pašu	pašas
L	pašā	pašos	pašā	pašās

Illustrations of use:
Pie mājas aug divi ozoli, abi tēva stādīti *At the house two oaktrees are growing, both (of them) planted by my father*
atrast citus draugus *to find other friends*
izlasīt grāmatu no viena gala līdz otram *to read a book from one end to the other*
To var izdarīt ikviens/katrs bērns *Every child can do that (even a child can do that)*
Ikviens te noder par palīgu *Everybody will be able to help*
visu dienu (acc.) *all day long, the whole day*
Blaumanis ir viens no svarīgākajiem latviešu rakstniekiem *Blaumanis is one of the most important Latvian writers*
Viss (for the gender, see p. 40) **ir kārtībā** *Everything is okay*
Ko dari, to dari pats! *What you do, do (it) yourself*
Pie paša mājas ir darziņš *Close to the house there is a small garden*
Es saku to pašu *I say the same*

Chapter 5

NUMERALS
(Skaitļa vārds)

Numerals are divided into *cardinal* and *ordinal numbers*, with *fractions* as a subgroup of the latter.

The inventory of both cardinal and ordinal numbers in Latvian are presented in the following table:

	Cardinal Numbers	**Ordinal Numbers**
0	nulle	nultais
1	viens	pirmais
2	divi	otrais
3	trīs	trešais
4	četri	ceturtais
5	pieci	piektais
6	seši	sestais
7	septiņi	septītais
8	astoņi	astotais
9	deviņi	devītais
10	desmit(s)	desmitais
11	vienpadsmit	vienpadsmitais
12	divpadsmit	divpadsmitais
13	trīspadsmit	trīspadsmitais
14	četrpadsmit	četrpadsmitais
15	piecpadsmit	piecpadsmitais
16	sešpadsmit	sešpadsmitais
17	septiņpadsmit	septiņpadsmitais
18	astoņpadsmit	astoņpadsmitais
19	deviņpadsmit	deviņpadsmitais
20	divdesmit	divdesmitais
21	divdesmit viens	divdesmit pirmais
22	divdesmit divi	divdesmit otrais
30	trīsdesmit	trīsdesmitais

40	četrdesmit	četrdesmitais
50	piecdesmit	piecdesmitais
60	sešdesmit	sešdesmitais
70	septiņdesmit	septiņdesmitais
80	astoņdesmit	astoņdesmitais
90	deviņdesmit	deviņdesmitais
100	simt(s)	simtais
200	divsimt/divi simti	divsimtais
300	trīssimt/trīs simti	trīssimtais
400	četrsimt/četri simti	četrsimtais
500	piecsimt/pieci simti	piecsimtais
1.000	tūkstoš/tūkstotis	tūkstošais
2.000	divtūkstoš/divi tūkstoši	divtūkstošais
5.000	piectūkstoš/pieci tūkstoši	piectūkstošais
100.000	simttūkstoš/simt tūkstoši	simttūkstošais
1.000.000	miljons	miljonais
2.000.000	divi miljoni	divmiljonais

Note: In the chart the forms of the (declinable) cardinal numbers are given in the masculine. The ordinal numbers are given in the masc. sg. of the long form.

1. Cardinal Numbers

For inventory, see table above.

A. Declension

The cardinal numbers in Latvian are partly *declinable*, partly *indeclinable*.

The *declinable* are all those with *flectional endings* (e. g. **viens/viena, divi/divas, deviņi/deviņas, simts, divi simti, tūkstotis**) whereas numbers *without flectional endings* (e. g. **desmit, vienpadsmit, divdesmit, simt, divsimt, tūkstoš**) are *indeclinable*.

a) Declinable:
Nulle is declined as a noun of the fifth declension.
Viens (masc.)/**viena** (fem.) is treated like the singular of short form adjectives (cf. p. 57 f. – type **labs/laba**). Plural forms are also

possible, namely in connection with plural nouns (cf. p. 51 f. above and p. 218 below).

Divi (masc.)/**divas** (fem.) is declined like the plural of short form adjectives (type **labi/labas**). The same is the case with **abi/abas** *both* (which is not really a numeral, cf. p. 73), **četri/četras, pieci/piecas, seši /sešas, septiņi/septiņas, astoņi/astoņas,** and **deviņi/deviņas**. The same also holds true for

Trīs, but this paradigm shows a couple of alternative contracted forms and should be given separately:

	M	F
N	trīs	trīs
G	triju	triju
D	tri(jie)m	tri(jā)m
A	trīs	trīs
L	trijos/trīs	trijās/trīs

Simts and **miljons** are declined as nouns of the 1st declension whereas **tūkstotis** follows the pattern of nouns of the 2nd declension. Observe the *t : š* shift: **tūkstotis**, but gen. **tūkstoša**, dat. **tūkstotim** etc. according to the principle valid for second declensional nouns (p. 44 f.).

b) Indeclinable
All other cardinal numbers are indeclinable.

B. Syntax

Declinable cardinal numbers (with the exception of **simts, tūkstotis, miljons**) have *adjectival* syntax, i. e. they agree in *gender, number* and *case* with an accompanying quantified noun: **man ir divi lati / divas grāmatas** *I have two lats / two books,* **es iedevu divus latus / divas grāmatas savam draugam** *I gave two lats / two books to my friend,* **viņš ir atbraucis uz Rīgu ar diviem latiem / divām grāmatām** *he has come to Riga with two lats / two books.*

Indeclinable cardinal numbers as well as **simts, tūkstotis,** and **miljons** have *substantival* syntax, i. e. they behave like nouns by requiring the genitive (plural) of the accompanying noun, e. g. **(man ir) desmit/vienpadsmit/divdesmit/simts/tūkstotis/miljons latu/grāmatu** *(I have) ten/eleven/twenty/hundred/thousand/one million lats/books* (like **ceļasoma latu/grāmatu** *a suitcase of lats/books*, cf. the partitive adnominal genitive, p. 169 below).

The claim that indeclinable numerals require a following genitive needs an important modification since

1) this rule is restricted to cases where the numeral – or to be more precise, the numeral + noun group – occupies a nominative or accusative position, i. e. as subject or object to a transitive verb (i. e. an accusative-governing verb) or in the function of an adverbial of time; in other oblique cases the following noun must be in the genitive, dative or locative, depending on the syntactic environment;

2) in nominative (and partly accusative) position the noun can also be in the nominative (or accusative with accusative representation).

Illustrations:

subject function:
gen. or nom. **atnāca desmit zēnu/meiteņu** or **zēni/meitenes**
ten boys / girls came

Note: the nominative construction is mandatory when a declinable attribute precedes the group, e. g. **visi desmit zēni/meitenes atnāca** *all ten boys/girls came*.

object function:
after transitive verbs:
gen. or acc. **mēs sastapām desmit zēnu/meiteņu** or **zēnus/meitenes**
we met ten boys/girls

When preceded by a declinable attribute, the group must be in the accusative case: **mēs sastapām visus desmit zēnus / visas desmit meitenes** *we met all ten boys / girls*.

adverbial of time:
preferably accusative **viņi bija / pavadīja desmit dienas Rīgā**
they were / spent ten days in Riga

genitive function:
desmit valstu okupācija
occupation of ten states

dative function:
> **viņš palīdzēja desmit zēniem / meitenēm**
> he helped ten boys/girls

locative function:
> **viņš atrada viņas fotogrāfiju desmit grāmatās**
> *he found her photograph in ten books*

Note: The numerals 10-20 are declined only in connection with the hours of the day (the clock), e. g. **viņa atnāca desmitos / ap desmitiem** *she came at ten / around ten (o'clock),* cf. the question **cikos viņa atnāca?** *at what time did she come?* Thus, constructions of the type ***ar desmitiem zēniem** *with ten boys,* ***desmitos dārzos** *in ten gardens* are impossible. For further expressions of hours of the day (the clock), see chapter 10.

In cases with quantifiers like **daudz** *much,* **maz** *little,* **vairāk** *more* and similar (cf. p. 170) a grammatical conflict may arise. The following guidelines should be given: the genitive governing power is lost in the plural after prepositions, cf. **ar daudz grāmatām** *with many books* (alternative construction: **ar daudzām grāmatām**). In the singular one will find **ar daudz naudas** *with much money,* but **ar daudz naudu** can also be heard.

In *compound* numbers only the *last unit is declined with respect to case*: **šī grupa sastāv no deviņi simti** (or **deviņsimt**) **piecdesmit sešiem cilvēkiem/no deviņsimt piecdesmit viena cilvēka** *this group consists of nine hundred and fifty-six/of nine hundred and fifty one people (persons).*

Finally, mention should be made of the use of nominative forms in object position, cf., for example **nopirkt divi kilogrami miltu** *buy two kilogrammes of flour.* Constructions of this type are somewhat archaic. The norm of contemporary Standard Latvian would prescribe: **divus kilogramus**. In a historical perspective the nominative in question is likely to reflect a (reinterpreted) dual form.

2. Ordinal Numbers

A. Declension

The ordinal numbers in Latvian are all declinable. They are inflected as *long form (definite) adjectives,* i. e. according to *number, gender and case.*

In a *compound* ordinal number only the last number is ordinal and is declined. The preceding numbers have the appearance of undeclined cardinal numbers, e. g. **tūkstoš deviņsimt deviņdesmit piektais (gads) / tūkstoš deviņsimt deviņdesmit piektā (gada)**, lit. *(the) one thousand nine hundred and ninety fifth (year)*.

B. Syntax

Ordinal numbers have adjectival syntax, i. e. they agree with the head noun in gender, number and case, e. g.

viņa jau desmitajā klasē *she is already in the tenth form*

Years and dates are expressed by ordinal numbers.
To answer the question *when?* the *locative* case is used for the *year*: **viņš ir dzimis tūkstoš deviņsimt deviņdesmit sestajā gadā** *he is born in the year 1996*.

The *locative* is also used for answering the *when*-question for *dates*, e. g. **viņš atbrauca piecpadsmitajā augustā** *he arrived on August 15*.

In the case of a *month-year combination* with a *when*-question, the *date* appears in the *locative case* whereas the year has the form of a *preposited adnominal genitive* (cf. p. 158 below): **viņš ir dzimis tūkstoš deviņsimt deviņdesmit sestā gada piecpadsmitajā augustā** *he is born on August 15, 1996*.

For translating a sentence like 'today is August 15, 1996' the *nominative*, not the locative, of the date expression must be used (because syntactically it occupies the function of a grammatical subject): **šodien ir tūkstoš deviņsimt deviņdesmit sestā gada piecpadsmitais augusts**.

In written exposition numerals are, of course, usually encountered instead of written-out number words.

3. Fractions

A. Non-decimal Fractions

Fractions in Latvian are formed with the *numerator* expressed by a cardinal number in the feminine gender and the *denominator* by an ordinal number also in the feminine gender (to agree with the noun **daļa** *part*), e. g. **divas trešdaļas** (or **divas trešās daļas**) *two third(s)*.

The noun of which something is a fraction, is in the *genitive (singular)* irrespective of the case in which the fraction occurs, e. g. **ar divām trešdaļām akcijas** *with two thirds of a share*.

Certain fractions (esp. 1 1/2, 2 1/2) are frequently expressed through the combination of the noun **pus-** *half* + (the genitive) of the *accented* ordinal number **-otr-**, e. g. (**šeit ir** / **viņš izdzēra**) **pusotra (litra (alus))** (here is / he drank) *one and a half (liters (of beer))* for the masc., (**šeit ir** / **viņš izdzēra**) **pusotras (pudeles)** *one and a half (bottles)* for the fem. gender.

If the group represents another case than the nominative or the accusative syntactically, the element **-otr-** appears in the appropriate case, e. g. **ar pusotrām pudelēm** (dat. pl.) **alus** (gen. sg.) *with one and a half bottles of beer*. The inflection is that of an adjective (type **labs/ laba**).

B. Decimal Fractions

There is, of course, also another way of handling fractions, namely as decimal units, e. g. 15.03, which is read **piecpadsmit komats** (comma) **nulle trīs**.

Chapter 6
THE VERB
(Darbības vārds)

Grammatical Categories

The grammatical categories of the Latvian verb are as follows:

1) *number*, i. e. singular and plural.

2) *person*. Latvian distinguishes between three persons: the 1st, 2nd and 3rd.
Note: a peculiarity of Latvian (as well as Lithuanian) is the lack of formal distinction between the 3rd p. sg. and pl.

3) *gender* which is marginal since it is relevant only for participle forms. Two genders are distinguished: *masculine and feminine*.

4) *tense*. The Latvian indicative has six tenses: three simple, the *present, past* and *future*; and three compound, the *present perfect, past perfect* and the *future perfect*.

5) *mood*. Beside the unmarked *indicative,* Latvian distinguishes the marked *imperative*, the *subjunctive*, the *relative* and the *debitive*.

6) *voice*: *active* and *passive*.

A seventh possible category in Latvian is that of *aspect*. Latvian has some evidence for establishing such a category (with an opposition between *perfective* and *imperfective* verb pairs). This question will be discussed below (p. 115 ff.).

Numbers 4-6 (7) are specific verbal categories whereas 1-3 were also encountered with nominal word classes.

Finite and Non-Finite Forms

The following forms – all present in Latvian – are labeled *non-finite*: *infinitive*, *participles* and *gerunds*, as well as the verbal noun. All other forms – including compound forms with participial constituents – are referred to as *finite*.

Verb Stems

To be able to form the inventory of the Latvian verb one must know:

1) the *infinitive* stem, 2) the *present* stem and 3) the *past (preterite)* stem.

On the basis of 1) the infinitive stem (which is found by dropping the *-t/-ties* of the infinitive) the following forms of the paradigm (in addition to the infinitive itself) are constructed:

- the simple future
- the (present) subjunctive
- the *dam*-gerund
- the past participle passive (*t*-participle)

From 2) the present stem (which is obtained through deletion of the stem suffix of the Ist, IInd and IIIrd conjugation respectively, see below) are formed:

- the simple present
- the imperative
- the debitive
- the present gerund in *-Vm*
- the present gerund (*ot*-gerund)
- the present participle active (*oš*-participle)
- the present participle passive (*m*-participle)

From 3) the preterite stem (which is obtained from the 3 p. preterite by dropping the *-a*) the following forms are constructed:

- the simple past
- the past gerund (*-is/-usi*-gerund)
- the past participle active (*-is/-usi*-participle)

It could be possible to work with two stems only, namely the present and infinitive, since the preterite stem is often identical with the infinitive stem or can be derived from it by relatively simple morphophonemic rules (i. e. such strategies as vowel lengthening and/or consonant change). Still, our experience has shown that most students seem to prefer a system with three stems.

The intervocalic *-j* causes a problem for the analysis of stems. Thus, one may, for example, speak of a present/preterite stem *jāj-* in opposition to the infinitive stem *jā-ride*, but it is equally possible to regard this *j* as an automatic glide for the purpose of avoiding "hiatus" (i. e. collision of two vowels not constituting a diphthong). A third possibility is to count it as part of the ending, e. g. *jā-jØ/V*, but this alternative should be rejected for structural reasons since there seems to be no clear evidence of *jā*-preterites.

Morphophonemic Rules
These rules are given in chapter 1 on phonology and will be referred to when necessary in the presentation below.

THE FINITE VERB

Introduction

For generalties, see p. 81 f. above.
Our disposition will be as follows:
After the presentation of the conjugational types, the formation of the simple tenses are given with focus on the simple present and past tenses, which for practical and pedagogical purposes will be presented side by side. Then follows a description of the formation of the simple future.

The next step is the description of the formation of the compound tenses wherupon the categories aspect and tense (with emphasis on the use of the tenses), further the marked moods (i. e. the formation and use of moods other than the indicative). Finally, the formation and use of the category of voice are presented.

Principal Forms

The *principal forms* of the Latvian verb are the following:
- the infinitive
- the (3rd p.) simple present
- the (3rd p.) simple past

Conjugational Types

The Latvian verb is customarily divided into three conjugations, referred to as the Ist, IInd and IIIrd respectively. The Ist conjugation may also be labeled the *short conjugation,* since the verbs of this conjugation are characterized through a *monosyllabic* stem in all principal forms, i. e. the infinitive, the present tense and the past tense, e. g. **nāk-, nāk-, nāc-** *come.*

The IInd conjugation is recognized through the feature 'more than one syllable' in all principal forms: **runā-t, runā-j-, runā-** *speak,* whence this conjugation is also properly called the *long conjugation.*

The IIIrd (with two subdivisions, A and B respectively, cf. p. 105) conjugation constitutes a kind of compromise between the short and the long conjugations, and is consequently labeled the *mixed conjugation,* since it has the characteristics of the short in the present tense, but the long in the past tense and the infinitive, e. g. **las-** (pres.) vs. **lasī-j-/lasī-t** *read.*

Conjugations II and (partly) III are the only *productive* classes, in contrast to I, which (irrespective of the large number of verbs belonging to this conjugation) has ceased to be *productive.*

This approach to the Latvian conjugations as the short, long and mixed is optimal from a pedagogical point of view, since the system is logical and easy to remember for the student.

Predicatability of Conjugational Type on the Basis of the Infinitive

As stated above all monosyllabics belong to the short conjugation. For examples, see above. Of the remaining verbs those ending in -ot belong (without exception) to the IInd (= long) conjugation, e. g. inf. **dzīvo-t**, 3 p. pres. **dzīvo**, 3 p. pret. **dzīvo-j-a**. To this conjugation further belong the absolute majority of the verbs ending in -āt, e. g. **runāt** *speak,* cf. above. Observe, however, that all verbs ending in -ināt are IIIrd conjugational (= mixed), e. g. **audzināt**, pres. **audzin-**, pret. **audzinā-** *bring up, educate.* The same holds true for the following three -āt-verbs: **dziedāt** *sing,* **raudāt** *cry, weep* and **zināt** *know.* The verb **sargāt** *guard* vacillates between the mixed and the long conjugation, but now tends to follow the latter.

To the IIIrd (mixed) conjugation further belong most of the verbs ending in -īt, cf. **lasīt** *read.* There are some exceptions, as in the denominative **cienīt** *respect, esteem* (: **ciena** *respect, esteem*), which follow the IInd conjugation.

Many verbs ending in -ēt belong to the IIIrd conjugation, e. g. **gribēt** *wish,* but there are also numerous -ēt verbs which are inflected according to the IInd conjugation, e. g. **zīmēt** *draw* (: **zīme** *sign*).

THE FORMATION OF THE TENSES OF THE INDICATIVE ACTIVE

Formation of the Simple Tenses
(Darbības vārda vienkaršo formu darīšana)

Formation of the Present and the Preterite
As pointed out above, it appears practical to deal with these two formations jointly, in order to emphasize the contrast between them.

Desinences
Two sets of endings are encountered:

Subset a):	Subset b):
SG	
1 p. -u	-u
2 p. -Ø/-i	-i
3 p. -Ø	-a
PL	
1 p. -am	-ām
2 p. -at	-āt
3 p. -Ø	-a

The functional distribution between the two subsets is as follows:

Subset b) is used in all preterite formations, as well as in the present tense of conjugation III B, whereas subset a) is encountered in the remaining cases. As is seen from the table, subset a) is split between zero ending and -*i* in the 2nd p. sg. For distributional rules on this point, see under the different types in the presentation below.

The zero endings in the 3 p. and the 2 p. sg. of subset a) are due to the loss of short -*a* and -*i* respectively, according to the rules given in the chapter on phonology p. 35 f.

The corresponding *reflexive* endings are:

Subset a):	Subset b):
SG	
1 p. -os	-os
2 p. -ies	-ies
3 p. -as	-ās
PL	
1 p. -amies	-āmies
2 p. -aties	-āties
3 p. -as	-ās

Note that in the reflexive subset a) has only one possible ending in the 2nd p. sg.

The endings of the reflexive can be derived from the non-reflexive through a set of lengthening rules (similar to those by which long adjective forms are derived from short forms, cf. p. 59), viz. *u* > *uo*, *-i*/Ø, 2nd p.) > *ie, a* /Ø, 3rd p. sg.) > *ā*.

The present tense can be characterized by specific present tense markers such as the *j*-suffix, the *n*-suffix or infix and the *st*-suffix. Such markers are found in certain verbs of the Ist conjugation. Thus, the *j*-formative is encountered in subclasses 3 and 4. The *-n-* infix is reflected in subclass 2, subgroups A b and C whereas the *-n* suffix is present in subclass 5 (with subgroups). Subclass 6 (with subgroups) is reserved for the *st*-marker. Due to diachronic changes the *j* has merged with consonants other than labials. Also, the *n*-infix has become "disguised" through history as a result of the loss of the sound *n* in the position between a vowel and consonant (cf. p. 32). However, the *-n-* has left a trace in the compensatory lengthening of the subsequent vowel (p. 32).

East Baltic, i. e. Latvian and Lithuanian, has known two different preterite formations, referred to as the *ā*- and *ē*-preterite respectively. Both have survived in Lithuanian whereas in Latvian the two types have merged into one, the *-ā*-preterite (cf. the endings of the 1st and 2nd p. plural of the preterite, i. e. *-ām, -āt*, as well as the 3 p. *-a* (< *-ā). However, the the *ē*-preterite has left certain traces in the timbre of the root vowel and the palatalization of *k* > *c, g* > *dz* in certain verbs of the Ist conjugation. Such cases are referred to below.

THE FIRST (SHORT) CONJUGATION

Of the three conjugations this is the only really problematic one, since it can involve such strategies as vocalic alternations (ablaut) and consonantal shifts, which in certain cases (see below) imply redundant differentiation of the forms of the present and the past tenses in addition to that offered by the desinences, cf. the set of endings for these two tenses presented above (p. 85).

When the *present tense* shows a *(historically) palatalized consonant* (cf. p. 25), it is always due to a former *j*-cluster (cf. chapter 1: Phonology, p. 25), whereby non-labials have merged with the *j* to form a single palatalized consonant. After labials the *j* is preserved. In past tense forms the corresponding non-palatalized consonant is encountered. Examples are given below.

The only palatalized consonants possible in the *past tense* are *c* and *dz,* which signalize that the corresponding consonants of the present tense and the infinitive are *-k* or *-g*. For examples, see below.

THE VERB: THE TENSES OF THE INDICATIVE ACTIVE

In the presentation of the Ist conjugation one has to work with a number of subclasses. We have chosen a system of 6 subclasses (1-6) with subgroups under some of them.

In order to facilitate the reading a chart should be given before the more detailed analysis is presented:

Subclass 1: Unchanged Stem in all Principal Forms
    Subgroup A: Stems ending in Postvocalic *-j*
    Subgroup B: Stems ending in a Dental or Velar Stop
    Subgroup C: Stems ending in *-c/-dz,* infinitives in *-kt/-gt*
    Subgroup D: Stems ending in *-in*
    Subgroup E: Stems with *-e-/-ē-*

Subclass 2: Different Stems in the Present and Past Tenses
    Subgroup A: Vowels *-e-, -ie-* or *-o-* in the Present Tense vs. *-i-* or *-a-* in the Past Tense
    Subgroup B: Short Vowel in the Present Tense vs. Corresponding Long in the Past Tense
    Subgroup C: Long Vowel (*-ī-* or *-ū-*) in the Present Tense vs. Short (*-i-* or *-u-*) in the Past Tense
    Subgroup D: Same Vowel, but Different Stem Final Consonant in the Present and Past Tenses

Subclass 3: Contrastive Palatalized Consonant in the Present Tense, Contrastive Long Vowel in the Past Tense

Subclass 4: Suffix *-j* in the Present Tense
    Subgroup A: Postconsonantal *-j*
    Subgroup B. Postvocalic *-j*

Subclass 5: Suffix *-n* in the Present Tense
    Subgroup A: The Verb **aut**
    Subgroup B: Verbs in *-iet*

Subclass 6: Verbs with *-st-*Suffix in the Present Tense
    Subgroup A: Verbs with unchanged Stem
    Subgroup B: Verbs with Preterites in *-j*
    Subgroup C: Verbs with Preterites in *-v*
    Subgroup D: Verbs with Preterites in *-n*
    Subgroup E: Verbs with *-s* in all Principal Forms
    Subgroup F: Verbs with *-z-* in the past Tense and the Infinitive

88 THE VERB: THE TENSES OF THE INDICATIVE ACTIVE

Subgroup G: Verbs with *-st* in the Present Tense and the Infinitive vs. Dental (*-t*/*-d*) in the Past Tense

The Irregular Verbs **būt, dot** and **iet**

Note: The student should carefully observe which subclasses have preserved the *-i* in the 2nd p. of the present tense and which have not. The ending of the 3rd p. is always zero in the Ist conjugation.

Subclass 1: Unchanged Stem in all Principal Forms
The following subgroups should be distinguished:

Subgroup A: Stems ending in Postvocalic -j
The *-j* appears here automatically in order to prevent vowel cumulation ("hiatus").

Infinitive	Present tense	Past tense
SG		
jāt *to ride*	1 p. **jā-j-u**	**jāj-u**
	2 p. *jā-j-Ø*	**jā-j-i**
	3 p. **jā-j-Ø**	**jā-j-a**
PL		
	1 p. **jā-j-am**	**jā-j-ām**
	2 p. **ja̅-j-at**	**jā-j-at**
	3 p. **jā-j-Ø**	**jā-j-a**

Other examples:
klāt *spread, set (table), cover*, **at-klāt** *discover*, **krāt** *collect*, **māt** *wave*, **rāt** *scold*, **at-stāt** *leave*; **dēt** (**dē-j-Ø, dē-j-a**) *lay (eggs)*, **spēt** (**spē-j-Ø, spēj-a**) *manage, be able*.

Here we can also put the type

Infinitive	Present tense	Past tense
SG		
mīt *to change*	1 p. **mij-u**	**mij-u**
	2 p. *mij-Ø*	**mij-i**
	3 p. **mij-Ø**	**mij-a**
PL		
	1 p. **mij-am**	**mij-ām**
	2 p. **mij-at**	**mij-āt**
	3 p. **mij-Ø**	**mij-āt**

where the *-ī-* of the infinitive is segmented into *-ij-* in both the present and past tenses (without any lengthening involved).

A parallel example is **vīt** *wind*.

THE VERB: THE TENSES OF THE INDICATIVE ACTIVE

For verbs in *-īt* with *-in-* in the present and past tenses, see 1 D below and for those with *st*-presents p. 101 ff.

Subgroup B: Stems ending in a Dental or Velar Stop
Examples of paradigms:

Dental stems:

Infinitive	Present tense	Past tense
SG		
sist *to beat*	1 p. **sit-u**	sit-u
	2 p. *sit-Ø*	sit-i
	3 p. **sit-Ø**	sit-a
PL		
	1 p. **sit-am**	sit-ām
	2 p. **sit-at**	sit-āt
	3 p. **sit-Ø**	sit-a

Velar stems:
sākt *to begin*

Infinitive	Present tense	Past tense
SG		
sākt *to begin*	1 p. **sāk-u**	sāk-u
	2 p. *sāc-Ø*	sāk-i
	3 p. **sāk-Ø**	sāk-a
PL		
	1 p. **sāk-am**	sāk-ām
	2 p. **sāk-at**	sāk-āt
	3 p. **sāk-Ø**	sāk-a

Observe the homonymy of forms in the 1 p. sg. present and preterite. The forms of the 1st and 2nd person plural differentiate the present tense from the past through desinences only. Note the zero endings of the forms of the 2nd person sg. and 3rd person present. The palatalized *c* in the second person present appears as the automatic result of the palatalization of **k > c* before the underlying (formerly present) *-i-* ending of this form. The infinitive **sist** has *-st < *-t-t* according to p. 27.

Examples of the same type as **sist** (only with an unchanged consonant) are **rist (ris-u,** preterite **ris-u)** *to bind* and **virt (vir-u, vir-u)** *to boil*. Inflected in the same way as **sākt** are (among others) **augt** *grow*.

Subgroup C: Stems ending in -c/-dz, Infinitives in -kt /-gt

This class has a stem with one of the consonants -c/-dz in both the present and past tenses in opposition to the infinitive which is in -k-t /-g-t.

Example of paradigm:

Infinitive	Present tense	Past tense
SG		
braukt *to travel*	1 p. **brauc-u**	brauc-u
	2 p. *brauc-Ø*	brauc-i
	3 p. **brauc-Ø**	brauc-a
PL		
	1 p. **brauc-am**	brauc-ām
	2 p. **brauc-at**	brauc-āt
	3 p. **brauc-Ø**	brauc-a

Here belong a good number of verbs, cf., for example, **plūkt** *pick, pluck*, **teikt** *tell, say*, **veikt** *carry out*, **beigt (beidzu, beidz; beidzu, beidzi)** *finish, complete*, **slēgt (slēdzu, slēdz; slēdzu, slēdzi)** *close, lock*, **sniegt (sniedzu, sniedzi; sniedzu, sniedzi)** *achieve, obtain*, and others.

The change to *c/dz* in the present tense is motivated by a former *j*-cluster (*kj/gj), the so-called *j*-present (on which see below). The appearance of *c/dz* in the forms of the preterite is due to an underlying *ē*-preterite, cf. pp. 31 and 91 below.

Example of a *reflexive* paradigm:

Infinitive	Present tense	Past tense
beigties *to end*	**beidz-a-s**	**beidz-ā-s**

Subgroup D: Stems ending in -in

Pattern:

Infinitive	Present tense	Past tense
SG		
mīt *to tread*	1 p. **min-u**	min-u
	2 p. *min-Ø*	min-i
	3 p. **min-Ø**	min-a
PL		
	1 p. **min-am**	min-ām
	2 p. **min-at**	min-āt
	3 p. **min-Ø**	min-a

In these verbs the infinitive ends in **-ī-t** (and not *-**in-t**), in accordance with the automatic rule of compensatory loss of preconsonantal *n* described in the chapter on phonology (p. 32).

Other examples are **pīt** *plait,* **tīt** *wind, wrap* and **trīt** *sharpen, grind.* One might also expect to find verbs in *-**un** (*-**ūt**) following the same pattern, but the author has not been able to trace any example.

Subgroup E: Stems with -e-/-ē-

This type is constituted by verbs with a vowel that is graphemically the same, but phonemically different in the present vs. the past tense, i. e. an open *e/ē* in the present tense is contrasted with a narrow *e/ē* in the past tense (and the infinitive).

Example of a paradigm:

Infinitive	Present tense	Past tense
	SG	
nest *to carry*	1 p. **nes-u**	**nes-u**
	2 p. ***nes-Ø***	**nes-i**
	3 p. **nes-Ø**	**nes-a**
	PL	
	1 p. **nes-am**	**nes-ām**
	2 p. **nes-at**	**nes-āt**
	3 p. **nes-Ø**	**nes-a**

The same occurs, for example, in **vest (ved, veda)** *lead,* **ēst (ēd, ēda)** *eat,* **degt (deg, dega)** *burn,* **bēgt (bēg, bēga)** *run away, flee.*

All forms of the present tense (except the second person singular, which has an underlying *-i*) are spoken with an open *e*. In the past tense a narrow *e* is pronounced in all instances – even in the 2nd p. sg. irrespective of the *-i* (which does not reflect *-*i*, but a diphthong). This distribution has become a rule in verbs of this type (structure *CVC* where the *-C* is represented by a stop or a sibilant). Note, however, that not every verb of this structure automatically follows the pattern of subclass 1E. Thus, for example, **sēsties** *sit down* is inflected according to 2 D c.

For general rules for the distribution of open vs. narrow *e/ē* in the chapter on phonology p. 30 f. Note the homonymy between the 1 p. sg. present and past tenses.

The student would expect the endings of the preterite to trigger the pronunciation of an open *e/ē* in the root. The reason for the unexpected narrow *e/ē*-sounds seems to be a former *ē*-preterite, cf. p. 31 which has been substituted by *ā*-preterite forms, i. e. *nes-ē-m -> *nes-ā-m*. The *ā*-preterite has been generalized in Standard Latvian, but the *ē*-preterite has left a trace in the timbre of the root vowel. Indirect reflexes of a former *ē*-preterite are also observed in verbs of the type **nākt, nāk, nāca**, see below.

Subclass 2: Different Stems in the Present and Past Tenses
Subgroup A: Vowels -e-, -ie- or -o- in the Stem of the Present Tense vs. -i- or -a- in the Past Tense and the Infinitive

a) The Pattern *-e- : -i-:*

A good number of verbs with the structure *CVR*, where R is a resonant (*l, m* or *r*), show an alternation *-i-* in the infinitive and the past tense as opposed to (an open) *-e-* in the present tense. In the 2 p. sg. of the present tense the *e* has a narrow pronunciation (due to an underlying syncopized *-i*).

Illustration:

Infinitive	Present tense	Past tense
	SG	
vilkt *to pull*	1 p. **velk-u**	**vilk-u**
	2 p. *velc-Ø*	**vilk-i**
	3 p. **velk-Ø**	**vilk-a**
	PL	
	1 p. **velk-am**	**vilk-ām** etc.

Other examples: **krimst (kremt, krimta)** *gnaw*. The *-st* of the infinitive has arisen from *t-t, cf. the presence of the dental in the present and past tenses.

Verbs in which *R = r* follow the same pattern except that the *e* of the present is lengthened to *ē* (in tautosyllabic position):

Infinitive	Present tense	Past tense
	SG	
pirkt *to buy*	1 p. **pērk-u**	**pirk-u**
	2 p. *pērc-Ø*	**pirk-i**
	3 p. **pērk-Ø**	**pirk-a**
	PL	
	1 p. **pērk-am**	**pirk-ām** etc.

Other examples:
cirpt (cērp, cirpa) *shear,* **cirst (cērt, cirta)** *chop.* For the *-st* of the infinitive, see comment to *krimst* above.

Basically the same pattern as in **pirkt** is observed in a case such as

Infinitive	Present tense	Past tense
	SG	
likt *to put*	1 p. **liek-u**	**lik-u**
	2 p. *liec-Ø*	**lik-i**
	3 p. **liek-Ø**	**lik-a**

PL

1 p. **liek-am**   **lik-ām** etc.

It should be noted that there are no examples of an ablaut *i : ei : i*. Only the pattern *i : ie : i* is encountered. For the pronunciation of *-ie-*, see chapter on phonology (p. 33).

Due to the loss of a preconsonantal *n* (cf. p. 32 above) and subsequent compensatory lengthening of *$*enC > ieC$*, a verb like **tikt** *get* has merged with the **likt**-type: **tikt (tieku, tiec, tiek; tiku, tiki, tika)**. The $*n$ infix was a former present marker on a par with such present tense markers as the *-j* and *-st* suffixes (see below).

b) The Pattern *-o- : -a-:*

Infinitive	Present tense	Past tense
SG		
tapt *to become*	1 p. **top-u**	**tap-u**
	2 p. *top-i*	**tap-i**
	3 p. **top-Ø**	**tap-a**
PL		
	1 p. **top-am**	**tap-ām** etc.

This *a : o : a* alternation is not an inherited ablaut, but represents a secondary one according to the formula $*-a-n-C$ with loss of a present tense *n*-marker with compensatory "lengthening" to *o* (p. 32).

Some analogous verbs: **plakt (plok, plaka)** *decrease*, **rakt (rok, raka)** *dig,* **smakt (smok, smaka)** *choke,* **sastapt (sastop, sastapa)** *meet,* **zagt (zog, zaga)** *steal*.

Observe that in verbs of the *a : o : a*-type the second person singular present is in *-i,* except in the verbs with infinitives in *-kt/gt* where *k/g* yield *c/dz* in the position before *-i,* which then undergoes a syncope. Thus, we have **top-i**, but **roc-Ø, zodz-Ø.**

Subgroup B: Short Vowel (-a- or -e-) in the Present Tense vs. Corresponding Long in the Past Tense

A frequent case is the alternation short vowel (*-a-* or *-e-*) in the infinitive and the present tense, vs. long vowel (*-ā-* or *-ē-*) in the preterite.

Illustrations:
a) of *a : ā*:

Infinitive	Present tense	Past tense
SG		
skart *to touch*	1 p. **skar-u**	**skār-u**
	2 p. *skar-Ø*	**skār-i**

THE VERB: THE TENSES OF THE INDICATIVE ACTIVE

PL	3 p. **skar-Ø**	**skār-a**
	1 p. **skar-am**	**skār-ām** etc.

b) of *e : ē*:

Infinitive	Present tense	Past tense
SG		
ŋemt *to take*	1 p. **ŋem-u**	**ŋēm-u**
	2 p. *ŋem-Ø*	**ŋēm-i**
	3 p. **ŋem-Ø**	**ŋēm-a**
PL		
	1 p. **ŋem-am**	**ŋēm-ām** etc.

Here we have the same contrast open *e* in all praesentic forms (but for the 2 p. sg. with an underlying *-i*) vs. closed *ē* in all forms of the preterite which was encountered in the **nest**-type mentioned above.

c) The **dzert**-type should be especially mentioned here.
The paradigm is as follows:

Infinitive	Present tense	Past tense
SG		
dzert *to drink*	1 p. **dzer-u**	**dzēr-u**
	1 p. *dzer-Ø*	**dzēr-i**
	2 p. **dzer-Ø**	**dzēr-a**
PL		
	1 p. **dzer-am**	**dzēr-ām** etc.

One would expect the same contrast of open vs. closed *e/ē* as in **ŋemt**. However, this is not the case: the closed pronunciation is met with in all forms not only of the preterite, but also in the present tense. The reason for this is that the *r* was originally palatalized (= *ŗ* < *rj*), cf. phonology p. 24 and p. 25. This pattern is followed in all verbs of the structure *-ert*, e. g. **ķert** *catch, seize,* **spert** *kick,* **tvert** *grasp, seize*.

d) Verbs in *-iet*.

The verbs in *-iet* (cf. also below) form the present tense in *-ej-*, whereas the preterite is characterized through lengthening: *-ēj-*.
Illustration:

Infinitive	Present tense	Past tense
SG		
smiet *to laugh*	1 p. **smej-u**	**smēj-u**
	2 p. *smej-Ø*	**smēj-i**
	3 p. **smej-Ø**	**smēj-a**

PL
1 p. **smej-am**   smēj-ām etc.

Other examples: **liet, lej, lēja** *pour*, **riet, rej, rēja** *bark*.
In this type (as in the following), *-ie-* appears in preconsonantal position, *-ej/ēj-* in prevocalic.

e) The verb **lēkt** *to jump* is inflected as follows:

Infinitive	Present tense	Past tense
lēkt	**SG**	
	1 p. **lec-u**	**lēc-u**
	2 p. *lec-Ø*	**lēc-i**
	3 p. **lec-Ø**	**lēc-a**
	PL	
	1 p. **lec-am**	**lēc-ām** etc.

Note that a narrow *e/ē* is spoken in all forms of the preterite as well as in the second p. sg. present. The *c* in the preterite forms has the same explanation as with **nāca** whereas the *c* in the present tense is due to a former **kj*-cluster.

Subgroup C: Long Vowel (-ī- or -ū-) in the Present Tense vs. Short Vowel (-i- or -u-) in the Past Tense

As pointed out (p. 32 the long vowel in the present tense is due to the loss of an *n* in the position between a vowel and a consonant:

a) Alternation *-ī- : -i-*:

Infinitive	Present tense	Past tense
krist[1] *to fall*	**SG**	
	1 p. **krīt-u**	**krit-a**
	2 p. *krīt-Ø*	**krit-i**
	3 p. **krīt-Ø**	**krit-a**
	PL	
	1 p. **krīt-am**	**krit-ām** etc.

[1] **krist** reflects earlier **krit-t-* (acording to p. 27)

Other examples:
pa-tikt (pa-tīk-Ø, pa-tik-a) *like*.

b) Alternation *-ū- : -u-*:

Infinitive	Present tense	Past tense
zust *to disappear*	**SG**	
	1 p. **zūd-u**	**zud-u**
	2 p. *zūd-i*	**zud-i**

	3 p. **zūd-Ø**	zud-a
PL	1 p. **zūd-am**	zud-ām etc.

Other examples:
just (jūt-Ø, jut-a) *to feel*.

Subgroup D: Same Vowel, but Different Stem Final Consonant in the Present and Past Tenses

a) the ver*b* **nākt** *to come*.

This verb is unique in that a velar stop in the present tense and the infinitive, alternates with -*c* in the preterite (as well as in the 2nd p. sg. pres.).

The **nākt**-paradigm has the following appearance:

Infinitive	Present tense	Past tense
	SG	
nākt *to come*	1 p. **nāk-u**	nāc-u
	2 p. ***nāc-Ø***	nāc-i
	3 p. **nāk-Ø**	nāc-a
	PL	
	1 p. **nāk-am**	nāc-ām
	2 p. **nāk-at**	nāc-āt
	3 p. **nāk-Ø**	nāc-a

As in a previous section (1 E), an indirect reflex of a former *ē*-preterite is observed. The presence of the (historically) palatalized *c* in the forms of the past tense is motivated through a shift from *k* > *c* before a front vowel, viz. **ē*. It seems legitimate to reconstruct a development of the type **nāk-ē-m* → **nāc-ē-m* -→ *nāc-ām*.

b) -*š-/-ž-* in the Present Tense, -*s/-z-* in the Past Tense and the Infinitive

Examples:

Infinitive	Present tense	Past tense
	SG	
plēst *to tear*	1 p. **pleš-u**	plēs-u
	2 p. ***ples-Ø***	plēs-i
	3 p. **pleš-Ø**	plēs-a
	PL	
	1 p. **pleš-am**	plēš-ām etc.

Here again a narrow *e/ē* is spoken in all forms of the paradigm.

Infinitive	Present tense	Past tense
	SG	
griezt *to turn*	1 p. **griež-u**	griez-u

THE VERB: THE TENSES OF THE INDICATIVE ACTIVE

	2 p. *griez-Ø*	griez-i
	3 p. griež-Ø	griez-a
PL		
	1 p. griež-am	griez-ām etc.

The same consonant change occurs in **bāzt** *shove, thrust*, **gāzt** *overturn*, **grauzt** *gnaw*, **lauzt** *break* and a number of others. The -ž- descends to *z+j.

c) -š-/-ž- in the Present Tense, -t-/-d- in the Past Tense and -s- in the Infinitive

Examples:

Infinitive	Present tense	Past tense
	SG	
ciest[1] *to suffer*	1 p. cieš-u	ciet-u
	2 p. *ciet-Ø*	ciet-i
	3 p. cieš-Ø	ciet-a
	PL	
	1 p. cieš-am	ciet-ām etc.

[1] with -st from *-tt (cf. p. 25)

A parallel example is **pūst (pūš, pūta)** *blow*.

The treatment of the voiced dental + *j* is illustrated in:

Infinitive	Present tense	Past tense
	SG	
kost[1] *to bite*	1 p. kož-u	kod-u
	2 p. *kod-Ø*	kod-i
	3 p. kož-Ø	kod-a
	PL	
	1 p. kož-am	kod-ām etc.

[1] **kost** has to be reconstructed as *kandti (cf. p. 27 and 32)

An analogous example is represented by **laist (laiž, laida)** *let*.

A reflexive paradigm is reflected in:

Infinitive	Present tense	Past tense
	SG	
sēsties *to sit down*	1 p. sēž-os	sēd-os
	2 p. *sēd-ies*	sēd-ies
	3 p. sēž-as	sēd-ās

PL

1 p. sēž-amies   sēd-āmies etc.

The -š- and -ž- of the present tense in types b) and c) originate from clusters *s+j, t + j, z + j and d + j (cf. p. 25). Note that the -s- is retained in the 2nd p. pres. (due to the underlying ending -i whereby no j is involved).

Subclass 3: Contrastive Palatalized Consonant in the Present Tense, Contrastive Long Vowel in the Past Tense

This is a complex type in that both the present tense and the past tense have contrastive markers, the former in the form of a palatalized consonant (vs. unpalatatalized in the past tense) while the latter has a distinctive long vowel.

Paradigm pattern:

Infinitive	Present tense	Past tense
SG		
celt *to lift, build* 1 p. **ceļ-u**		cēl-u
2 p. *cel-Ø*		cēl-i
3 p. **ceļ-Ø**		cēl-a
PL		
1 p. **ceļ-am**		cēl-ām etc.

Treated in the same manner as **celt** are **dzelt** *sting, bite*, **šķelt** *split*, **(no)pelt** *criticize*, **smelt** *scoop*, **-zvelt** *hit*, **velt** *roll*, **zelt** *become green*.

The ļ is due to a former cluster *l + j which resulted in a palatalized single phoneme /ļ/. The situation was the same with verbs with stem final r (type **kart, dzert** above), but the ŗ was subsequently hardened (cf. p. 24 and 25). For *n + j > ņ no relevant cases have been found.

The remaining three subclasses are characterized by a suffix, -j, n- and -st respectively, in the present tense.

Subclass 4: Suffix -j in the Present Tense

Subgroup A: Postconsonantal -j

Unlike other consonants, clusters of labials + j did not merge into a single palatalized phoneme, but were kept intact, such that one can speak of a j-suffix on a synchronic level.

For the verbs in 1 C, 2 B c) and e), 2 D b) and c) and in 3 we have a (postconsonantal) j-suffix in a diachronic perspective.

a) *-p/-b+j:*

Infinitive	Present tense	Past tense
	SG	
glābt *to save*	1 p. **glāb-j-u**	**glāb-u**
	2 p. *glāb-j-Ø*	**glāb-i**
	3 p. **glāb-j-Ø**	**glāb-a**
	PL	
	1 p. **glāb-j-am**	**glāb-ām** etc.

Other examples:
slēpt (**slēp-j-Ø, slēp-a**) *hide*, **kāpt** (**kāpj-Ø, kāp-a**) *climb*.

b) verbs with *m + j* in the present tense have a lengthened vowel in the past tense, e. g.

Infinitive	Present tense	Past tense
SG		
vemt *to vomit*	1 p. **vem-j-u**	**vēm-u**
	2 p. *vem-Ø*	**vēm-i**
	3 p. **vem-j-Ø**	**vēm-a**
	PL	
	1 p. **vem-j-am**	**vēm-ām** etc.

The verb **lemt** *decide* is inflected in the same way as **vemt**.

Infinitive	Present tense	Past tense
	SG	
jumt *to roof*	1 p. **jum-j-u**	**jūm-u**
	2 p. *jum-Ø*	**jūm-i**
	3 p. **jum-j-Ø**	**jūm-a**
	PL	
	1 p. **jum-j-am**	**jūm-ām** etc.

The verb **stumt** *push* is treated similarly.

Subgroup B: Postvocalic -j
Here we find monosyllabics in a) *-ūt* and b) *-aut*

a) Verbs in -ūt

These verbs (with the exception of the irregular **būt**, see p. 103, and **dabūt,** which follows the second (long) conjugation) have *-ūj* in the present tense and *-uv* in the past tense, i. e. *-ū-* is preserved before *-j* (= preconsonantal position), but is segmented into *-uv* before the vocalic desinences of the past tense.

Illustration:

Infinitive	Present tense	Past tense
SG		
skūt *to shave*	1 p. **skūj-u**	**skuv-u**
	2 p. *skū-j-Ø*	**skuv-i**
	3 p. **skū-j-Ø**	**skuv-a**
PL		
	1 p. **skū-j-am**	**skuv-ām** etc.

Other example: **šūt** *sew*.

For verbs in *-ūt* with the formative *-st-* in the forms of the present tense, cf. p. 102 f. below.

b) Verbs in -aut

These verbs show the following pattern:
Illustration:

Infinitive	Present tense	Past tense
SG		
kraut *to pile*	1 p. **krauj-u**	**krāv-u**
	2 p. *krauj-Ø*	**krāv-i**
	3 p. **krauj-Ø**	**krāv-a**
PL		
	1 p. **krauj-am**	**krāv-ām** etc.

Other examples: **bḷaut** *shout*, **graut** *destroy; thunder*, **jaut** *knead*, **kaut** *kill*, **maut** *moo*, **raut** *pull, pluck*, **skaut** *embrace*, **spḷaut** *spit*.

As seen in the above paradigm, *-au* appears in preconsonantal position, whereas *-au* renders *-av* with concomitant lengthening to *-āv* in prevocalic position.

Subclass 5: Suffix *-n* in the Present Tense
Subgroup A: The verb aut

This verb is treated like the preceding verbs in *-aut*, except that it has *-n* instead of *-j* in the forms of the present tense:

Infinitive	Present tense	Past tense
SG		
aut *to put on*	1 p. **au-n-u**	**āv-u**
	2 p. *au-n-Ø*	**āv-i**
	3 p. **au-n-Ø**	**āv-a**
PL		
	1 p. **au-n-am**	**āv-ām** etc.

THE VERB: THE TENSES OF THE INDICATIVE ACTIVE

Subgroup B: Verbs in -iet
Part of the verbs in *-iet* take an *n*-suffix in the present tense. As with the other verbs in *-iet* (cf. above) the preterite ends in *-ēj*.
Illustration:

Infinitive	Present tense	Past tense
SG		
skriet *to run*	1 p. skrien-u	skrēj-u
	2 p. *skrien-Ø*	skrēj-i
	3 p. skrien-Ø	skrēj-a
PL		
	1 p. skrien-am	skrēj-ām etc.

Other examples: **siet, sien, sēja** *bind*, **sliet, slien, slēja** *prop*.

Subclass 6: Verbs with *st*-Suffix in the Present Tense
As pointed out (p. 86 above) *-st* is a present tense marker on a par with the *-j*-suffix and the *n*-infix/suffix. Observe that are dealing with an *-st*-verb only when this element is found in the present tense. Thus, **līt, līst, lija** *rain* counts as a *st*-verb whereas, for example, **nest, nes, nesa** *carry* does not.

Several subgroups of *st*-verbs should be distinguished, viz.

Subgroup A: Verbs with Unchanged Stem
a) the numerous verbs of the **alkt, alkst, alka** (*to long for*)-pattern:

Here belong among others **dzimt, dzimst, dzima** *be born*, **ģībt, ģībst, ģība** *faint*, **ilgt, ilgst, ilga** *last*, **mirt, mirst, mira** *die*, **pampt, pampst, pampa** *swell*, **plaukt, plaukst, plauka** *flourish*, **reibt, reibst, reiba** *become giddy*, **rimt, rimst, rima** *calm down*, **rūgt, rūgst, rūga** *ferment*, **salt, salst, sala** *get cold*, **skumt, skumst, skuma** *grieve*, **saslimt, saslimst, saslima** *become ill*, **sapīkt, sapīkst, sapīka** *get annoyed*, **slāpt, slāpst, slāpa** *thirst*, **sprāgt, sprāgst, sprāga** *burst*, **svilt, svilst, svila** *get scorched*, **trūkt, trūkst, trūka** *be lacking*, **tūkt, tūkst, tūka** *swell*, **tvīkt, tvīkst, tvīka** *blush*.

b) the small **izsīkt, izsīkst, izsīka to** *(to become exhausted)* -type:
This type has a long root vowel in all forms.

Subgroup B: Verbs with Preterites in -j
Pattern:
inf. **līt**, 3rd pres. **līst**, 3rd pret. **lija** *to rain*. Another example of this type is **dzīt, dzīst, dzija** *heal*.

Subgroup C: Verbs with Preterites in -v
inf. **kļūt, kļūst, kļuva** *to become*. Other examples: **gūt, gūsta, guva** *obtain*, **sa-grūt, sa-grūst, sa-gruva** *collapse*, **pūt, pūst, puva** *rot*, **žūt, žūst, žuva** *become dry*.

In 6 B and C the long preconsonantal root vowel of the infinitive and the present tense (-*ī*- and -*ū*-) has been segmented into -*ij*- and -*uv*- respectively before the vocalic desinences of the preterite.

Subgroup D: Verbs with Preterites in -n
Pattern:
inf. **pa-zīt**, 3rd pres. **pa-zīst, pa-zina** *to know, recognize*. Other examples are **at-zīt** *acknowledge* and **tīt** *wind, wrap*.

The long -*ī*- in the infinitive and present tense is due to the loss of -*n*- in preconsonantal position (cf. p. 32).

Subgroup E: Verbs with -s- in all Principal Forms
Pattern:
aiz-mirst, aiz-mirst, aiz-mirsa *to forget*.
Other examples: **ap-klust, ap-klust, ap-klusa** *grow silent*, **aust, aust, ausa** *dawn*, **karst, karst, karsa** *grow hot*.

In the **aiz-mirst**-type the root ends in an -*s*, to which is added -*t* in the infinitive, yielding -*st*. In the present tense one would expect *-*s*+*st*. This sequence has been simplified to -*st*.

Note the verb **kust, kūst, kusa** *thaw* with a distinctive long vowel in the present tense. This length must be due to secondary superposition of the -*st* suffix on a form with the *n*-infix, i. e. *ku-n-s- > *$kūs$- + st, resulting in **kūst**.

Subgroup F: Verbs with -z- in the Past Tense and the Infinitive
The two verbs in -*zt*, namely **birzt** *to crumble* and **lūzt** *to break*: pres. **birst, lūst** vs. **birza, lūza,** behave in the same way as -*st*-verbs.

Here the group *-*z*-*st* of the present tense has been simplified to -*st*.

In conclusion, it should be emphasized that the second person singular of the present tense of -*st*-verbs always has the ending -*i*, as opposed to the zero ending of the 3rd person: **pazīsti, kļūsti : pazīst, kļūst**.

Subgroup G: Verbs with -st in the Infinitive and the Present Tense vs. Dental (-t/-d) in the Past Tense
Model:
vīst, vīst, vīta *to fade*
svīst, svīst, svīda *to sweat*

This means that the clusters *-t-st/-d-st* from the present tense have been simplified to *-st*. The *-st* in the infinitive originates from *-t/d-t*.

The Irregular Verbs *būt*, *dot* and *iet*
Finally, the paradigms of the three irregular verbs **būt** *be*, **dot** *give* and **iet** *go* should be given:

Infinitive		Present tense	Past tense
	SG		
būt *to be*		1 p. **es-mu**	**bi-j-u**
		2 p. **es-i**	**bi-j-i**
		3 p. *ir*	**bi-j-a**
	PL		
		1 p. **es-am**	**bi-j-ām**
		2 p. **es-at**	**bi-j-āt**
		3 p. *ir* (neg. form *nav*)	**bi-j-a**

Note the suppletivism **es- : ir : bi-j**.

In colloquial speech as well as older writings the shortened form **bij** is frequently encountered in the 3rd person.

Infinitive		Present tense	Past tense
	SG		
iet *to go*		1 p. **ej-u**	**gā-j-u**
		2 p. *ej-Ø*	**gā-j-i**
		3 p. *ie-t*	**gā-j-a**
	PL		
		1 p. **ej-am**	**gā-j-ām**
		2 p. **ej-at**	**gā-j-āt**
		3 p. *ie-t*	**gā-j-a**

Observe the zero ending in the 2 p. pres. sg. as well as the alternation *ej-* (prevocalic position) : *ie-* (preconsonantal position) and the ending -*t* in the 3 p. As in the case of **būt** there is suppletivism between the present and past tenses.

Infinitive	Present tense	Past tense
	SG	
dot *to give*	1 p. **dod-u**	**dev-u**
	2 p. **dod-Ø**	**dev-i**
	3 p. **dod-Ø**	**dev-a**
	PL	
	1 p. **dod-am**	**dev-ām**
	2 p. **dod-at**	**dev-āt**
	3 p. **dod-Ø**	**dev-a**

Note the zero ending of the 2 p. sg. pres. and the radical difference between the stems of the present and past tenses.

THE SECOND (LONG) CONJUGATION

As pointed out (p. 84 above) the infinitives of this conjugation end in -*ot* (**dzīvot** *live*), -*āt* (**runāt** *speak*), (quite rarely) -*ēt* (**zīmēt** *draw*), -*īt* (**cienīt** *respect*) or -*ūt* (only one verb: **dabūt** *get*). Since these verbs are treated in the same way, only one paradigm, namely that of **mazgāt** *wash* will be given:

Infinitive	Present tense	Past tense
	SG	
mazgāt *to wash*	1 p. **mazgā-j-u**	**mazgā-j-u**
	2 *p.* *mazgā-Ø*	**mazgā-j-i**
	3 p. **mazgā-Ø**	**mazgā-j-a**
	PL	
	1 p. **mazgā-j-am**	**mazgā-j-ām**
	2 p. **mazgā-j-at**	**mazgā-j-āt**
	3 p. **mazgā**	**mazgā-j-a**

Note the zero ending in the 2 p. sg. pres. as well as the total merger of the forms of the 1 p. sg. in the present and the past tenses. The same merger was observed also with certain verbs of the Ist conjugation (viz. subclass 1), cf. above.

The -*j*- appears automatically to prevent *hiatus* (i. e. combination of two vowels which do not constitute a diphthong). It can be analyzed either as a glide (which we prefer), as part of the stem or (less attractively) as part of the desinence.

Reflexive verbs of this conjugation end in *-oties, -āties, -ēties* and *-īties*. A sample of the paradigm ist that of **mazgāties** *wash oneself*:

Infinitive	Present tense	Past tense
SG		
mazgāties	1 p. mazgā-j-os	mazgā-j-os
	2 p. *mazgā-j-ies*	mazgā-j-ies
	3 p. mazgā-j-as	mazgā-j-ās
PL		
	1 p. mazgā-j-amies	mazgā-j-āmies
	2 p. mazgā-j-aties	mazgā-j-āties
	3 p. mazgā-j-as	mazgā-j-ās

THE THIRD (MIXED) CONJUGATION

Here two subclasses must be distinguished, since IIIrd conjugation verbs in *-ēt* follow one pattern (III A), and those in *-īt and -ināt* another (III B). The verbs **gribēt** *wish* and **lasīt** *read* illustrate these paradigms:

III A:

Infinitive	Present tense	Past tense
SG		
gribēt *to wish*	1 p. grib-u	gribē-j-u
	2 p. *grib-i*	gribē-j-i
	3 p. grib-Ø	gribē-j-a
PL		
	1 p. grib-am	gribē-j-ām
	2 p. grib-at	gribē-j-āt
	3 p. grib-Ø	gribē-j-a

Observe the depalatalized consonant (*-k-*) of the verb **mācēt** *know* in all forms (including the 2nd p. sg.) of the present tense, i. e. **māk-u, *māk-i*, māk-Ø, māk-am, māk-at** (vs. **mācēju, mācēji** etc. in the past).

III B:

Infinitive	Present tense	Past tense
SG		
lasīt *to read*	1 p. las-u	lasī-j-u
	2 p. *las-i*	lasī-j-i
	3 p. las-a	lasī-j-a
PL		
	1 p. las-ām	lasī-j-ām
	2 p. las-āt	lasī-j-āt
	3 p. las-a	lasī-j-a

Observe that both subclasses have the ending *-i* in the 2 p. sg. Note the contrast in the desinences of the present tense forms of III A (= -Ø, *-am*, *-at*) as compared to III B (= *-a*, *-ām*, *-āt*). The status of the *-j-* in forms of the past is the same as that commented upon in connection with the IInd conjugation.

Note that the verb **sacīt** *say* has a depalatalized consonant (*-k-*) in the present tense, i. e. **sak-u,** *sak-i,* **sak-a, sak-am, sak-at** (vs. **sacīju, sacīji** etc. in the past tense). The verb **mācīt(ies)** learn, however, has *-c-* in all forms of the present tense, i. e. **mācu,** *māci,* **māca** etc. The reflexive paradigm is given below.

All verbs in *-ināt* are inflected according to the **lasīt**-pattern..

Two verbs of the IIIrd conjugation must be treated separately, namely **sēdēt** *sit* and **gulēt** *sleep; lie*:

Infinitive	Present tense	Past tense
SG		
sēdēt *to sit*	1 p. **sēž-u**	**sēdē-j-u**
	2 p. *sēd-i*	**sēdē-j-i**
	3 p. **sēž-Ø**	**sēdē-j-a**
PL		
	1 p. **sēž-am**	**sēdē-j-ām**
	2 p. **sēž-at**	**sēdē-j-āt**
	3 p. **sēž-Ø**	**sēdē-j-a**

According to the principles set forth above (p. 29 ff.) a narrow *ē* is spoken in all forms of *sēd-/sēž* (both in the present and past tense forms).

Infinitive	Present tense	Past tense
SG		
gulēt *to sleep*	1 p. **guļ-u**	**gulē-j-u**
	2 p. *gul-i*	**gulē-j-i**
	3 p. **guļ**	**gulē-j-a**
PL		
	1 p. **guļ-am**	**gulē-j-ām**
	2 p. **guļ-at**	**gulē-j-ā***t*
	3 p. **guļ**	**gulē-j-a**

Note the alternation between *ž* and *d*, and *ļ* and *l* in the present tense, where the unpalatalized *d* and *l* are found in the position before *-i*, i. e. in the 2 p. sg.

THE VERB: THE TENSES OF THE INDICATIVE ACTIVE

The *ž* and the *ļ* reflect *dj and *lj respectively. Such palatalizations (cf. chapter on phonology, p. 25) are otherwise restricted to the present tense of the Ist conjugation (see p. 86 ff.).

Reflexive paradigms have the following appearance (**vēlēties; mācīties**):

Infinitive	Present tense	Past tense
SG		
vēlēties *to wish*	1 p. vēl-os	vēlē-j-ās
	2 p. *vēl-ies*	vēlē-j-ies
	3 p. vēl-ās	vēlē-j-ās
PL		
	1 p. vēl-amies	vēlē-j-āmies
	2 p. vēl-aties	vēlē-j-āties
	3 p. vēl-ās	vēlē-j-ās

Infinitive	Present tense	Past tense
SG		
mācīties *to learn*	1 p. māc-os	mācī-j-os
	2 p. *māc-ies*	mācī-j-ies
	3 p. māc-ās	mācī-j-ās
PL		
	1 p. māc-āmies	mācī-j-āmies
	2 p. māc-āties	mācī-j-āties
	3 p. māc-ās	mācī-j-ās

Conjugations I-III: The Ending of the 2nd Person Sg.
Here rules must be given in order to regulate:
a) the choice between the endings *-Ø* (zero) and *-i*,
b) the quality of the consonant preceding the ending,
c) the timbre of the vowel *-e-* when it occurs in the present tense.

First it should be stated that the *past tense* is unproblematic: the ending is here always *-i* and the consonant is the same as in all other forms of the paradigm.

In the *present tense* the ending is *-Ø* (zero) in the II (long) conjugation (e. g. **runā** *you speak*, **dzīvo** *you live*). The ending is *-i* with unchanged consonant in all verbs of the IIIrd (mixed) conjugation (i. e. both subtype A): **gribi** (: **gribēt**) *you wish* and subtype B) **lasi** (: **lasīt**) *you read*. Thus, it is the Ist conjugation which poses difficulties. Here the ending is *-Ø* (zero) except in the verbs with the special present tense markers, the *-st* (= suffix) with variants (cf. p. 101 ff.) or the **-n-* (nasal infix). The *st*-element is present in the "surface structure", e. g. **kļūsti** (: **kļūt**) *you become*, whereas the nasal infix has disappeared (p. 32), but has left a trace in the compensatory lengthening of the preceding vowel, whereby these present-tense forms show a distinctively lengthened vowel *-ī-, -ū-, -o-* as opposed to the (corresponding) short vowels *-i-, -u-, -a-* in the past tense and the infinitive, e. g. **krīti** *you fall* (vs. **kriti** *you fell* and the inf. **krist** *fall*), **jūti** *you feel* (vs. **juti** *you felt* and the inf. **just** *feel*) and **proti** *you understand* / **topi** *you become* (vs. **prati** *you understood* / **tapi** *you became* and the inf. **prast** *understand* / **tapt** *become*.

Verbs with roots / stems ending in *-k* or *-g* always shift these to *-c* and *-dz* in the 2nd p. of the present tense (but never in the past tense) and – irrespective of type – always have zero ending in the 2nd person of the present tense, e. g. **roc** *you collect* (: **rok** 3 p., **raku** *I collected*, **raki** *you collected*, inf. **rakt** *collect*), **zodz** *you steal* (: **zog** 3 p., **zagu** *I stole*, **zagi** *you stole*, inf. **zagt** *steal*), **sāc** *you begin* (: **sāk** 3 p., **sāku** *I began*, **sāki** *you began*, **sākt** *begin*), **liec** *you put, place* (: **liek** 3 p., **liku** *I put, placed*, **liki** *you put, placed*, inf. **likt** *put, place*), **pērc** *you buy* (: **pērk** 3 p., **pirku** *I bought*, **pirki** *you bought*, inf. **pirkt** *buy*), **bēdz** *you flee* (: **bēg** 3 p., **bēgu** *I fled*, **bēgi** *you fled*, **bēgt** *flee*).

With consonants other than *-k* and *-g* the following rule applies: the 2nd p. sg. of the present tense always has the same consonant as in the past tense, i. e. retains the unchanged ("unpalatalized", see p. 25) consonant in cases where there is a consonant shift between the present and the past tense, cf., for example, **glāb** *you save* (: other forms of the present **glābj-**, past tense **glāb-**, inf. **glābt**), **cel** *you lift, raise* (: other forms of the present **ceļ-**, past tense **cēl-**, inf. **celt**), and finally **griez** *you turn* (: other forms of the present **griež-**, past tense **griez-**, inf. **griezt**).

In terms of closed vs. open *-e-* the 2nd p. sg. present is always pronounced with a closed *-e-*, e. g. **tu dzen** [dzen] *you chase* : **dzen-** [dzɛn] in the other forms of the present tense.

Finally, the reflexive ending of the 2nd p. sg. is always *-ies*. The rules determining the quality of a preceding consonant are the same as in a corresponding non-reflexive form – irrespective of whether this ending is *-i* or *-Ø* (zero).

> The historical explanation for the exceptional position of the 2nd p. sg. in the paradigm of the present tense in Latvian is that an *-i* has been partly retained, partly lost. The present marker *-j-* which is found in many verbs of conjugation I triggers "palatalization" of consonants (i. e. **zj > ž, l > ļ, b > bj* etc.), but is lost before the **-i*, which explains the unchanged ("unplatalized") consonant of the 2nd person present. "Palatalized" consonants in the 2nd sg. present are restricted to *-c* and *-dz* alone, which reflect **-ki* and **-gi* (as, for example in **sāc** /< **sāci < *sāki/* vs. **sāk-** in the other forms of **sākt** *begin*) or **kji > *ki > c* and **-gji > *-gi > -dz* (e. g. **nāc** *you come* where the rest

THE VERB: THE TENSES OF THE INDICATIVE ACTIVE

of the paradigm also has *-c-* due to *-*kj*). The only case where -*k* and -*g* are encountered in the 2nd person present is in verbs of conjugation III, e. g. **saki** *you say* (: past tense stem **sacīj-**, inf. **sacīt**); this -*i* derives from a diphthong *-*ai* (-*āi*) which did not trigger a shift from a velar stop to an affricate. The -*i* in the 2nd sg. of the past tense also originates from *-*ai* (-*āi*).

Forms of the type **runā** *you speak* and **dzīvo** *you live* represent the earlier forms ***runāji** and **dzīvoji** (and the forms of the 3rd person ***runāja** and **dzīvoja**, respectively). The reason why the corresponding forms of the past tense **runāji**, **runāja** and **dzīvoji**, **dzīvoja** have retained -*ji* and -*ja* is that these endings reflect *-*jāi* and *-*jā*, respectively.

Formation of the Future Tense

The future tense is formed from the infinitive stem (cf. p. 81) which is arrived at by dropping the -*t* of the infinitive. To this stem is added an *s*-formative (with the allomorph -*š*- in the 1st p. sg.). The -*s*/*š*- is followed by the following endings:

		Non-reflexive	*Reflexive*
SG	1 p.	-u	-os
	2 p.	-i	-ies
	3 p.	-Ø	-ies
PL	1 p.	-im	-imies
	2 p.	-i(e)t	-i(e)ties
	3 p.	-Ø	-ies

The -*š*- allomorph originates from *-*sj+u* < *-*s-i-u*, i. e. the *j reflects the same -*i*- which is encountered in other forms of the future paradigm.

In order to arrive at correct forms one has to distinguish between 1) vocalic stems, and 2) consonantal stems.

1. Vocalic Stems

Vocalic stems encompass all verbs of the IInd and IIIrd conjugations, plus some verbs of the Ist conjugation (type **spē-t** *to be able to*).

Examples of paradigms:
IInd conjugation:

infinitive	**runā-t** *speak*	**dzīvo-t** *live*	**zīmē-t** *draw*
SG			
1 p.	runā-š-u	dzīvo-š-u	zīmē-š-u
2 p.	runā-s-i	dzīvo-s-i	zīmē-s-i
3 p.	runā-s-Ø	dzīvo-s-Ø	zīmē-s-Ø
PL			
1 p.	runā-s-im	dzīvo-s-im	zīmē-s-im
2 p.	runā-s-i(e)t	dzīvo-s-i(e)t	zīmē-s-i(e)t

3 p. **runā-s-Ø**   **dzīvo-s-Ø**   **zīmē-s-Ø**

IIIrd conjugation:
infinitive **gribē-t** *to wish*   **lasī-t** *to read*
SG
1 p. **gribē-š-u**   lasī-š-u
2 p. **gribē-s-i**   lasī-s-i
3 p. **gribē-s-Ø**   lasī-s-Ø
PL
1 p. **gribē-s-im**   lasī-s-im
2 p. **gribē-s-i(e)t**   lasī-s-i(e)t
3 p. **gribē-s-Ø**   lasī-s-Ø

Ist conjugation:
infinitive **spē-t** *to be able to*
SG
1 p. **spē-š-u**
2 p. **spē-s-i**
3 p. **spē-s-Ø**
PL
1 p. **spē-s-im**
2 p. **spē-s-i(e)t**
3 p. **spē-s-Ø**

2. Consonantal Stems
A. Stems ending in Labials and Velars

Verb stems ending in labials and velars form future tense forms in the same way as vocalic stems, e. g.

infinitive **vem-t** *vomit* **glāb-t** *save* **teik-t** *say* **bēg-t** *run away, flee*

SG
1 p. **vem-š-u**   **glāb-š-u**   **teik-š-u**   **bēg-š-u**
2 p. **vem-s-i**   **glāb-s-i**   **teik-s-i**   **bēg-s-i**
3 p. **vem-s**   **glāb-s-Ø**   **teik-s-Ø**   **bēg-s-Ø**
PL
1 p. **vem-s-im**   **glāb-s-im**   **teik-s-im**   **bēg-s-im**
2 p. **vem-s-i(e)t** **glāb-s-i(e)t teik-s-i(e)t bēg-s-i(e)t**
3 p. **vem-s-Ø**   **glāb-s-Ø**   **teik-s-Ø**   **bēg-s-Ø**

B. Sibilant Stems

Besides labials and velars, only the sibilants *s* and *z* can occur before the *-t* of the infinitive.

Infinitives ending in *-st* are ambigous since they can reflect 1) *-s-t* (as, for example in **nest** *carry*, pres. 1 p. sg. **nesu**, pret. 1 p. sg. **nesu**), 2) **-t-t* (cf. p. 25, for example, in **mest** *throw*, 1 p. sg. pres. **metu**, 1 p. sg. pret. **metu**), or 3) **d-t* (like, for example, in **vest** *lead*, pres. 1 p. sg. **vedu**, pret. 1 p. sg. **vedu**). In these cases the vowel *-ī-* is inserted between the original stem's final consonant (*-s, -t* or *-d*) and the ending (i. e. the *s/š*-formative + the desinences proper). In this way (normalized) vocalic stems are obtained, and assimilations and dissimilations which would have led to unclear forms are avoided.

Examples of paradigms:

infinitive	**nes-t** to carry	**mes-t** to throw	**ves-t** to lead
SG			
1 p.	**nes-ī-š-u**	**met-ī-š-u**	**ved-ī-š-u**
2 p.	**nes-ī-s-i**	**met-ī-s-i**	**ved-ī-s-i**
3 p.	**nes-ī-s-Ø**	**met-ī-s-Ø**	**ved-ī-s-Ø**
PL			
1 p.	**nes-ī-s-im**	**met-ī-s-im**	**ved-ī-s-im**
2 p.	**nes-ī-s-i(e)t**	**met-ī-s-i(e)t**	**ved-ī-s-i(e)t**
3 p.	**nes-ī-s-Ø**	**met-ī-s-Ø**	**ved-ī-s-Ø**

The same formational principle is followed in *-zt*-verbs, e. g.

infinitive	**lauzt** break
SG	
1 p.	**lauz-ī-š-u**
2 p.	**lauz-ī-s-i**
3 p.	**lauz-ī-s-Ø**
PL	
1 p.	**lauz-ī-s-im**
2 p.	**lauz-ī-s-i(e)t**
3 p.	**lauz-ī-s-Ø**

It is important to be aware that the original stem is found by looking at the stem consonant in the past tense, and not the present, since this could lead to the formation of incorrect forms. Thus, the above verb **lauzt** has **lauž-** in the present tense, which would generate the incorrect form *****lauž-ī-s/š**. The same complication exists in the case of verbs in *-st*, cf., for example, **plēs-t** *tear* which has **plēš-** in the present tense, as opposed to **plēs-** in the past. From the former an incorrect form *****plēš-ī-s/š-** would be derived, and not the correct **plēs-ī-s/š-**.

Finally, it should be mentioned that the three irregular verbs **bū-t**, **do-t** and **ie-t**, (cf. p. 103-104), form the future tense in a regular way, i. e. **bū-š-u, bū-s-i; do-š-u, do-s-i; ie-š-u, ie-s-i** etc.

Examples of Reflexive Paradigms
In conclusion, a couple of reflexive paradigms should be given:

infinitive	**mazgaties** *to wash oneself*	**cel-ties** *rise*
SG		
1 p.	**mazgā-š-os**	**cel-š-os**
2 p.	**mazgā-s-ies**	**cel-s-ies**
3 p.	**mazgā-s-ies**	**cel-s-ies**
PL		
1 p.	**mazgā-s-imies**	**cel-s-imies**
2 p.	**mazgā-s-i(e)tis**	**cel-s-i(e)tis**
3 p.	**mazgā-s-ies**	**cel-s-ies**

Formation of the Compound Tenses
(Darbības vārda salikto formu darīšana)

As pointed out above (p. 81) the compound tenses in Latvian are the *present perfect*, the *past perfect* and the *future perfect*. (Alternative terms would be the *compound present*, the *compound past* and the *compound future*.)

These forms are constructed with the help of the simple present, past and future tenses of the auxiliary **būt,** followed by the nominative case of the past active participle in the appropriate gender and number. This participle (for more detailed formation of which, see p. 151 f.) is in *-is* and *-uši* for the masculine singular and plural respectively, while the corresponding forms of the feminine are in *-usi* and *-ušas*. For alternative forms in older writings, see p. 154.

The *reflexive* endings are as follows:
-ies (masc. sg.), *-ušies* (masc. pl.), *-usies* (fem. sg.) and *-ušās* (fem. pl.).

The Present Perfect
After the introduction just given to the compound tenses one example should be sufficient to illustrate the formation of the present perfect:

Non-reflexive:

         M F
SG **es esmu / tu esi / viņš/viņa ir strādājis/strādājusi**
I/ you have / he/she has worked

PL **mēs esam / jūs esat / viņi/viņas ir strādājuši / strādājušas**[1]
we/ you/they (masc. & fem.) *have worked*

Reflexive:

         M F
SG **es esmu / tu esi / viņš/viņa ir cēlies/cēlusies**
I/you have / he/ she has risen (gotten up)

PL **mēs esam / jūs esat / viņi/viņas ir cēlušies/cēlušās**[1]
we/you have / he/she has risen (gotten up)

[1] in polite form (to one person): **jūs esat strādājis/strādājusi / cēlies/cēlusies**

The Past Perfect

Non-reflexive:

         M   F
SG **es biju / tu biji / viņš : viņa bija strādājis / strādājusi**
I / you have / he / she had worked

             M
PL **mēs bijām / jūs bijāt/ viņi : viņas bija strādājuši/**
             F
             strādājušas[1]
we/ you/they (masc. & fem.) *had worked*

Reflexive:

         M F
SG **es biju / tu biji / viņš/viņa bija cēlies/cēlusies**
I/ you / he/ she had risen (gotten up)

PL **mēs bijām / jūs bijāt / viņi/viņas bija cēlušies/cēlušās**[1]
we/ you/they (masc. & fem.) *had risen (gotten up)*

[1] in polite form (to one person): **jūs bijāt strādājis/strādājusi / cēlies/cēlusies**

The Future Perfect

Non-reflexive:

SG   M   F
SG   es būšu / tu būsi / viņš/viņa būs strādājis / strādājusi
I shall / you / he : she will have worked

PL   M
PL   mēs būsim / jūs būsi(e)t / viņi/viņas būs strādājuši/
       F
       strādājušas[1]
we shall / you/they (masc. & fem.) will have worked

Reflexive:

SG   M   F
SG   es būšu / tu būsi / viņš/viņa būs cēlies/cēlusies
I shall / you / he/she will have risen (gotten up)

PL   M
PL   mēs būsim / jūs būsi(e)t / viņi/viņas būs cēlušies/
       F
       cēlušās[1]
we shall / you/they (masc. & fem.) will have risen (gotten up)

[1] in polite form (to one person): **jūs būsi(e)t strādājis/strādājusi / cēlies/cēlusies**

ASPECT AND TENSE
(Veids un laiks)

Introduction

The disposition will be as follows:

I   Aspect (with the subsection *Aktionsarten*)
II Tense

It is natural to introduce aspect before the description of the use of the tenses since it appears practical to present tense with some view also to aspect. Although principally different, aspect and tense are intimately interwoven.

I Aspect

It is not easy to give a precise overall *definition* of the notion of aspect. It says something about *how* an action is performed according to two parameters labeled imperfective *(nepabeigtais veids)* and perfective *(pabeigtais veids)* respectively.

The *perfective* perspective implies that the action is looked upon as *accomplished*, or, to put in a more abstract way, is observed in its *totality*.

The *imperfective* perspective is that of an action in process, i. e. *not accomplished*, *not* viewed in its *totality*. This meaning is expressed in English by the so-called progressive with the auxiliary *be* + *-ing*-form of the main verb.

The participation of two members, perfective and imperfective, makes it possible to regard aspect as a *binary* (privative) opposition whereby only one member of the opposition is defined in positive terms, *in casu* the perfective, which is said to be *marked*, i. e. has the feature [+ totality], in contrast to the imperfective which is *unmarked* with respect to this feature.

The following question arises: Can aspect be regarded as a *grammatical category* of Latvian?

Grammaticalization implies a *mandatory* formal (morphological) expression of some definite semantic function. The requirements of both a specific *form* and *function* are crucial to the question of grammaticalization.

Let us test the question of the existence of a grammaticalized aspect in Latvian by considering the following two verb forms: **rakstīja** *was/were writing* and **uz-rakstīja** *wrote*. From a *functional-semantic* point of view they are clearly distinct, cf. their translations into the English *continuous* (progressive) vs. *non-continuous* (non-progressive) respectively, which reflect an aspectual opposition. *Formally* they differ through the absence vs. presence of a prefix. So far the requirements for assuming grammaticalization of aspect in Latvian seem to be fulfilled.

Prefixation is a regular strategy in Latvian for deriving verbs with perfective meaning from unprefixed verbs. The latter are as a rule imperfective. The verb **rakstīt** can take several prefixes, but **uz-** is the only one which does not supply this verb with an essentially new meaning. With **rakstīt uz-** may be said to be an empty (or near to empty) prefix in contrast to, for example, **pār-** which in combination with the verb in question creates a new verb semantically distinct from the basic one: **pār-rakstīt** *to rewrite*. The verb **pār-rakstīt** must be regarded as neutral with respect to the opposition perfective : imperfective. It is biaspectual. In contrast to the situation in many Slavic languages (cf., for example, Russian **pere-pisat'** : **pere-pisyvat'** *to rewrite*) and to some extent also in Lithuanian (e. g. **per-rašyti** : **per-rašinėti** *to rewrite*), Latvian does not allow secondary imperfectives to be formed with the help of suffixation. On the other hand, however, Latvian has developed a system of formally distinguished aspectual pairs according to the formula prefixed verb (= prefective) vs. unprefixed verb + adverb (= imperfective). This strategy, however, is limited to cases where the prefix shows a concrete (= local or directional) sense like for instance in:

iet *to go* → **ie-iet** *to enter* (prefix **ie-** *in*) = Russian **vo-jti** (pf.)
iet iekšā *to enter* (adverb **iekšā** *in*) = Russian **v-chodit'** (ipf.)

braukt *to go, travel* → **at-braukt** *to arrive* (pf.)
  braukt šurp *to arrive* (ipf.)

slēgt *to lock* → **at-slēgt** *to unlock, open* (pf.)
  slēgt vaļā *to unlock, open* (ipf.)

Both pairs **iet/ieiet, atbraukt/braukt šurp** and **atslēgt/slēgt vaļā** have complete tense paradigms, i. e. simple as well as compound forms.

What kind of proof do we have in support of the tenet that the prefixed verbs of the above type are really perfective whereas the unprefixed verbs accompanied by an adverb are imperfective?

Let us examine the following example:
Viņš ieiet istabā, apsēžas pie galdas un paņem rokās grāmatu

He enters the room, sits down at the table and takes a book in his hands

All three Latvian verbs (**ieiet, apsēžas, paņem**) are in the present tense. If one accepts that **paņemt** and **apsēžas** are perfective verbs according to the strategy described in connection with prefixation above, it seems legitimate to argue that also the remaining coordinate **ieiet** is perfective. My informants rejected the possibility of replacing **ieiet** in the above sentence with ***iet iekšā** which I take as an additional neat hint at the imperfective character of the latter. In the above example we have to do with the stylistic device which can be labeled *praesens dramaticum (historicum)*, cf. the functions of the perfective present described on p. 119.

What we observe in oppositions like **ieiet** : **iet iekšā** and similar cases is an *embryonic* grammaticalized system of oppositions of perfective vs. imperfective forms restricted to specific prefixes and adverbs in combination with a lexically specific set of verbs. The combination of unprefixed verb + adverb may be regarded as a kind of periphrastic construction which can be included in the morphology. However, the conclusion about the status of the oppositions of the type **ieiet** vs. **iet iekšā** is complicated by the existence also of the combination **ieiet iekšā**.

> The opposition prefixed verb vs. unprefixed verb + adverb may have originated from interference between the Finno-Ugric language Livonian and Latvian where the Indo-European language Latvian may have supplied Livonian with prefixation (unknown in Finno-Ugric) and Livonian in its turn Latvian with the adverb phrase which is known from Balto-Finnic (and other Finno-Ugric) languages. The result is a combination of the two strategies in both languages which seems to have led to an embryonic grammatical aspect opposition in Latvian. One could also think of influence from German, but the pattern *eingeht* vs. *geht ein* has a different distribution and is aspectually irrelevant.

Perfectivization

Perfectivization is as a rule expressed with the help of different prefixes. The commonest prefix for creating neutral perfectives, i. e. perfectives which do not obtain a radically new meaning in comparison with the corresponding unprefixed verb is **no-**, but also other prefixed (**pa -, uz-** etc.) are encountered in this function. The situation varies with the verb, cf. **darīt** : **padarīt** to *do*, **rakstīt** : **uzrakstīt** *to write*, **beigt** : **nobeigt** *to end*. The **no-** prefix is also used as a means of perfectivization with verbs of foreign origin, e.g. **nofotografēt, noregulēt**.

Imperfectivization

As pointed out above suffixation seems to be irrelevant as an aspect forming strategy in Latvian. Imperfectives are the bulk of unprefixed verbs (and in the case of verbs of motion: unprefixed verb + adverb).

Aktionsarten
(Procedurals)

In today's linguistics a distinction is made between *aspect* and *aktionsart* (there is no commonly accepted term in English for the latter although "procedurals" has been suggested).

The notion of *aktionsarten* is somewhat loose, which means that a universally accepted definition has not yet been arrived at. Many investigators would, however, subscribe to the following concept: Like aspect, the term *aktionsarten* also says something about *how* an action is performed, but contrary to aspect, *aktionsarten* is conceived as a lexical, and not a grammatical category. The 'aktionsart' *modifies the lexical meaning of the verb in question*. Thus, a verb like, for instance, **pastāvēt** can hardly be conceived as a neutral perfective to **stāvēt** *stand*, since **pa-** in this case is not felt to be semantically empty, but has the meaning '(for) a little (while) / some time', whence **pastāvēt** is said to belong to the *limitative aktionsart*. The relationship between **pārrakstīt** and **rakstīt** can also be determined as one of *aktionsart* since **pār-** modifies the meaning of **rakstīt**. Thus, Latvian prefixes have a double function, namely 1) to derive neutral perfectives from unprefixed imperfectives and 2) to modify the lexical meaning of the basic verb.

Most investigators would probably hold that the situation in Latvian is more properly described as one dominated by lexicalized *aktionsarten* rather than grammaticalized aspect.

II Tense

As pointed out above (p. 81) there are six tenses in Standard Latvian, namely *three simple* (i. e. the present, past and future) and *three compound* (the present perfect, the past perfect and the future perfect). Thus, for the indicative active the following concrete paradigm for the verb **(uz)rakstīt** *to write* in the 3rd p. (masc. sg.) can be presented:

	Past	*Present*	*Future*
IPF	rakstīja	raksta	rakstīs
PF	uzrakstīja	uzraksta	uzrakstīs

	Past Perfect	*Present Perfect*	*Future Perfect*
IPF	bija rakstījis	ir rakstījis	būs rakstījis
PF	bija uzrakstījis	ir uzrakstījis	būs uzrakstījis

The *formation* of the tenses has been dealt with above (p. 85-114). In the following the meaning and use of the tenses will be described.

Simple Tenses

1. The Present Tense
(Vienkāršā tagadne)

Consider the following sentence pairs:

Viņš raksta vēstuli : Viņš uzraksta vēstuli

The former corresponds to English 'he is writing a letter (just now)' whereas the latter should be extended with an adverbial like, for instance, **katru dienu** *every day* to sound natural. Thus, unlike Slavic, the perfective present of Latvian does not obtain future meaning, but retains a present tense meaning, however, in a more *abstract* or *general* sense than the *concrete hic et nunc* function of the imperfective present.

It should be observed that Latvian can make use of the "inclusive" (imperfective) present in cases like **viņš dzīvo šeit jau gadu** *he has been living here for a year (already)*, i. e. it has the same solution as German, Slavic and Romance languages, cf. *ich wohne hier seit einem Jahr, ja živu zdes' uže god* and *je demeure içi depuis une année*, but it is also possible to say **viņš ir (no)dzīvojis šeit jau gadu**, i. e. using the present prefect tense as English and (broadly speaking) the Nordic languages.

The *meaning* of the present tense in Latvian (and many other languages) can be expressed through the formula:

$$E \text{ simul } S$$

which reads 'E is simultaneous with S' where E stands for 'event' and S for 'moment of speech'.

2. The Past Tense
(Vienkāršā pagātne)
Compare the above presentation of the present tense and contrast the following sentence pairs:

Viņš rakstīja vēstuli   **: Viņš uzrakstīja vēstuli**
He was writing a letter   *: He wrote a letter*

The meaning of the Latvian past can be illustrated in the following way:

E before S

3. The Future Tense
(Vienkāršā nākotne)
Much of the same that has been said about the simple past above in terms of aspectuality can be repeated for the future tense.
Contrast the following sentence pair:

Viņš rakstīs vēstuli   **: Viņš uzrakstīs vēstuli**
He will be writing a letter   *: He will write a letter*

The basic meaning of the Latvian simple future can be diagrammed in this way:

E after S

Modal Uses of the Simple Future
Finally, mention should be made of the fact that the (simple) future (as in many other languages) can acquire *modal* nuances (see also section on mood), cf., for example **iesim!** *let us go!*

Compound Tenses

The compound tenses denote the result of a past event projected into the present, past or future respectively.

As a result of interference from Russian (with only one form to cover meanings related to the past) an increase in the use of simple forms instead (especially) of past forms has been observed among Latvian speaking people in Latvia in many cases where compound forms would traditionally have been expected. Thus, comparisons which have been made between works of Soviet Latvian authors and of Latvian exile authors have revealed significant differences in this respect.

1. The Present Perfect
(Saliktā tagadne)

This tense denotes a past event seen from the perspective of the present (a kind of indefinite past).

The meaning of this form can be diagrammed in the following way:

$$(Ea \text{ before } R) + (Es \text{ simul } R)$$

where the symbol Ea refers to the verbal action ('event action'), R to "reference point" and Es to a state resulting from that action ('event').

2. The Past Perfect
(Saliktā pagātne)

Let us start with the following autentical example:
Viņš bija nācis vakar, bet es nebiju mājās

The main clause of this compound sentence cannot be translated by the pluperfect into English:
*He had come yesterday, but I was not at home

Thus, it looks legitimate to call this tense the past perfect rather than the pluperfect in Latvian because it seems to differ from the English and Scandinavian pluperfect. However, in Ceplīte & Ceplītis 1991, p. 70 the following definition of the compound past is given: "[it indicates that] an action has taken place prior to another action which has occurred in the past" (our translation). This definition which could be valid for English and the Nordic languages as well, is accompanied by the following example: **es biju gājis kādu kilometru, kad apjautu savu kļūdu** *I had gone some kilometer when I discovered my error*. My Latvian informants okayed the insertion of **jau** *already* in this example, but claimed that this would not be necessary to express the meaning of a pluperfect in the English sense. Thus, one feels somewhat puzzled about the situation. It is possible that the Latvian compound past is more "flexible" than, say, the English and Scandinavian pluperfect and could be adequately described both according to a *bipartite* formula, namely E *before* R *before* S as in English and Scandinavian and a *tripartite* formula

$$(Ea \text{ before } R) + (Es \text{ simul } R) + (R \text{ before } S)$$

where the symbols *Ea* and *Es* are explained under point 1) above. The former may perhaps be regarded as basic, the latter as an additional characterization. At any rate, the compound past of Latvian is not used when a specific time reference is given. Thus, a sentence like **es esmu paņēmis vēstuli vakar* is incorrect as is its English counterpart: **I have received a letter yesterday.*

3. The Future Perfect
(Saliktā nākotne)
As a typical example of the compound future in a main clause may serve:
Viņš būs uzrakstījis vēstuli (līdz 1. decembrim)
He will have finished the letter till (by) December 1.

The basic meaning of the Latvian compound future can probably be expressed by the following formula:

$$E \text{ before } R \text{ after } S$$

where *R* denotes a 'reference point'. The reference point is the event expressed in the main clause.

If this description of the Latvian compound future is correct and the meaning of the simple future is adequately described as *E* after *S*, one should expect the compound future to occur predominantly in compound sentences with *sequential* actions, whereas the simple future could be characterized as unmarked since it should be able to express both sequence and simultaneity (probably limited by aspect). This conception seems to hold true.

Modal Uses of the Future Perfect
Finally, it should be mentioned that, like the simple future, also the compound future can acquire *modal* nuances as shown by the following example:
Viņi laikam būs jau atbraukuši
They have possibly/presumably arrived.

Limitations
The above presentation has been confined to the active voice and the finite verb. For tense in the passive voice as well as in the non-finite verbal system, i. e. participles and gerunds, see sections on voice and the non-finite verb. For tenses in the marked moods, see section on mood.

MOOD
(Izteiksme)

Mood is *an expression of the speaker's attitude towards the content of the verb (utterance).*
As stated above (p. 81), Latvian has the following moods:

1. the **indicative** *(īstenības izteiksme)*
2. the **imperative** *(pavēles izteiksme)*
3. the **subjunctive** *(vēlējuma izteiksme* or *kondicionālis)*
4. the **debitive** *(debitīvs* or *vajadzības izteiksme)*
5. the **relative** mood *(atstāstījuma izteiksme)*

The indicative can be regarded as the unmarked mood in opposition to the rest which are labeled marked moods.

The rationale for considering the debitive and the relative as moods can be questioned on formal grounds (not least in view of the fact that they have almost as many tenses as the unmarked indicative).

1. The Indicative

The indicative has already been described from the point of view of its morphological characteristics in connection with the different tenses above (simple present, simple past, simple future, present perfect, past perfect, future perfect). For the use of these tenses, see section on tense. Functionally the indicative is in contrast with the other moods, in that it expresses something real which either has taken place, is taking place or undoubtedly will take place: **Jānis studēja/ir studējis/studē/ studēs filoloģiju Latvijas universitātē** *John studied/has studied/is studying will be studying philology at the University of Latvia.*

2. The Imperative

As shown in the table on p. 82, the imperative is formed on the basis of the present stem.
The imperative proper is limited to one person, i. e. the 2nd (singular and plural).
In the singular it is *identical in form with the 2nd p. sg. of the present tense.* Since the 2nd sg. present shows certain irregularities, the guidelines formulated on p. 107 ff. should be consulted.

Examples:
non-reflexives:
runā! *speak!*
lasi! *read!*
saki! *say!*
nes! *carry!*
piedod! *forgive!*
nāc! *come!*
bēdz! *run away, flee!*
esi! *be!*
jūti! *feel!*

Reflexives:
mazgājies! *wash yourself!*
celies! *rise (get up)!*

To form the plural, the ending *-iet* (non-reflexive) or *-ieties* (reflexive) are added to the form of the second sg. imperative:
runā-j-iet!
lasiet!
sakiet!
nes-iet!
piedodiet!
nāc-iet!
bēdz-iet!
es-iet!
jūt-iet!

mazgā-j-ieties!
celieties!

Note that an automatic *j*-glide is inserted before the ending *-iet(ies)* when the 2nd sg. imperative ends in a vowel (*-ā, -ē* or *-o*).

It should further be emphasized that the 2nd p.plural imperative always has the consonant of the 2nd p. sg. present and not that of the 2nd plural present. This is to prevent the student from constructing incorrect imperative forms like, for example, ***nākiet** instead of the correct **nāciet**.

Finally, it should be emphasized that with imperatives with an *-e-/-ē-* in the root (e. g. **esi! esiet! bēdz! bēdziet!**) a narrow *-e-/-ē* is spoken (as should be expected according to the rules, cf. p. 29 ff.).

THE VERB: MOOD

The *use* and *meaning* of the imperative has been sufficiently illustrated through the examples given.

Besides the second person forms of the imperative, there is also a form called *adhortative,* which is identical in form with the 1st person indicative of the future tense:
runāsim! *let us speak!*
nesīsim! *let us carry!*
With the same meaning also the 1 p. pl. indicative of the present tense is used:
runājam! *let us speak!*, **nesam!** *let us carry!*
An imperativelike function is also encountered in the 3 p. This function is expressed through the particle **lai** (cf. **laist** *to let*) + the *nominative* sg. of the personal pronoun + the 3 p. of the indicative present tense:
lai viņš/viņa/viņi/viņas nāk! *may he/she/they* (masc. & fem.) *come!*
lai dzīvo Latvija/ karalis! *long live Latvia / the king!*
svētīts lai top tavs vārds *hallowed be Thy name.*

3. The Subjunctive

A. Formation
Latvian distinguishes between a present and a past subjunctive, the latter being a compound formation.

1) The *present* subjunctive is formed on the basis of the infinitive stem, to which is added the ending *-tu* (non-reflexive), *-tos* (reflexive), irrespective of the person or number referred to.
Examples:
non-reflexives:
runā-t *speak* → **runā-tu**
gribē-t *wish* → **gribē-tu**
pirk-t *buy* → **pirk-tu**
brauk-t *go, travel* → **brauk-tu**
bū-t *be* → **bū-tu**
reflexives:
mazgā-ties *wash oneself* → **mazgā-tos**
cel-ties *rise (get up)* → **cel-tos**

Illustration of a paradigm:
es/tu/viņš/viņa/mēs/jūs/viņi/viņas runātu/celtos

In accordance with the general rules (p. 29 ff.), an *-e/-ē* before *-tu/-tos* has the open pronunciation (in contrast to the infinitive, where a narrow *-e/-ē* is spoken).

2) the *past* subjunctive is formed by combining the past active participle (in the appropriate form masc./fem.; sg./pl., cf. p. 153 below)

with the present subjunctive of **būt** *be* in the function of an auxiliary, e. g:

         M   F   M   F
SG **būtu runājis/runājusi / cēlies/cēlusi**
PL **būtu runājuši/runājušas / cēlušies/cēlušās**

The *difference in meaning* between the present and the past subjunctive may be illustrated through the following example:
    Ja man būtu nauda (pašlaik), es brauktu uz Rīgu (pašlaik)
    If I had money (now), I would go to Riga (now)
                            vs.
    Ja man būtu bijusi nauda (tai laikā/tad), es būtu braucis uz Rīgu (tai laikā)
    If I had had money (then / at that time), I would have gone to Riga (then / at that time)

There is also a *subjunctive passive,* which is formed with the help of one of the auxiliaries **taptu/būtu** + the *t*-participle, see section on voice as well as non-finite verb forms (passive participles). One example will suffice here for illustration:
    Ja šis velosipēds būtu nupirkts pagājušajā gadā, jis būtu bijis lētāks, nekā tagad
    If this bicycle had been bought last year, it would have been cheaper than now.

B. Some Major Functions

The subjunctive is encountered in main clauses, in main *and* subordinate clauses or in subordinate clauses alone.

a) The Subjunctive in Main Clauses
- To express a *wish:*
Kaut arī mums būtu tik daudz naudas! *If even we had that much money!*
- In *polite request*:
Vai tu varētu man palīdzēt? *Could you help me?*
Vai jūs man lūdzu atslēgtu šis durvis? *Could you please shut/close this door?*
Es gribētu nopirkt [...] *I would like to buy [...]*
(Compare also the corresponding subjunctive formula in German *ich möchte (gern) [...],* in French *je voudrais (bien) [...],* in Russian *ja chotel(a) by [...].*)

THE VERB: MOOD

b) The Subjunctive both in the Main and the Subordinate Clauses

• This subjunctive is used in *conditional clauses* if the content is *hypothetical*:

Ja mums būtu bijis daudz naudas, mēs būtu braukuši uz Ameriku
If we had had a lot of money, we would have gone to America

NB. In conditional clauses of a non-hypothetical nature, the indicative must be used:

Ja sestdien būs skaidrs laiks, mēs brauksim uz Jūrmalu
If there will be nice weather on Saturday, we will go to Jurmala

c) The Subjunctive in Subordinate Clauses

• In order to express *purpose*, the conjunction **lai** + the subjunctive is used, e.g.

Lai drusku atpūstos, mēs nedēļas nogalē aizbrauksim uz Jūrmalu
In order to rest a little, we shall go to Jurmala at the end of the week

Note: Foreigners frequently make mistakes by using an infinitive construction in this function, which is not tolerated in this function in Latvian, cf. pp. 145 and 210.

• A *wish* (after the verb form **vēlos** *I wish*, the verb + noun combination **izsacīt vēlēšanos** *express the wish*) is expressed by **lai** + the subjunctive:

Es vēlos, lai darbība tiktu īstenota
I wish that the action shall be carried out
Darbības vārds vēlējuma izteiksmē izsaka vēlēšanos, lai darbība tiktu īstenota, vai arī norāda, ka darbība ir iespējama
The verb in the subjunctive mood expresses the wish that the action shall be carried out, or it can show that the action is possible

Note the shift between conjunctions **lai** and **ka** (on which see immediately below) in this example.

• Close to the function of the subjunctive described in the preceding point is the following:

Ir svarīgi, lai tu nāktu
It is important that you come
Vajag (present tense from the verb **vajadzēt** *must, need*), **lai tu nāktu**
It is necessary that you come

• After verbs or expressions implying a *command*, the construction **lai** + the subjunctive is also used:

Viņš sacīja, lai es tulīt nāktu
He said (so) (in order that) that I should come at once
Note: The construction with **lai** + the subjunctive after a *verbum dicendi* (verb of saying) implies, however, only a *vague command* whence the relative mood (on which see below) is preferred instead:
Viņš sacīja, lai es tulīt nākot
He said that I should come at once
Observe that two constructions in Latvian correspond to the English *that*: either **ka** + *the indicative/relative mood* or: **lai** + *the subjunctive/the relative mood* (on which, see below). The choice between the two constructions depends on the character of the utterance. Thus, contrast the following two constructions:
Viņš sacīja, ka ir/esot skaidrs laiks
He said that the weather was nice
        and
Viņš sacīja, lai es tulīt nāktu/nākot
The fundamental difference between the **ka-** and **lai-**constructions after *verba dicendi* is that in the former a *description* (state) is expressed, while in the latter the verb of saying implies a *wish* or a *command*. In direct speech the wish/command is expressed with the help of an imperative phrase:
Viņš sacīja: "Nāc tulīt!"
He said: "Come at once!"
whereas the construction
Viņš sacīja, ka ir/esot skaidrs laiks
corresponds to an indicative construction in direct speech:
Vinš sacīja: "Laiks ir skaidrs"
He said: "The weather is nice".

- The subjunctive is also used in *concessive* subordinate clauses with a *hypothetical* meaning, e.g.

Lai kur es dzīvotu, es nekad neaizmirsīšu savo dzimto pusi
Wherever I would be living, I shall never forget my native place

- Its use is also obligatory in hypothetical comparisons, e.g.

Mežā bija tik klusu, it kā vāja nemaz nebūtu
It was so quiet (silent) in the forest as if there were no wind at all

- A subtle area is the use of the subjunctive in certain relative clauses after a *negated* main clause:

Visā manā valstī nav cilvēka, kas mani mīlētu
In all my country there is not a person who would love me
The *hypothetical* character of this sentence is clearly felt.
The same is the case in:

- **Arī man kādreiz gribas drauga, par ko es būtu drošs**

I, too, at times (some time) (would like) like (to have) a friend whom I could trust.

Observe the generalizing adverb **kādreiz** which eliminates the possibility that the utterance refers to a single concrete event which would require the use of the indicative.

A similar case with a generalizing meaning is encountered in:
- **Es nekad neesmu dzirdējis, ka viņa tā dziedātu**
I have never heard that she has sung like this (heard her singing like this)
- After verbs and expressions which express *fear lest* something should happen, a construction with the subjunctive (with a mandatory pleonastic ('superfluous') **ne**) can be used, e.g.
Vecāki baidījās, kaut bērns nesaslimtu
The parents feared that the child would fall ill
A construction with **ka** + the indicative (without the negational particle **ne**) can be used with the same meaning:
Vecāki baidījās, ka bērns saslims
For the student the latter construction is preferable in active use, but he/she must know the alternative construction in order to be able to interpret it correctly when encountered in texts.

> The pleonastic **ne** in the subjunctive construction is motivated in historical syntax (through the development from *parataxis* (coordination) to *hypotaxis* (subordination), cf. **Lai bērns nesaslimtu! Vecāki baidījās** *May the child not fall ill! The parents feared/were afraid* → **Vecāki baidījās, kaut bērns nesaslimtu.** Cf. similar constructions in Romance, Slavic and other languages, e.g. French *je crains, qu'il ne vienne* 'I am afraid that he will come', Russian *ja bojus′, čtoby on ne prišël* 'I am afraid that he will come'. Here again we find the pleonastic **ne** + the subjunctive.
> Observe that the construction with the subjunctive in expressions of fear cannot be used if the main clause is negated. Thus, for instance after **(es) nebaidījos** *I am not afraid* only the indicative is possible.

4. The Debitive

A. Formation

The debitive is a specific formation of Latvian alone. It is formed with the help of the *proclitic particle* **jā-** (of obscure origin) + the *3rd p. of the present tense indicative*, e.g. **jārunā** (< **runāt** *to speak*) / **jāsāk** (< **sākt** *to begin*).

An exception is the verb **būt**, where the debitive is formed on the basis of the infinitive: **jābūt**.

The debitive distinguishes all six tenses of the indicative, cf. the following paradigm:

simple present:	(**ir**) **jārunā**
simple past:	**bija jārunā**
simple future:	**būs jārunā**
present perfect:	**ir bijis jārunā**
past perfect:	**bija bijis jārunā**
future perfect:	**būs bijis jārunā**

The debitive has two sub-moods, namely those of the subjunctive and the relative mood, cf.

the subjunctive in:
man būtu (pres.) / būtu bijis (past) jārunā
I should have / have had to speak

and the relative mood in:
man esot (pres,) / būšot (pret.) jārunā
I (am said) to have to be saying

The status of the debitive as a marked mood could be questioned on the following grounds: first, it has as many tenses as the indicative, whereas a marked mood is characterized through a poorer inventory of tenses (for example, the imperative with only one tense, or the subjunctive with two); second, it distinguishes sub-moods which again could be taken as an argument against its status as a marked mood or a mood at all.

B. Syntax

The (logical) *subject* of the debitive is in the *dative case*, e.g.
Man (ir) jārunā *I must/have to speak*.

Note also that in sentences with an *adjective in the function of a predicative*, the adjective must be in agreement with the dative subject and therefore appear in the *dative case*, e.g.
Studentiem jābūt uzmanīgiem
The students have to be attentive

Moreover, the object of a transitive verb appears in the *nominative*, and not the accusative case, e.g.
man jālasa *avīze* *I have to read the newspaper*

Note: The accusative should, however, be used in two contexts, namely after a transitive infinitive or if the object is a pronoun of the 1st or 2nd person, cf.
Man jāsāk lasīt *avīzi* *I have to begin to read the newspaper*
Ojāram būs *mūs* jāapmeklē *Ojars will have to look for us*

Observe that when the dative subject is deleted, a general meaning (English "one". German/Nordic "man", French "on") is obtained:
Kad ūdens smeļas mutē, jāmācās peldēt (Latvian proverb)

When the water is streaming into the mouth, one has to learn to swim.

C. Alternative Constructions

The debitive meaning can also be rendered in other ways, namely by:

a) the impersonal verb (cf. p. 206) **vajadzēt** (pres. **vajag**, pret. **vajadzēja**), e.g. **viņam vajag strādāt** *he must work*, **šo uzdevumu vajag padarīt** *this task has to be done* (observe the accusative **šo uzdevumu** due to its object function dependent on **(vajag) padarīt** – in contrast to the example quoted under c) where **šis uzdevums** is in the position of a grammatical subject and therefore appears in the nominative case),

b) the impersonal verb **nākties** (pres. **nākas**, pret. **nācās**): **mums nākas aizbraukt** *we have to leave (go)*,

c) the passive *m*-participle: **šis uzdevums ir padarāms** *this task has to be done.*

Whereas the debitive construction implies *objective necessity*, the **vajadzēt**-construction designates *obligation* or *moral necessity* (English *shall/should*). Classical contrastive illustrations are **jums jādzer tēja** *you have to drink tea* (because there is no coffee) and **jums vajag dzert tēju** *you have to (= should) drink tea* (because it is healthy/good for you). The **nākties**-construction as a rule expresses *inevitability* (like the impersonal verb *prichodit'sya* in Russian).

5. The Relative Mood

A. Formation

The so-called relative mood, i. e. a mood which expresses second-hand information, is – as in Lithuanian – formed with the help of (most frequently active) petrified participle forms (present *-ot*, refl. *-oties*, future *-šot*, refl. *-šoties*) in the function of a finite verb. (For the formation of these participles/gerunds, see p. 148)

The relative mood in Latvian distinguishes *four tenses*, namely *two simple* (viz. the present and the future), e.g. **lasot** (*read*) and **lasīšot** respectively, and *two compound* (viz. the present perfect and the future perfect), e.g. **esot lasījis/lasījusi/lasījuši/lasījušas** and **būšot lasījis/lasījusi/lasījuši /lasījušas**. As can be seen from the examples, the compound tenses are constructed with the help of the auxiliary **būt** in the (undeclinable) relative mood plus the main verb in the form of the nominative (masc., fem., sg. and pl.) of the past active participle.

In comparison with the indicative mood the inventory of the past tenses in the relative mood are reduced to the present perfect alone, and the simple past and the past perfect are lacking. Still, the relative mood is characterized through a relatively rich system of tenses, which could put into question the status of the relative mood as an independent mood, cf. our comments in connection with the debitive above.

B. Use

The relative mood is used when the speaker/writer wishes to make explicit that he/she has not witnessed the message himself/herself.

This implies two areas of usage:

a) *indirect speech*
b) *rendering of rumours and unsure claims*

The relative mood is used after *verba dicendi* (verbs of saying) and similar.

It seems legitimate to distinguish between the present and future meanings on the one side, and that of the past on the other.

Illustrations of the *present and future tenses of the relative mood*:

Anda teica, ka drīz *došoties* brīvdienās uz Latviju *apciemošot* draugus. Mēnesi vēlāk viņa *braukšot* atpakaļ uz Norvēģiju

Anda said that she would go to Latvia during the holidays and see friends. A month later she would return to Norway.

Observe the logical time reference in Latvian (in opposition to the automatic principle of the so-called *consecutio temporum* in English). Note also that the relative mood can be found in whole passages (as in the above example) and thus go beyond the subordinate clause introduced by the conjunction **ka** (*that*) after the *verbum dicendi*.

Observe further that the relative mood seems to have developed a kind of sub-mood, namely that of the imperative (or rather subjunctive), cf., for example:

Viņš sacīja, lai es tulīt nākot
He said that I should come at once.

In direct speech this corresponds to a construction with the imperative, i. e.:

Viņš sacīja: "Nāc tulīt!"
He said: "Come here at once!"
Cf. under the subjunctive above.

Illustration of the *past tense of the relative mood*:

Here it seems possible to distinguish between three functions, namely:

1. the "narrative", whereby the past participle of the main verb alone is used without the **būt**-auxiliary in the form of the relative mood, e.g. This strategy covers function a) above.

Anda *devusies* brīvdienās uz Latviju un *apciemojusi* draugus. Mēnesi vēlāk viņa *atbraukusi* uz Norveğiju

Anda is said to have gone for Latvija during her vacations to see friends. After a month she is said to have returned to Norway.

In negated form **nav** + the past active participle is used, e.g.

Anda nav devusies [...].

2. the "dubitative" which implies the use of the **būt**-auxiliary + the past participle of the main verb:

Anda *esot devusies* brīvdienās uz Latviju un *[esot] apciemojusi* draugus. Mēnesi vēlāk viņa *esot atbraukusi* uz Norvēğiju.

In *negated* form **ne**- (not **nav**) is used, i. e. **neesot devusies** etc.

The dubitative is used in function b), cf. the table above.

3. the "folkloristic narrative" which involves the same technique as in 1, except that in negated form **ne** is used (as in 2 and not **nav** as in 1). The following illustration is taken from a tale / legend:

Netālu no Dobeles Lielbērzes muižā *kūluši* labību. Kādu rītu strādnieki *gājuši* kult. *Redzējuši*, ka Velns sēd uz bedres malas un šuj zābakus. Bikses *karājušās* uz ārda gala. Strādnieki *paņēmuši* sprigulus un *dzinuši* Velnu ārā. Velns *negājis*. Te *dziedājis* gailis. Velns *pakampis* ārdu ar biksēm un *aizskrējis* uz purvu. Tur tas *nogrimis*. Tikai ārda gals *palicis* ārā. Vēl tagad šo purvu sauc par Velna līci.

On the Lielberze estate not far from Dobele grain was being threshed. One morning the workers went to thresh grain. They saw that the Devil was sitting at the edge of a pit and sewing a pair of boots. His trousers were hanging on the end of a stackstand. The workers took the beaters and started chasing the Devil away. The Devil wouldn't go. At that moment) the cock crowed. The Devil seized the stackstand with the trousers and ran into the marsh. There he drowned. Only the end of the stackstand stuck out. This marsh is called the Devil's Bay up to the present day.

The relative mood has been claimed to be in a state of decline since World War II, which has been ascribed to interference from Russian, where this mood is lacking. However, the relative mood is flourishing in today's press in Latvia. If the alleged decline of the debitive is correct, it now seems to experience a period of renaissance, at least in the language of the press, cf. the following example:

LR vēstniecība Briselē ziņo, ka V.Birkavs *iepazīstinājis* S. Balančino ar iekšpolitisko situāciju Latvijā un *raksturojis* ieceres valsts aizsardzības nostiprināšanā, kuras paredzēts realizēt ar Partenerattiecību mieram starpniecību.
V.Birkavs *esot apmeklējis* ari Latvijas vēstniecības vajadzībām iegadāto ēku Briselē, kurā Ārlietu ministrija drīzumā *plānojot* uzsākt remontdarbus [...].
The embassy of the Republic of Latvia in Brussels reports that V.Birkavs informed S.Balancino about the political situation within Latvia and has presented plans for strengthening of the national defense, which are supposed to be realized with Partnership for peace as an intermediary.
V. Birkavs has also (reportedly) visited the building acquired for the Latvian embassy in Brussels, where the Ministry of Foreign Affairs is (reportedly) planning to start restoration work in the near future.

In many (but far from all cases, cf. the examples just quoted) the relative mood can be rendered in English by 'is said to' (or 'reportedly'), in Norwegian by 'skal være' (or 'angivelig'), in Swedish by 'lär vara' e.g. **viņš esot slims** *he is said to be ill / han skal være syk / han lär vara sjuk.* See also examples above.

In Slavic the relative mood of Baltic has a kind of parallel in the Bulgarian *renarrated mood* (formally equally expressed through an active participle) as well as the so-called *Referatskonjunktiv* in German (type: *Hans sagt, dass er krank sei*). The relative mood is also encountered in Balto-Finnic languages (Estonian).

VOICE
(Darbības vārda kārta)

Latvian distinguishes between the *active* and the *passive*. This voice section will deal with both the morphology and use of voice with special emphasis on the passive.

Definitions

From a semantic point of view, a *passive* construction can be defined as *an utterance in which the grammatical subject refers to the patient* (literally 'the suffering'), i. e. the one against whom the action is directed. For example, in 'I was bullied (by him)', in contrast to an *active,* where *the grammatical subject* ('he') *refers to the agent*, i. e. the performer of the action: 'he bullied me'. (An alternative is to define the passive in positive terms and the active in negative by stating that all constructions which are not passive, are active.)

In the *active* sentence quoted above, the agent is expressed by the grammatical subject *he*, the patient by the object *me*. In the *passive* it is the other way around: the patient is expressed by the subject *I* whereas the (optional) agent is reflected in the complement *by him*.

The examples just quoted demonstrate that in English the verb is morphologically different in the active voice than in the passive. The same is also the case in Latvian.

Morphology of the Active Voice

The morphological make-up of active verb forms has been illustrated on pp. 85-114 above.

Use of the Active Voice

The active voice is encountered far more frequently than the passive, and it must be used when the conditions for using a passive construction are not present, cf. p. 139 f. below.

Morphology of the Passive Voice

1. Expression of the Passive Voice in Latvian
A. *The Indicative*
For expression of the passive voice, Latvian has at its disposal two *auxiliaries:* **tikt** (or more rarely **tapt** or **kļūt**) *to become* and **būt** *to be,* which are combined with the *t*-participle of the main verb (for the formation of this participle, see p. 155). This formational strategy will be referred to as the *formal* passive.

To some extent, the formal passive in Latvian can also be expressed through *reflexive* verbs (as is true in the Nordic, Slavic and Romance languages); see p. 141 f.

As in the active, in the passive *six tenses* are distinguished, namely, *the present, the past, the future, the present perfect, the past perfect* and *the future perfect*. The **tikt** (or **tapt/kļūt**) auxiliary is used to form the the first three, whereas **būt** is reserved for the perfect tenses.

We will avoid using the terms "simple" vs. "compound" forms (tenses) in connection with the passive, since all forms must necessarily be compound. Other grammars of Latvian, however, often use these terms with the present, past and future referred to as simple forms, and the present, past and future perfect as compound. The full forms of the present, past and future perfect would be **esmu/biju/būšu ticis/tikusi mazgāts/mazgāta / esam/bijām/būsim tikuši/tikušas mazgāti/mazgātas**. The forms **ticis/tikusi/tikuši/ti-kušas**, however, are as a rule omitted (deleted). The (underlying) fuller forms in practice are the reason for considering the forms of the present, past and future perfect (more) compound than the forms of the present, past and future.

The distributional criteria for **tikt** and **būt** as auxiliaries in the passive have now been given. There remains, however, one more parameter to be considered (besides that between "simple" and "compound"), namely that between passive participles with a *verbal function,* and passive participles which *function as adjectives*. In the former case **tikt** is used, in the latter **būt**; for example, **kareivis tiek ievainots** *the soldier is (being) wounded* vs. **kareivis ir ievainots** *the soldier is wounded*. What we see here is an opposition of action (so-called "Handlungspassiv") vs. state (= "Zustandspassiv").

The Latvian passive reminds one of the German and the Nordic passive, in that two auxiliaries (with the meanings "become" vs. "be") are used in combination with the past passive participle, cf. German *wird gewaschen* vs. *ist gewaschen,* Norwegian *bli vasket* vs. *være vasket,* and further in the possibility of deletion of the *werden / bli* auxiliary in the present, past and future perfect; e. g., German *ist gewaschen (worden),* Norwegian *er (blitt) vasket*. In German and the Nordic languages an opposition between "Handlungs-" and "Zustandspassiv" is also present.

Sample of a passive paradigm in the indicative mood:

Infinitive: **tikt/būt mazgātam** (note: dative!) *to be washed*

	Present	*Past*	*Future*
SG 1	**tieku mazgāts** *I am being washed*	**tiku mazgāts** *I was being washed*	**tikšu mazgāts** *I am going to be washed*
2	**tiec mazgāts**	**tiki mazgāts**	**tiksi mazgāts**
3	**tiek mazgāts**	**tika mazgāts**	**tiks mazgāts**
PL 1	**tiekam mazgāti**	**tikām mazgāti**	**tiksim mazgāti**
2	**tiekat mazgāti**	**tikāt mazgāti**	**tiksit mazgāti**
3	**tiek mazgāti**	**tika mazgāti**	**tiks mazgāti**

	Present Perfect	*Past Perfect*	*Future Perfect*
SG 1	**esmu mazgāts** *I have been washed*	**biju mazgāts** *I had been washed*	**būšu mazgāts** *I will have been washed*
2	**esi mazgāts**	**biji mazgāts**	**būsi mazgāts**
3	**ir mazgāts**	**bija mazgāts**	**būs mazgāts**
PL 1	**esam mazgāti**	**bijām mazgāti**	**būsim mazgāti**
2	**esat mazgāti**	**bijāt mazgāti**	**būsi(e)t mazgāti**
3	**ir mazgāti**	**bija mazgāti**	**būs mazgāti**

For the sake of convenience, the participle is given only in the masculine (sg. and pl.) in the table above. The complete paradigm reads: **tieku/tiku/tikšu /esmu/biju/būšu mazgāts** (masc.) / **mazgāta** (fem.) etc., **tiekam/tikām/tiksim mazgāti** (masc.) / **mazgātas** (fem.) etc.

The reason for the appearance of the participle in the dative case in the infinitive is to be found in the section on syntax, p. 146.

For the choice of aspect, i. e. the prefixed (perfective) form of the participle vs. the unprefixed (imperfective) form, see the general principles set forth in the section on Aspect (and Tense), p. 115 ff.

B. *Other Moods than the Indicative (Marked Moods)*

Beyond in the indicative mood, the passive can also be expressed in the subjunctive, the relative, the imperative (rarely) and (extremely rarely) the debitive.

Examples of paradigms of the subjunctive and relative passive

The same formational principle which was demonstrated in connection with the indicative passive is encountered here as well, namely the combination of the auxiliaries **tikt/būt** (in the proper form) with the *t*-participle in the masculine/feminine, singular/plural, as appropriate.

The Subjunctive

	Present		*Past*	
SG 1		**mazgāts-/ta**		**mazgāts/-ta**
2		"		"
3	**tiktu**	"	**būtu**	"
PL 1		**mazgāti/-tas**		**mazgāti/-tas**
2		"		**mazgāti/-tas**
3		"		**mazgāti/-tas**

As in the active voice, two tenses of the subjunctive are distinguished in the passive. For the forms of the auxiliaries **tiktu** and **būtu** which are the same in all three persons and both numbers, see section on (the formation of) the subjunctive, p. 125.

The Relative Mood

	Present		*Future*	
SG 1		**mazgāts/-ta**		**mazgāts/-ta**
2		"		"
3	**tiekot**	"	**tikšot**	"
PL 1		**mazgāti/-tas**		**mazgāti/-tas**
2		"		"
3		"		"

	Past (Present Perfect)		*Future Perfect*	
SG 1		**mazgāts/-ta**		**mazgāts/-ta**
2		"		"
3	**esot**	"	**būšot**	"
PL 1		**mazgāti/-tas**		**mazgāti/-tas**
2		"		"
3		"		"

As is seen in the table above, the number of tenses in the relative passive is the same as in the relative active, namely four. In comparison with the indicative system (both active and passive), the number of tenses with a time reference in the past have been reduced from three to one.

For the forms of the auxiliaries **tiekot/tikšot** and **esot/būšot**, see the section on formation of the relative mood, p. 131 and p. 148.

2. Expression of the Passive Voice in English

In the interest of a contrastive perspective, a couple of words should also be said about the formation of the passive in English.

In English the passive voice is expressed through the combination of *one* auxiliary *(be)* with one participle (i. e. the past passive participle, see the English translations in the above paradigms.

The Romance languages and (most of) the Slavic also have a passive morphology of the same type as English.

The morphological make-up of the German and the Nordic passive has already been dealt with on p. 136.

Motivations for choosing Passive Constructions. General Considerations

Generally speaking, there are two important motivations for choosing a passive construction over an active:

1. Passive constructions have *a different functional sentence perspective* (FSP) than the corresponding active, called *"theme-rheme"* structure.

2. Passive constructions admit *deletion (omission) of the agent*

1. Functional Sentence Perspective (FSP)

The following two sentences have differing functional sentence perspectives:

(1) The workmen are building a house
(2) The house is being built by workmen

In (1) 'the workmen' belongs to the *theme* (i. e. is part of the given information) whereas 'a house' is *rhematic* (i. e. brings new information). In (2) the situation is the reverse: 'the house' is *thematic*, 'workmen' *rhematic*.

In context-bound, non-emphatic sentences, *the theme appears at the beginning of the utterance, the rheme at the end.* This theme-before-rheme order should be considered as a general rule. Furthermore, in *article languages* (English, Nordic, Romance) a *thematic* noun will appear with *a definite article* whereas a *rhematic* noun is usually accompanied by *an indefinite article*. In *non-article languages* (such as Latvian), the criterion for recognition of the *theme* is in fact its *initial position*; see p. 221. The same is observed in English with proper names, cf. *Peter* (thematic) *beat Paul* (thematic) vs. *Paul* (thematic) *was beaten by Peter* (rhematic).

2. Agent Deletion

Agent deletion occurs under the following circumstances:

a) when the agent is *self-evident, of little relevance or difficult to express*; for example, 'the glue should be applied carefully' (by whom? the owner/purchaser / user of the tube?); 'a person who has committed a crime, will be sentenced to x days in prison' (by the judge/court/community/state?),

b) when the agent is avoided on purpose (so-called "agent-hiding"): 'Major heavily attacked yesterday' (by one MP / a few MPs / the entire Opposition / all MPs?).

In such cases, languages with an active:passive opposition (Latvian, English etc.) will use a passive (or passive-equivalent) construction; see below.

The Equivalents of English Passives in Latvian

Constructions with an Agent

The previously mentioned active sentence *the workmen are building a house* (with the word order subject-verb-object, or SVO) could be translated into Lithuanian by an equally active SVO construction: *Darbinieki ceļ māju*.

The passive SVO-sentence 'the house is being built by workmen' should be expected to be rendered by the passive SVO construction ***māja tiek celta darbinieku / darbinieku celta**. However, *formally passive sentences with an explicitly expressed agent are extremely rare in Latvian*, and should be avoided. A formally active sentence with the word order object-verb-subject (OVS) is used instead: **māju ceļ darbinieki** (an exception to this rule is noun phrases, cf. pp. 169 and 227. The sentence **māju ceļ darbinieki** has the same *theme-rheme* structure as the English passive sentence 'the house is being built by workmen'. The same holds true for *Pāvilu sita Pēteris* in relation to *Paul was beaten by Peter*.

OVS-structures are far more common in case languages than in caseless ones, since in the former sentence members in initial position are identified as either object or subject by virtue of their grammatical *form,* while in the latter where the initial position is earmarked for the function of the subject, both in active and passive sentences.

Constructions without an Agent

As mentioned above, *agentless passive* sentences in English can be translated by formally passive constructions in Latvian. Thus, the sentence 'he is bullied every day' corresponds to Latvian **viņš tiek apcelts katru dienu** (where the participle agrees in gender, number and case [nominative] with the subject **viņš**). However, it is also possible to use a formally active one-part sentence (cf. p. 205 ff.) with the structure OV: **viņu apceļ katru dienu** with a formally active OV-structure. Both solutions have the patient (**viņš/viņu**) in the thematic initial position.

Verb in the 3rd Person Active without an explicitly expressed Subject

A quite analogous example is **biļetes tiek pārdotas kasē** *tickets are (being) soldat the cashier's desk,* i. e. a formally passive construction which can be replaced by the isofunctional active solution **biļetes pārdod kasē**. In the latter case the 3rd p. of the verb is used without an explicitly expressed subject, corresponding to *man*-sentences in German or Nordic (cf. German *man verkauft Karten in der Kasse*) or to a formally passive construction: *Karten werden in der Kasse verkauft, tickets are sold in the cash-box.*

Constructions of the Type 'it is/was confirmed that [...]'

The standard way of rendering such cases in Latvian is to use the above mentioned construction, i. e. 3rd p. active of the verb without a subject: **apstiprināja, ka** [...] *it was confirmed that [...].* A parallel example is: **šo jautājumu apspriež** (or: **šis jautājums tiek apspriests**) *this issue is being discussed.*

Reflexive Passives

As mentioned above (p. 136), Latvian admits formal *reflexive passives,* but only within considerable constraints. Thus, reflexive passives are not used where the role of an agent is important, e. g. in *****biļetes pārdodas kasē** or *****plāns izpildās veiksmīgi**. This use of the reflexive in the function of a passive is felt to be a "Russianism" and is avoided. In the former example one would have to choose one of the two constructions mentioned above (i. e. **biļetes tiek pārdotas kasē** or **biļetes pārdod kasē**). The same holds true for the latter, i. e. **plāns tiek izpildīts veiksmīgi** or **plānu izpilda veiksmīgi** ('the plan is carried out successfully').

The reflexive passive construction is possible in cases such as **grāmatas glabājas bibliotēkā** *books are kept in the library* and **nazis pilnīgi nolietojies** *the knife is totally worn out* (both cases quoted from Ceplīte & Ceplītis 1991).

Formal Passives with Intransitive Verbs

In a caseless language like English, passive participles are formed from transitive verbs, i. e. verbs with an object. In case languages the formation of passive participles is as a rule equally limited to *transitive* verbs, but the definition of transitivity is different, since here transitive verbs are understood to be verbs with an object in the *accusative* case. A peculiarity of Latvian, however, is that formally "passive" constructions are also possible with intransitive verbs.

Thus, "passive" constructions of this type are frequently encountered in Latvian. They must be in the form of a *one-part impersonal sentence* (cf. p. 206) with the participle in the (unmarked) *masculine* (singular) form (see p. 40). A much quoted example in grammars of Latvian is **diezgan jau ir staigāts** lit. *it has been walked quite a lot already*. A parallel example would be **visu nakti bija dejots**, lit. *it was danced all night long*. Note the correspondence with English constructions with a formal (semantically empty subject) *it*.

These were examples of intransitive (or intransitively used) verbs. A verb such as *threaten* is transitive in English. Its Latvian correspondence **draudēt** is intransitive, since it requires a dative, not accusative, object. To translate a sentence like *he was threatened* into Latvian, one would prefer to say **viņam draudēja**, i. e. use a formally active construction with the verb in the 3rd p. and no subject.

REFLEXIVE AND NON-REFLEXIVE VERBS
(Atgriezeniskie und tiešie darbības vārdi)

In this section the functions and meanings of the reflexive verbs in contrast with non-reflexive verbs will be described. For the formal expression of reflexives and non-reflexives, see pp. 85-114 above.

The reflexive verbs of Latvian show a variety of functions.
1. In the first place there is a small group of *reflexiva tantum*, i. e. reflexives without any non-reflexive counterpart, like, for example, **brīnīties** *wonder, be surprised*, **dusmoties** *be angry*, **atcerēties** *remember*, **ilgoties** *long (for)*, **kavēties** *be delayed*, **pateikties kādam** (dat.) *thank sby*, **rotaļāties** *play*, **spēlēties ar lellēm** *play with dolls* (vs. **spēlēt futbolu, mūzikas instrumentu** *play football/an instrument*), **smieties** *laugh* (vs. non-reflexive **smaidīt** *smile!*), **steigties** *hurry*, **censties** *endeavour, try*.
2. All remaining reflexives (prefixed and non-prefixed) have non-reflexive (transitive) counterparts:

a) the *reflexives proper*, i. e. cases like **celties** *rise, get up (after sleep)* : **celt ko** (acc.) *lift, raise sby / sth.*, **mazgāties** *wash oneself* : **mazgāt ko** (acc.) *wash sby / sth.* **ģērbties** *dress oneself* : **ģērbt ko** (acc.) *dress sby / sth.*, **skūties** *shave oneself* : **skūt ko** *shave sby*, **gatavoties** *prepare oneself* : **gatavot ko** (acc.) *prepare sth.*, **sauļoties** *sunbathe*, **mācīties** *study (learn oneself)* : **mācīt kādam** (dat.) **ko** (acc.) *teach sby sth.* Here can also be mentioned cases like **baidīties** *fear, be afraid*, **nobīties** *get frightened* vs. **baidīt ko** (acc.) *frighten sby*.

Note: In certain cases a reflexive verb can be combined with an accusative object, e. g. **pirkties ko** *by oneself sth.* As is seen from this example, however, the reflexive indicates that the action is taking place within the subject's own sphere of interest. Moreover, in a non-reflexive situation a dative (of the addressee, cf. p. 177) would have taken the place of the reflexive: **pirkt ko draugam** *buy sth. to a friend*.

b) the *passive* reflexives. Here belong cases like those mentioned in the section on voice (p. 141 above), e. g. **glabāties** *be kept/preserved*. Between such verbs and the reflexives in a) are cases of the type **atvērties** *open / be opened* vs. the transitive **atvērt**, **slēgties** *close, be closed* vs. the transitive **slēgt** *close*, **apstāties** *stop* vs. the transitive **apstādināt** *stop*, **sākties** *begin, start* : **sākt ko** (acc.) *start sth.*, **turpināties** *continue* : **turpināt ko** (acc.) *continue sth.*, **beigties** *stop / finish* : **beigt ko** (acc.) *stop/finish sth.*

Illustrations:
durvis slēdzas *doors close* : **viņš slēdz durvis** *he is closing the doors*, **automašīna apstājās** *the car stopped* : **policists apstādināja**

automašīnu *the policeman stopped the car*, **stunda sakās (turpinājās, beidzās)** *the lesson started (continued, finished)* : **skolotājs sāka (turpināja, beidza) stundu** *the teacher started (continued, finished) the lesson.*

c) this group is constituted by *reciprocal* verbs. Some examples: **iepazīties** *become acquainted* : **iepazīstināt ko ar ko** *make sby acquainted with sby*, **satikties/sastapties** *meet (each other / one another)* : **satikt/sastapt ko** *meet sby*, **redzēties** *see (each other / one another)* : **redzēt ko** (acc.) s*ee sby / sth.*, **sarakstīties (ar kādu)** *to correspond (with sby)*, **sarunāties (ar kādu)** *talk/speak (with sby)*, **skupstīties** *kiss* : **skupstīt ko** *kiss sby*, **kauties** fight (each other / one another),

d) *impersonal* (for definition, see p. 206) *reflexives*: **man liekas** *I think / it seems to me*, **man gribas** *I wish.* **Kā Jums klājas?** *How are you getting along?*

THE NON-FINITE FORMS OF THE VERB

As mentioned on p. 81, the non-finite forms of the verb are the *infinitive*, the *gerunds* and *participles* and the *verbal noun*.

I The Infinitive
(Nenoteiksme)

Formal Characteristics
A. Active
The infinitive is formed from the infinitive stem with the infinitive marker *-t*, or *-ties* for the relative verbs: **runāt** *to speak*, **dzīvot** *to live*, **zīmēt** *to draw*, **lasīt** *to read*, **nākt** *to come*, **iet** *to go*, **sarakstīties** *to correspond*, **celties** *to rise, get up (from the bed)*, **smieties** *to laugh*.

With Ist conjugational verbs with roots ending in *-t* or *-d*, the infinitive is in *-st* (according to p. 27), e.g. **sist** (root **sit-**) *to beat*, **vest** (root **ved-**) *to lead*.

The infinitive is not declined.

It can appear both in imperfective and perfective forms, e.g. **darīt** : **padarīt** *do*.

B. Passive
The passive infinitive is normally given in the form of the passive *t*-participle (see p. 155) preceded by the infinitive **būt** *to be* or **tikt** *to become*, e.g. **būt apceltam** *to be mobbed (be made fun of)*, cf. below.

Syntax
The Latvian infinitive can be 1) grammatically *independent* or 2) *dependent*, cf. p. 207.

1) is found in the *dative + infinitive* construction, which can be used in (modal) questions (both direct and indirect):
   Ko mums (pa)darīt? *What can we do?* (lit. *what for us to do?*);
   Viņa jautāja, ko viņai (pa)darīt *She asked what she should do.*

2) is found after various types of *finite* verbs:
   a) *phasal* verbs, i. e. verbs with the meaning of *beginning, continuation* and *stopping*: **viņš sāka/turpināja/beidza dziedāt** *he began/continued/stopped singing.*
   b) certain *auxiliary* modal verbs like **varēt** *be able*, **vēlēt** *wish*,
   c) a good number of other verbs; for example, **solīt** *promise*, **patikt** *like*, **mēģināt** *try*, **censties** *endeavour, try*, **gatavoties** *prepare*: **viņi**

solīja atbraukt šodien *they promised to come today*, **man patīk runāt latviski** *I like to speak Latvian*.

The infinitive can also be used after certain "adjectival adverbs", such as: **grūti** *difficult*, **viegli** *easy*, **žēl** *sad*, e.g. **man grūti runāt latviski** *it is difficult for me to speak Latvian*, **man žēl šo dzirdēt** *I feel sad to hear this*.

Note that the English construction *in order to + infinitive* is not rendered with an infinitival construction in Latvian, only with **lai** + *the subjunctive*, see p. 127 f.

The participle component of the *passive infinitive* is in the dative case if a logical subject in the dative case is referred to. The same holds true for general statements (with omission of the dative subject).

Examples:
Skolniekiem nav labi būt apceltiem
It is not good for schoolchildren to be mobbed (made fun of);
Nav labi būt apceltam
It is not good (for anyone) to be mobbed.

With reference to a nominative subject, i. e. grammatical subject, however, the participle must also appear in the nominative case, e.g.
Skolnieki negrib būt apcelti
Schoolchildren don't like to be mobbed.

The rules for the choice of aspect are the same as with finite forms, cf. p. 115 ff.

II Gerunds and Participles
(Nelokamie un lokamie divdabji)

Latvian has a rich inventory of gerunds and participles. In tabular form the system can be presented in the following way:

1 a) Indeclinable gerunds:

Voice / Stem	Present stem	Infinitive stem
Active	-ot	-šot[1]
	-Vm[2]	

[1] although derived from the infinitive stem this gerund has a future reference (cf. below; it will be recalled, see p. 82, that also finite future tense forms are derived from the infinitive stem). Observe that reflexive forms are not included in the table, and that the indeclinable gerunds are all active in meaning.

[2] V symbolizes a vowel (*-a-* or *-ā-*, depending upon the class)

b) Partly declinable gerunds:

Voice / Stem	Infinitive stem	Past stem
Active	-dam-s/-dam-a/-dam-i/-dam-as[1]	-is/-usi/-uši/-ušas[1]

[1] reflexive forms are not included in the table.

2) The participles form a symmetrical system with the following inventory:

Voice / Stem	Present stem	Past stem
Active	-oš-	-us/-uš-[1]
Passive	-m-	-t-

[1] the masc. sg. nom. ends in -is. In the active voice reflexive forms can also be encountered. Such forms are not included in the table above.

By virtue of their functions, the indeclinable and partly declinable participles may be labeled gerunds.

1. THE GERUNDS

As mentioned above (p. 146), two indeclinable gerunds are discerned, namely:
a) the gerund in -Vm, refl. -Vmies,
b) the gerund ending in -ot, reflexive -oties

There exists also a third indeclinable gerund with the -šot/-šoties ending, which is often omitted in grammars of Latvian because its use is very specialized (see p. 150).

Formation

A. Indeclinable Gerunds

a) The gerund ending in -Vm, refl.-Vmies is formed from the *stem of the present tense* (cf. p. 76) where $V = \bar{a}$ with the -īt(ies) and -ināt(ies) verbs of the IIIrd (mixed) conjugation and = a with all others.

Examples:
runāj-u → **runāj-am** (: runāt *speak*), **glāb-u** → **glāb-jam** (: glābt *save, rescue*), **gatavoj-os** → **gatavoj-amies** (: gatavoties *prepare oneself*), **māc-u** → **māc-ām** (: mācīt *teach*), **māc-os** → **māc-āmies** (**mācīties** *learn, study*)

b) The *-ot*, refl.*-oties* gerund is in accordance with the table given on p. 76, formed on the basis of the present tense stem.

Examples:
runāj-u → **runāj-ot** (: **runāt** *speak*), **glābj-u** → **glābj-ot** (: **glābt** *save, rescue*), **gatavoj-os** → **gatavoj-oties** (**gatavoties** *prepare oneself*).

Historically the gerund ending in *-ot/-oties* reflects a petrified form (derived from the dative case of the masc. sg.) of the present active participle, whereas the gerund ending in *-Vm/-Vmies* represents a petrified form (originating in the accusative sg.) of the present participle, which is likely to have been originally indifferent with respect to voice.

c) The above-mentioned gerund ending in *-šot/-šoties* is in fact – as indicated by the *š*-formative – a *future tense* gerund. Accordingly, it is formed on the basis of the infinitive stem.
Examples:
stāvē-t → **stāvē-šot** (: **stāvēt** *stand*), **bū-t** → **bū-šot** (: **būt** *be*); **beig-t** → **beig-šoties** (: **beigties** *end*).

B. Partly Declinable Gerunds

Here it is customary to include only the *-dam*-formation. However, it appears practical also to add an *-us*-formation, which can have gerundival function.

Thus, two formations are arrived at, namely

a) the *dam*-gerund,
b) the *us/uš*-gerund

a) The *dam*-gerund is formed from the *infinitive stem* (cf. p. 82). It is declined in *gender* and *number* as an adjective, e.g. from **lasīt** *read* the forms **lasī-dams** (masc. sg.), **lasī-dama** (fem. sg.), **lasī-dami** (masc. pl.), **lasī-damas** (fem. pl.) are obtained.

Reflexive forms end in *-damies* for the masc. sg., in *-damās* for the fem. sg., in *-damies* for the masc. pl. and *-damās* for the fem. pl., cf., for example, **cel-damies, cel-dama, cel-damies, cel-damās** (: **celties** *rise, get up*).

Note: With infinitives ending in *-st* (cf. p. 27), the *-s-* is written *-z-* before *-dam-* if the original consonant (which is preserved in the past tense) is *-t* or *-d*, e.g. **siz-dam-** (: preterite **sit-**, inf. **sist** *to beat*), **atraz-dam-** (: preterite **atrad-**, inf. **atrast** *to find*). If the original consonant is *-s*, an *-s-* is written, cf., for example **nes-dam** (but according to the voicing rule (p. 26), of course, spoken as -z-) due to the preterite **nes-** (: inf. **nest** *carry*).

b) The *-us/-uš*-gerund is – as illustrated in the table on p. 82 – formed on the basis of the *past stem*. Like the *dam*-gerund, it is declined in *gender* and *number*. Thus, the following forms are encounterted: *-usi* for the fem.sg., *-ušas* for the fem. pl., *-uši* for the masc. pl. The masc. sg. has a deviating form, *-is*. The corresponding reflexive forms are: *-usies, -ušās, -ušies* and *-ies*. For further comments on the morphological make-up of these forms, see under the past active participle, p. 153 f.

A concrete example is the verb **atnākt** *come, arrive*: **atnācis** (masc. sg.), **atnākusi** (fem. sg.), **atnākuši** (masc. pl.), **atnākušās** (fem. pl.). This verb has been chosen for illustration for two reasons: first, it shows the alternation between *c* and *k* with stems ending in *k* (paralleled by that of *dz* and *g* with *g*-stems, e.g. **no/beidzis** vs. **nobeigusi** : **no/beigt** *finish*), second, because of the *tendency* (NB not absolute rule!) to form partly declinable past stem gerunds from *perfective* verbs (cf. section on aspect, p. 115 ff.), while those from the present stem are formed from *imperfective* verbs (cf. the imperfective **lasīt** above). This opposition is utilized in a tense-aspect perspective (see under next point).

Syntax and Semantics of the Gerunds

The *meaning* of the gerunds is illustrated through their English translations in examples under points A and B below.

The *-am(ies)*-gerund expresses *simultaneity* with the action (state) described by the finite verb.

The *-šot(ies)*-gerund refers to an event taking place in the future.

From the *functional* point of view, these gerunds (with dependent members) are equivalent to adverbial clauses (most frequently time clauses).

The *-ot(ies)*-gerund is *neutral* with respect to the parameters *simultaneousness* and *anteriority* and can cover both meanings.

The *-dam(ies)* gerund (usually in imperfective, i. e. unprefixed form) expresses actions which occur *simultaneously* with those of the verb in the main clause, while the *-us-/-uš*-formation (usually in perfective, i. e. prefixed form) denotes an action which is not simultaneous, but *anterior* to that of the verb in the main clause. To express an action which is posterior to the action expressed by the verb in the main clause, the alternative construction with a subordinate clause must be used.

A. Indeclinable Gerunds
a) *-Vm,* refl.*-Vmies:*
This gerund is used with an accompanying accusative object after *verbs of perception (verba sentiendi) and similar*:
Dzirdēju Almu *atbraucam* uz Stokholmu
I have heard that Alma has come to Stockholm (lit. *I (have) heard Alma coming to Stockholm).*

The construction is parallel to the one indicated in the word-for-word translation into English. In Old Latvian, the participle was declinable and occurred in the accusative case in the construction in question, since syntactically it occupied the function of an apposition (cf. p. 202) which was in agreement with the object (**Almu** in the above example). The construction corresponds to the so-called "accusativus cum infinitivo"-construction in Latin, German, Nordic and certain other languages: *audīvi eum venīre, Ich hörte ihn kommen,* Norwegian *jeg hørte ham komme,* expressed in English by *I heard him coming.*

Note! the *-Vm(ies)*-gerund cannot be replaced by the *-oš*-participle (on which see below), but a subordinate *ka*-clause (*that*-clause) can be used instead:
Dzirdēju, ka Alma esot atbraukusi uz Stokholmu
I have heard that Alma has come to Stockholm

b) *-šot,* refl. *-šoties*
This gerund seems to be restricted to the relative mood, cf. example on p. 132.

c) *-ot,* refl. *-oties*
The function (so-called "absolute function") of this gerund is to *replace adverbial clauses* (see p. 211 ff.) *if the grammatical subject of the adverbial and the main clauses are not identical/not co-referential (contrast with B below). The logical subject of the participle construction (clause) is in the dative case,* e.g.
Tuvojoties dienesta laikam, Grīnis (viņš) atgriezās Latvijā
(quoted from A. Eiche 1983)
When the time for military service drew nearer, Grīnis (he) returned to Latvia.

From a diachronic perspective, both the noun (or the pronoun) and the gerund (which represents a petrified participle form) will have been in the dative case. Such a construction, labeled "the absolute dative" or "double dative" construction, is found also in Lithuanian and has a parallel in Slavic. In other Indo European languages cases other than the dative may be used to form gerundival clauses functionally equivalent to subordinate clauses. Thus, in Latin the (double) ablative is used, in Greek the (double) genitive and in Sanskrit the (double) locative.

The participle construction can be replaced by a subordinate clause with a finite verb:
Kad dienesta laiks tuvojās, Grīnis [...]
If the dative member is absent, a general meaning ("one") is assumed:
***Vertējot* konstrukcijas ar datīvu, vajadzētu ņemt vērā vismaz divus faktus**
When evaluating constructions with the dative, one has to consider at least two facts (..., at least two facts have to be considered).
Outside this "absolute" function, the *-ot(ies)*-gerund can alternate with the *dam(ies)*-gerund, on which see below. Observe that these gerunds – irrespective of aspect – always express *simultaneity* (not anteriority or posteriority), in relation to the finite verb of the main clause, as illustrated by the following example with a perfective (cf. p. 115 f.) gerund: **Jānim uzrakstot vēstuli, Sarma atnāca** which cannot be translated as **when John had written (had finished writing) the letter, Sarma came*, but only as *when John was finishing writing the letter, Sarma came*. Thus, Latvian has a gap in the system on this point. In order to translate *when John had written the letter, Sarma came*, a subordinate clause must be used:
Kad Jānis norakstīja vēstuli, Sarma atnāca.

B. Partly Declinable Gerunds

The partly declinable gerunds can *replace adverbial clauses, the grammatical subject of which is identical to (co-referential with) that of the main clause*. Thus, the *-dam(ies)*-gerund is used to express *simultaneity* with the action of the verb in the main clause, whereas the *-us(ies)*-gerund is used to denote an action which is *anterior* to that of the verb in the main clause. In order to express posteriority the alternative construction with a subordinate clause of time must be chosen. Thus, the relationship between these two gerunds is one of *complementary distribution*.

This is in contrast to the indeclinable *-ot(ies)* gerund in function A 3 above, which has no counterpart to express [non-simultaneity].

Examples:
-dam-:
Gerda nopietni skatījās, *mēģinādama* saprast (quoted from A. Eiche 1983)
Gerda looked at him seriously, trying to understand

As mentioned on p. 151 the *-dam-*gerund can be replaced by the *-ot-*gerund (provided that the logical subjects of both the participle construction and the main clause are identical, as in the above case):
Gerda nopietni skatījās, mēģinot saprast.

-us-/-uš-:
Aizgājusi mājās, Edīte pārvilka sausas drēbes (quoted from A. Eiche 1983)
When Edīte came home, she changed into dry clothes.

2. THE PARTICIPLES

The inventory of Latvian participles has been given in the table on p. 147. As shown in this table, there are two active (present and past) and two passive (also present and past) participles. Only the formatives of these participles are indicated in the table.

Formation

A. Active Participles
a) The present participle
This participle (see the table on p. 82) is formed on the basis of the *present stem* by adding the formative *-oš-*. The declension is that of an adjective (cf. p. 57 f.). As in the case of adjectives both *short* (indefinite) and *long* (definite) forms are distinguished:

Paradigm from **ziedoš-** *blossoming* (: **ziedēt** *to blossom*):

	Short forms		**Long forms**	
	masculine	*feminine*	*masculine*	*feminine*
SG N	zied-oš-s	zied-oš-a	zied-oš-ais	zied-oš-ā
G	zied-oš-a	zied-oš-as	zied-oš-ā	zied-oš-ās
D	zied-oš-am	zied-oš-ai	zied-oš-aj-am	zied-oš-aj-ai
A	zied-oš-u	ziede-oš-u	zied-oš-o	zied-oš-o
L	zied-oš-ā	zied-oš-ā	zied-oš-aj-ā	zied-oš-aj-ā
PL N	zied-oš-i	zied-oš-as	zied-oš-ie	zied-oš-ās
G	zied-oš-u	zied-oš-u	zied-oš-o	zied-oš-o
D	zied-oš-iem	zied-oš-ām	zied-oš-aj-iem	zied-oš-aj-ām
A	zied-oš-us	zied-oš-as	zied-oš-os	zied-oš-ās
L	zied-oš-os	zied-oš-ās	zied-oš-aj-os	zied-oš-aj-ās

THE VERB: NON-FINITE FORMS

Vocative forms are used only with the long forms. The formational rules are the same as those given under the adjective (p. 62, point 5).

For the rules for deriving long forms from the corresponding short, see p. 59.

Reflexive forms of the present active participle seem to be rare. The paradigm is defective. Only the following forms are encountered:

SINGULAR

	masculine	feminine
G		-ošās
A	-ošos	-ošos

PLURAL

	masculine	feminine
N	-ošies	-ošās
G	-ošos	-ošos
A	-ošos	-ošās

The rules for deriving reflexive forms from the corresponding non-reflexive are given on p. 86 above.

Note that reflexive forms can be constructed only from short forms, not long.

The *-oš-* participle of Latvian reflects *-ont-j- (cf. pp. 25 and 32) and is thus cognate with with the *-nt-*participles in other IE languages (Slavic, Germanic, Latin, Romance, Greek and so on).

b) The past participle

This participle is formed on the basis of the *preterite stem* (cf. p. 82) by adding the ending *-is* for the masc. nom. sg., and the formative *-us/š-* + adjectival endings for the remaining forms of the paradigm:

Paradigm from **pieaugt** *to grow up*

		Short forms		Long forms	
		masculine	feminine	masculine	feminine
SG	N	pieaudz-is	pieaug-us-i	pieaug-uš-ais	pieaug-uš-ā
	G	pieaug-uš-a	pieaug-uš-as	pieag-uš-ā	pieaug-uš-ās
	D	pieaug-uš-am	pieaug-uš-ai	pieaug-uš-aj-am	pieag-uš-aj-ai
	A	pieauguš-u	pieaug-uš-u	pieaug-uš-o	pieaug-uš-o
	L	pieaug-uš-ā	pieaug-uš-ā	pieaug-uš-aj-ā	pieaug-uš-aj-ā

PL N	pieaug-uš-i	pieaug-uš-as	pieaug-uš-ie	pieaug-uš-ās
G	pieaug-uš-u	pieaug-uš-u	pieaug-uš-o	pieaug-uš-o
D	pieaug-uš-iem	pieaug-uš-ām	pieaug-uš-aj-iem	pieag-uš-aj-ām
A	pieag-uš-us	pieaug-uš-as	pieaug-uš-os	pieaug-uš-ās
L	pieaug-uš-os	pieaug-uš-ās	pieag-uš-aj-os	pieaug-uš-aj-ās

Comments on the paradigm:

Observe that the ending *-is* of the masc. sg. triggers the *k > c* (e. g. **plaucis** (: **plaukt** *blossom*) vs. nom. fem. sg. **plauk-us-i**) and *g > dz* shift (cf. p. 25). Note further that the nom. sg. masc. long form is based not on the deviating form of the nom. masc. sg., but on the normalized (generalized) formative *-uš-* + the common ending *-ais*. It should also be observed that the fem. sg. has the formative *-us-* (not *-uš-*), accompanied by an unusual ending *-i* (also found in certain pronouns) in the nom. The corresponding long form ends in *-us-ī* or normalized *-uš-ā*. The rules for deriving long forms from short forms are given on p. 59.

In older writings (Blaumanis and others) forms ending in *-use* in the fem. sg. are encountered, e.g. **snieguse, bijuse, piegājuse, darījuse,** refl. **apdomājusēs.**

The *reflexive* paradigm (restricted to short forms only) is defective, with (roughly) the same cases missing as with the present active participle, cf. p. 153.

SINGULAR
masculine   feminine

	masculine	feminine
N	-ies	-us-ies
G	-ušās	-ušās
A	-ušos	-ušos

PLURAL
masculine   feminine

	masculine	feminine
N	-ušies	-ušās
G	-ušos	-ušos
A	-ušos	-ušās

The forms are easily deductible from the model presented under the present active participle.

This participle has also cognates in other IE languages (Slavic etc.). The *-is* (= *-ęs* in Lithuanian, cf. pp. 32 and 35) of the masc. sg., however, lacks evident parallels outside Baltic and may be the result of an internal arrangement within this branch. The *-š* in *-uš-* originates from *$*s+j$*. The *s* is preserved in the nom. sg. fem. The paradigm of the fem. reflects an old *$*ī/jā$*-declension (subtype of the *ā*-declension) whereas the masc. paradigm represents the *$*-jos$*-type. Both are well attested in IE languages.

B. Passive Participles

a) The present participle:

This participle (see the table p. 82) is formed from the present tense stem with the formative suffix *-ām-* (for IIIrd conjugational verbs in *-īt* and *-ināt*), or *-am-* for all others + the adjectival endings, as in the case of the active participles dealt with above.

Here again both short and long forms are distinguished.

Paradigm from **lasīt** *to read:*

	Short forms masculine	feminine	Long forms masculine	feminine
SG N	las-ā-m-s	las-ā-am-a	las-ā-m-ais	las-ā-m-ā
G	las-ā-m-a	las-ā-m-as	las-ā-m-ā	las-ā-m-ās
D	las-ā-m-am	las-ā-m-ai	las-ā-m-aj-am	las-ā-m-aj-ai
A	las-ā-m-u	las-ā-m-u	las-ā-m-o	las-ā-m-o
L	las-ā-m-ā	las-ā-m-ā	las-ā-m-aj-ā	las-ā-m-aj-ā
PL N	las-ā-m-i	las-ā-m-as	las-ā-m-ie	las-ā-m-ās
G	las-ā-m-u	las-ā-m-u	las-ā-m-o	las-ā-m-o
D	las-ā-m-iem	las-ā-m-ām	las-ā-m-aj-iem	las-ā-m-aj-ām
A	las-ā-m-us	las-ā-m-us	las-ā-m-os	las-ā-m-os
L	las-ā-m-os	las-ā-m-ās	las-ā-m-aj-os	las-ā-m-aj-ās

b) The past participle:

The basis for the formation of this participle is the *infinitive stem* (cf. p. 82). The formative suffix is *-t-*, to which are added adjectival endings. Both short and long forms are distingushed.

Paradigm from **lasīt** *to read:*

	Short forms masculine	feminine	Long forms masculine	feminine
SG N	lasī-t-s	lasī-t-a	lasī-t-ais	lasī-t-ā
G	lasī-t-a	lasī-t-as	lasī-t-ā	lasī-t-ās
D	lasī-t-am	lasī-t-ai	lasī-t-aj-am	lasī-t-aj-ai
A	lasī-t-u	lasī-t-u	lasī-t-o	lasī-t-o
L	lasī-t-ā	lasī-t-ā	lasī-t-aj-ā	lasī-t-aj-ā
PL N	lasī-t-i	lasī-t-as	lasī-t-ie	lasī-t-ās
G	lasī-t-u	lasī-t-u	lasī-t-o	lasī-t-o
D	lasī-t-iem	lasī-t-ām	lasī-t-aj-iem	lasī-t-aj-ām
A	lasī-t-us	lasī-t-as	lasī-t-os	lasī-t-os
L	lasī-t-os	lasī-t-ās	lasī-t-aj-os	lasī-t-aj-ās

Syntax

Participle forms used in *adverbial function(s)* have been treated as gerunds. Thus, this function has already been described (p. 150 ff.).

Participle forms are further used as *parts of the verbal predicate* in compound tenses of the indicative and subjunctive active and passive. For these functions, see pp. 112 ff., 120 ff., 126 and 137 f.

We are then left with two functions of the participles, namely 1) the *attributive* and – its close cognate – (2) the *appositive,* which coincide with functions also found under the adjective, cf. pp. 57 and 60 above. Like the adjective, the participle agrees with the head noun in gender, number and case. All fully declinable participles – both active and passive – are used in these functions.

A. Active Participles
a) *Attributive function*

Examples:
-ošs:
Es iedomājos Solvītu [...] brienam pa *ziedošu* pļavu [...] (quoted from A. Eiche 1983)
I imagined Solvīta [...] wading through a flowering meadow[...]
-is (-us-/-uš-):
Vajadzēs [...] iet uz pirti nomazgāt *sasvīdušo* seju [...] (quoted from A. Eiche 1983)
She will have [...] to go to the bath-house to wash her sweaty face

In both examples there is *agreement in gender, number and case between the participle modifier* (i. e. **ziedošu** and **sasvīdušo** respectively) *and the head noun* (**pļavu** and **seju**)

b) *Appositive function*

An apposition (p. 202) is close in function to the attribute. In this function, too, full agreement (i. e. in gender, number and case) between the participle and the governing noun has to be observed. The apposition is separated from the head noun through a pause in speech or a comma or dash in written texts, cf. examples below.

Examples:
-ošs:
Nāk tramvajs – zils un *spīdošs* kā zviņaina līdaka (quoted from A. Eiche 1983) *here comes a tram – blue and shining like a scaly pike*

-is (-us-/-uš-):
To vakaru viņi ilgi nosēdēja salauzti, *izmisuši*
(quoted from A. Eiche 1983)
That evening they sat for a long while, broken with despair

B. Passive Participles
In the same way as with the attributively and appositively used active participles, *agreement with respect to gender, number and case* between the participle modifier and the head noun must be observed.

a) *Attributive function*
Examples:
-Vm-:
Dzilnu pārņēma [...] *neciešama* **sajūta [...]** (quoted from A. Eiche 1983)
Dzilna was overwhelmed [...] by an insufferable feeling
-t-:
Senāk pat bija pircis vācu *ilustrētos* **žurnālus [...]** (quoted from A. Eiche 1983)
Formerly he had even bought German illustrated magazines
Note that the *-Vm*-participle denotes either *possibility* (e. g. **dzeramais ūdens** *potable water*) or *necessity* (e. g. **mazgajāmi šķīvji** *plates to be washed*). Purely passive meanings are rare in contemporary Latvian.

b) *Appositive* function
-Vm-:
Akā bija ūdens, *dzeramais* **and garšīgs**
In the well there was water, potable and tasty
-t-:
Bet ķīvīte kliedz par šo pašu vienīgo (= ligzdu], *izpostīto*
(quoted from A. Eiche 1983)
But the peewit cries about the heron's nest which has been destroyed;
***Gaismas* pievilktas, mušas riņķoja ap lampu** *Attracted by the light, the flies were circling around the lamp.*
In the last example the apposition is pre-posited.

Concluding Remarks on Participles
Like the adjectives, the *attributively* and *appositively* used participles can be encountered in indefinite (short) or definite (long) form.
Long forms of *reflexives* are avoided.

The distribution between *perfective* and *imperfective* participles follows the principles set forth in the section on aspect (p. 107 ff.).

Participles in the Funtion of other Word Classes

Pariticiples in the function of substantives were exemplified on p. 59 (under adjectives). Furthermore, they can function as adverbs (p. 154 ff.), cf., for example, **iznīcinoši** (: **iznīcināt** *to destroy*) in the sentence **20. gadsimts uz līviem ir iedarbojies iznīcinoši** *the 2oth century has had a destructive effect on the Livonians.*

III. The Verbal Noun

The candidate *par excellence* for this function is the noun in -šana, refl. -šanās which can be formed on the basis of the infinitive of any verb in Latvian, e.g.

lasī-t *to read* → **lasī-šana**,
brauk-t *to travel, go* → **brauk-šana**
satik-ties *to meet (each other)* → **satik-šanās** etc.

Note that with infinitives ending in *-st* and *-zt*, the *-s-* and *-z-* are dropped before the *-š-* in *-šana*, e.g.

kris-t *to fall* → **kri-šana**,
bāz-t *to thrust, shove* → **bā-šana**.

The *meaning* of the nouns ending in *-šana/-šanās* is that of a *nomen actionis*, i. e. *(the act of) reading, travelling, meeting (each other), falling, shoving* etc.

The *-šana/-šanās* nouns are declined according to the fourth declension (cf. p. 46). The paradigm of the reflexive noun is defective, in that dative and locative forms are lacking (cf. p. 50 f.). Plural reflexive forms are rare, but can be encountered.

THE VERB: WORD FORMATION

Suffixation

Common suffixes are: *-ā* (inf. *-āt)*, *-ē* (inf. *-ēt)*, *-ī* (inf. *-īt)*, *-o* (inf. *-ot)* and *-inā* (inf. *-ināt)*. In addition, there are also *-alē* (inf. *-alēt)*, *-elē* (inf. *-elēt)* and a couple of other *l*-extensions.

With the help of the suffix *-ināt* transitive verbs with factitive (causative) meaning can be derived from intransitives, cf., for example **augt** *grow* (intrans.) : **audzināt** *grow, bring up*, **degt** *burn* (intrans.) : **dedzināt** *burn* (trans.), **mosties** (*st* < **d-t*, cf. p. 27) *wake* (intrans.) : **modināt** *wake* (trans.).

This suffix derives factitives not only from verbs, but also from adjectives and to some extent also from nouns: **asināt** *sharpen* (: **ass** *sharp*), **mazināt** *reduce* (: **mazs** *small*), **stiprināt** *strengthen* (: **stiprs** *strong*), **mierināt** *comfort* (: **miers** *peace*).

The suffixes *-ā, -o, -ē* and *-ī* were covered under the presentation of the conjugations. In the paragraph on predictability of conjugational class from the infinitive (p. 84) derivational mechanisms were also commented upon. It should be added that the suffixes *-ā, -ī* and *-alē* can have iterative meaning, e.g. **braukāt** (: **braukt** *go, travel*), **skraidīt/skraidelēt** (: **skriet** *run*).

Prefixation. Verb Prefixes

Latvian distinguishes the following 11 verb prefixes: *aiz-, ap-, at-, ie-, iz-, no, pa-, pār-, pie-, sa-* and *uz-*. Out of these, 7 have corresponding prepositions (viz. *aiz, ap, no, pa, pār, pie* and *uz*).

With verbs of motion these prefixes obtain a perfectivizing function and correspond with adverbs + unprefixed verb in imperfective (ipf) function, cf. section on aspect, p. 115 ff.

Under the presentation of aspect, the double function of Latvian prefixes was mentioned (p. 118), namely 1) that of modifying the meaning of the corresponding unprefixed verb (as in English, German, Scandinavian etc.) and 2) that of forming perfective counterparts to imperfective simple verbs (without affecting the lexical meaning).

1. The prefix *aiz-* denotes a) *away, off*: **aizbraukt** *drive off*, **aiziet** *go away*, **aiznest** *carry away*, **aizslaucīt** *sweep away*, b) *obstruction, coverage*: **aizaugt** *become overgrown*, **aizklāt** *cover over*, **aizslēgt** *lock*, **aizvērt** *close*.

It corresponds with the adverbs **pro(jā)m** *away* and **cieti** *firmly*, e.g. **aiziet** (pf.) : **iet pro(jā)m** (ipf.) *go away*, **aizvērt** (pf.) : **vērt cieti** (ipf.) *lock*.

2. *ap-* means a) *around*: **apiet** *go around (*e. g. **apiet ap birzi** *go around the grove)*, **apjāt** *ride around*, **apstāt** *surround (***zēni apstāja skolotāju** *the boys surrounded the teacher*).

The corresponding adverb in imperfectivizing function is **apkārt**, cf. **apskriet** (pf.) : **skriet apkārt** (ipf.) *run around*;

3. *at-* has the following meanings: a) (motion) *towards*: **atbraukt** *arrive*, **atnākt** *come, arrive*, b) *away* (the opposite meaning of a) in some instances: **atiet** *depart* (e. g. **autobuss/vilciens/kuģis atiet pulksten divpadsmitos** *the bus/train/ship departs at twelve o'clock*), **atņemt** *take away*, **atvadīties** *bid farewell*, c) *repetition*: **atkārtot** *repeat*; d) *returning to former state*: **atspirgt** *feel better*.

It corresponds with the adverbs **šurp** *here, hither* (cf. **atnākt** pf. : **nākt šurp** ipf *come here*), **nost** *away, off* (cf. **atraut** pf. : **raut nost** ipf. *tear away*), **atpakaļ** *back* (cf. **atdot** pf. : **dot atpakaļ** *give back, return)* and **vaļā** *open* (untranslatable, cf. **atslēgt vaļā** *unlock)*.

4. *ie-* corresponds to English *in*: **ienākt** *come in (***ienākt istabā** *come into the room,* for the use of the locative, see p. 180*)*, **ieskriet** *run in*, **iebērt** *pour in*, **ieelpot** *inhale*. Moreover, this prefix can signalize the *beginning* of an action: **iemigt** *fall asleep*, **iemīlēt** *become fond of*. Finally, with some reflexive verbs it can designate a sudden action, e.g. **iekliegties** *shout out*, **iesmieties** *burst out laughing*.

Corresponding adverb: **iekšā** *inside* (cf. **ieiet iekšā** *go in*).

5. *iz-* *out (of)* is very frequently the opposite of **ie-**. Examples: **iznākt** *come out*, **izskriet** *run out*, **izbērt** *pour out*. Further, opposite to **ie-**, it can denote the (full) *completion* of an action: **izēst** *eat up* (to the end), **izsmēķēt** *smoke (to the end)*.

Corresponding adverb: **ārā** *outside* (e. g. **skriet ārā** *run out*).

6. *no-* in most cases correspond to English a) *down*: **nokāpt** *climb down*, **nodegt** *burn down*, but it can also mean b) *off* (**noaut** *take off (shoes)*, **nogriezt** *cut off*, **nolauzt** *break off* and c) *completion* (**nolietot** *wear out)*.

The most frequently corresponding adverb is **nost** *away, off* (e. g. **nokāpt nost** *climb down*).

7. *pa-* can have a (pure) perfectivizing sense (like the preceding *no:* **padarīt** *do*), but it can also denote an *attenuating aktionsart* (cf. p. 118), i. e. *a little*: **pagulēt** *sleep a little/for a while*, **parunāties** *chat a little/for a while*. This preposition lacks corresponding adverb(s).

8. *pār-* has a variety of meanings. It frequently corresponds to a) *over (*in the meaning *too much)* : **pāraugt** *overgrow*, **pārplūst** *overflow*, **pārstrādāties** *overwork*, **pārlidot** *fly over*, b) *doing a sth. over again*

(possibly in another way): **pārrakstīt** *rewrite*, **pārģērbties** *change one's clothes*, **pārveidot** *reform*, c) *transformation*: **pārmainīt** *change*, **pārtulkot** *translate*, d) *through*: **pārdzīvot** *live through*, **pārziemot** *hibernate*, e) *movement homewards*: **pāriet** *go home*, **pārnākt** *come home*, **pārbraukt** *drive home*, f) *mis-* (wrong): **pārprast** *misunderstand*, **pārrakstīties** *make an error (in writing)*.

Corresponding adverbs are **pāri** *over* (e. g. **lidot pāri** *fly over*) and **mājās** *home* (e. g. **iet mājās** *go home*).

9. *pie-* expresses a) *approaching* (**piebraukt** *drive up to*, **pieiet** *go up to*; it is accompanied by the preposition **pie**, e.g. **pienākt pie**, cf. **vilciens pienāca pie perrona** *the train came up to the platform*), b) *adding or putting together* (**piespraust pie** *pin to*, **piešūt pie** *sew on*, cf. **piešūt mētelim pogas** *sew buttons on the coat* (NB dative without preposition).

Corresponding adverb: **klāt** *near* (e. g. **nākt klāt** *approach*).

10. *sa-* denotes a) *(motion) together, coalescence*: **saaugt** *grow together*, **sasaukt** *call together*, b) *collapse into pieces*: **sabirzt** *fall to pieces*, **sagriezt** *cut to pieces*.

Corresponding adverb: **kopā** *together* (e. g. **nest kopā** *carry together*).

11. *uz-* often corresponds to English *(up)on*: **uzspļaut** *spit up-(on)*, **uzziest** *smear on* (cf. **uzziest sviestu uz maizes** *smear butter on the bread*), **uzgriezt** *switch on (electricity)*.

Corresponding adverb: **augšā** *upstairs* (**celties augšā (no krēsla)** *get up (from a chair)*.

Chapter 7

THE ADVERB
(Apstākļa vārds)

The adverb is a rather heterogeneous word class. Except for possible degrees of comparison, the adverb is indeclinable.

The bulk of adverbs in Latvian end in *-i* (see below), but there are many also ending in *-u* (cf. below), *-am/-ām* (e. g. **tiešām** *really*), as well as other types.

There are a good number of adverbs which can be said to be formed on the basis of adjectives (e. g. **labi** *well* vs. **labs/laba** *good*) and participles (e. g. **draudoši** *threateningly*), whereas others have common roots with pronouns – the so-called pronominal adverbs, for example: **k-ur** *where*, cf. **k-as** *who, what*.

Degrees of Comparison

Many adverbs ending in *-i* and *-u* allow the formation of comparative and superlative forms. The former take the suffix *-āk*, whereas the superlative forms are constituted by the comparative supplied with a prefix *vis- (all)*.

positive degree	comparative	supelative
lab-i *well*	**lab-āk** *better*	**vis-lab-āk** *best*
vēl-u *late*	**vēl-āk** *later*	**vis-vēl-āk** *latest*

Comparatives and superlatives are also formed from a number of adverbs with zero ending in the positive degree, e.g.

drīz *soon*	**drīz-āk** *sooner*	**vis-drīz-āk** *soonest*
maz *little*	**maz-āk** *less*	**vis-maz-āk** *least*

The antonym of **maz** *little*, **daudz** *much*, makes use of *suppletive* forms in the comparative and superlative: **vairāk** *more* and **visvairāk** *most*.

Syntax and Semantics

From a *semantic* point of view adverbs can be divided into:
- *of manner* (**ātri** *fast*, **patīkami** *pleasantly*),
- *of place* (e. g. **te** *here*, **kur** *where*),
- *of time* (**vienmēr** *always*, **iepriekš** *before*),
- *of cause and purpose* (**tādēļ** *therefore*).
- *interrogative* (**cik?** *how much/many?*, **kur?** *where?*, **kad?** *when?*)
- *indefinite* (**kaut kad** *sometime*, **kaut kur** *somewhere*)
- *negative* (**nekad** *never*, **nekur** *nowhere*)

Syntactically, adverbs can serve as *modifiers of a verb* (**iet ātri** *walk fast*), another *adverb* (/**iet**/ **ļoti ātri** *walk very fast*) or an *adjective* (**ļoti garšīgas pusdienas** *a very tasty dinner*).

Illustrations of the use of the comparative and the superlative: **Pēteris skrien ātri, Ojārs ātrāk, bet Jānis visātrāk** *Peter runs fast, Ojārs faster, but John fastest (of all).*

The formal appearance of an adverb also has the the *i*-form in adjectival function, found in cases like: **man bija auksti** *I felt* (lit. *was*) *cold* : **man bija aukstāk** *I felt colder*, cf. p. 179 and 208.

While the adverb in the positive can be *strengthened* by **ļoti** *very*, in the comparative **daudz** *much* must be used. Compare: **ļoti labi** *very well* : **daudz labāk** *much better*. More bookish synonyms for **daudz** before a comparative are **krietni** and **ievērojami,** both of which may be translated into English by *considerably*.

The Latvian equivalent of English "than" in comparisons is in most cases **nekā** (**kā** after a negated verb), e.g. **Jānis skrien ātrāk nekā Pēteris** *John runs faster than Peter,* **Jānis neskrien ātrāk kā Pēteris** *John does not run faster than Peter.*

The syntax of *indefinite* and *negative* adverbs is parallel to that described under indefinite and negative pronouns, see p. 70 ff. Observe constructions of the type **man nav kur iet** *I have nowhere to go* vs. **es nekur neeju** *I don't go anywhere, I go nowhere.*

The Negation

The Latvian negation is **ne** which in most cases is written together with the word which is negated, most frequently a verb, e.g. **viņš nerunā latviski** *he doesn't speak Latvian*. The negated counterpart of **ir** *is, are* is **nav**, cf. **Latvijā nav lauvu** (for the genitive, see p. 171f.) *in Latvia there are no (are not any) lions* (positive statement: **Afrikā ir lauvas** *in Africa there are lions*), **viņa nav studente** *she is not a student* (positive statement: **viņa ir studente** *she is a student*). Note the mandatory nominative **studente**, since **nav** in this example has the function of a copulative verb and not that of an existential one as in **Latvijā nav lauvu** where a genitive construction is required because of the *existential* verb **nav**.

Beside verbs the negation can also accompany other parts of speech, e.g. adjectives (**negudrs** *unwise, silly*), participles (**nepazīstams** *unknown*, **negaidīts** *unexpected*) and adverbs (**nelabi** *not well, bad(ly)*).

The negational element **ne-** is further encountered with negative pronouns (p. 72) and adverbs (see above), e.g. **neviens** *nobody*, **nekas** *nothing*, **nekur** *nowhere*. In this case it has to be repeated by another **ne-** before a verb, so-called *double negation*, e.g. **neviens no jums nezina** *none of you knows*.

English *neither nor* is rendered in Latvian by **ne ne** or **nedz nedz**. Illustrations: **ne šā, ne tā** *neither this way nor that way*, **to nezina ne viņš, ne tu** *neither he nor you will know that* (notice the double negation in the latter example).

Chapter 8

CASE
(Locījums)

Introduction

A chapter on case should include both prepositional and non-prepositional use. However, certain considerations – both practical and theoretical – have led the author to treat prepositional functions in a separate chapter under the heading "Prepositions".

The syntactic functions of the oblique cases in Latvian, i. e. all cases except the nominative and the vocative, can be of three kinds:

1) *adnominal* (= governed by a *nominal* word class, i. e. a noun, an adjective, a pronoun or a numeral),
2) *adverbal* (= governed by a verb),
3) *adverbial* (= with the same function as an adverb)

We consider this disposition a practical and adequate one despite the fact that 3) is not parallel with 1) and 2), since adverbial does not mean *governed by* an adverb, but *functioning as* an adverb. An alternative and in a way more consistent solution would have been to work with the notions 'government' (Latv. *pārvaldījums*, see p. 200) and 'juxtaposition' (or 'adjunction', Latv. *piekļāvums*, cf. p. 200), but in that case we would have had to put under the government heading that which is dealt with both under 1) and (the bulk of) 2) above, which in our view would have meant a less transparent and practical disposition. Furthermore, the notion of *primykanie* ("juxtaposition") – well known in Russian and Latvian (and other East European) grammatical traditions, but less in the West – would be unfamiliar to many readers.

A second alternative, namely to follow a scheme *object* vs. *adverbial* relations would not have paid due attention to point 1).

We will proceed below according to the scheme 1 - 3 and describe the functions of the cases in the following order: the genitive, the accusative, the dative and the locative. The description will also include a small typed note on the instrumental, for the status of which, see p. 41. Finally, the functions of the two non-oblique cases, the nominative and the vocative, will be dealt with.

THE GENITIVE

This is a widely used case in Latvian, which is encountered both with and without prepositions (for prepositional use, see chapter 9: "Prepositions").

The genitive has adnominal and adverbal functions, while the adverbial seems to be absent.

Under both the adnominal and adverbal types a *partitive* and *non-partitive* function should be distinguished. The partitive genitive expresses a part of a certain quantity, as for example in **tasīte tējas** *a cup of tea* (adnominal type) and **ēst sēņu** *to eat mushrooms* (adverbal type).

I Adnominal Function

1. Non-Partitive Genitive

The governing word can here be a *noun* or an *adjective*.

A. The governing Word is a Noun

In this case the genitive is in pre-position. The following functional types should be distinguished:

a) The Possessive Genitive

The meanings of this genitive are those of *possession* and *belonging*:

māsas grāmata *sister's book*, **koka zari** *the branches of the tree*.

It is worth noting that where an adjective would appear in languages like Slavic, Germanic and Romance, Latvian will often use a noun in the genitive case, e.g. **latviešu valoda** *the Latvian language* (lit. 'the language of the Latvians').

b) The Subjective and c) the Objective Genitive

The governing words are here exclusively *verbal* nouns.
Examples of the *subjective genitive*:
skolnieka atbilde *the pu-pil's answer*, **armijas aplenkums** *the siege of the army*, **Kolumba atklājums** *Columbus' discovery*, cf. the corresponding verb phrases **skolnieks atbild** *the pupil answers*, **armija aplenc** *the army is besieging* and **Kolumbs atklāja** *Columbus disco-*

vered with **skolnieks** and **Kolumbs** in the function of subjects. As is seen from the illustrations, the subjective genitive is found with verbal nouns derived both from intransitive and transitive verbs.

An example of the objective genitive is **Amerikas atklāšana** *the discovery of America*, cf. **atklāt Ameriku** *to discover America* with **Amerika** as object. Observe that only verbal nouns which correspond with *transitive* (i. e. non-prepositional accusative governing) verbs can be construed with the objective genitive. Other examples: **bērnu audzināšana** *upbringing of children* (: **audzināt bērnus**), **armijas aplenkšana** *the siege of the army*, i. e. *the army is besieged* (: **armija ir aplenkta**).

The subjective and objective genitive can be combined in Latvian, although many Latvians will find such constructions rather clumsy, cf. for example **Kolumba Amerikas atklāšana** *Columbus' discovery of America / the discovery of America by Columbus*.

The combination of these two genitives does not seem to be possible in Slavic; thus, the Russians must replace the subjective genitive by the instrumental case, and the Poles by the preposition *przez* which is parallel to the German solution with *durch* (*die Entdeckung Amerikas durch Kolumbus*).

For the grammarian the question arises whether the genitive **Kolumba** in the locution **Kolumba Amerikas atklāšana** represents the subjective genitive or the agentive (since the performer of actions in the passive voice in Latvian is in the genitive, see p. 168f. below). What we envisage here is the neutralization between two functions.

d) The Descriptive Genitive

This genitive is illustrated by examples like **goda vīrs** *a man of honour*, **pienākuma cilvēks** *a man of duty (dutiful man)*, **pirmās klases viesnīca** *a first class hotel*, **labākās markas vīns** *wine of the best quality*.

Instead of the genitive an adjective may sometimes be used: **pirmklasīga viesnīca**.

e) *genitivus definitivus (explicativus)*

As illustrated in the following examples, this type of genitive is more widely used in Latvian than in many other languages:
Daugavas upe *the river Daugava*, **Rīgas pilsēta** *the city of Riga*, **latviešu tauta** *the Latvian people*, **Kalniņa kungs** *Mr. Kalniņš*, **Kalniņa kundze** *Mrs Kalniņš*, **profesora kungs** *Herr Professor* (lit. 'Mr. Professor'), **profesores kundze** *Frau Professor* (observe, however: **profesors Ošiņš, profesore Šiliņa** with appositional agreement between the two components, cf. pp. 202 and 219).

This genitive is labeled "definitivus" because the above noun phrases can be transformed into verb phrases of the following *defining* character: **Daugava ir upe** *Daugava is a river*, **latvieši ir tauta** *the Latvians are a people*, **Kalniņš ir kungs** *Kalnins ist ein Herr* (lit. *Kalnins is a mister*) etc. It follows from this test that a word group like **Latvijas universitāte** *The university of Latvia* does not belong to group e), but can only be interpreted as a).

f) The Genitive of Material

This genitive denotes the material which something consists of: **zelta gredzens** *a gold(en) ring/ring of gold*. Alternative constructions are possible, cf. **gredzens no zelta** (prepositional solution) and **zeltains gredzens** (adjectival solution).

g) The Genitive of Purpose

Here belong examples of the type **tējas tasīte** *a tea cup* (i. e. a cup intended for tea). Observe the contrast **tējas tasīte** *a cup of tea* : **tasīte tējas** *a cup of tea* (partitive function, for which see below).

h) The Genitive of Reinforcement (Emphasis)

Examples:
gadu gadiem (adverbialized) *for years and years*, **ķeniņu ķeniņš** *King of Kings*.

B. The governing Word is an Adjective
Here belong the adjectives **cienīgs** *worthy (of)*, **kārs** *greedy (of)*, **vērts** *worth*.
Examples:
uzmanības cienīgs *deserving attention*, **naudas kārs** *greedy of money*, **labs padoms ir zelta vērts** *a good piece of advice is worth its weight in gold*.

C. The Agentive
This function may be said to be on the borderline between the adnominal, the adverbal and adverbial functions. For matters of convenience we have placed it here after the adjective, since it is conditioned by a participle, which syntactically has much in common with the adjective, cf. p. 156.

The agentive (or agent) which is the performer of the action in formally passive constructions, is expressed in Latvian by the genitive: **direktora parakstīta vēstule** *a / the letter written by the director (ein /der vom Direktor geschriebene Brief)*. Observe that the agentive is limited almost exclusively to noun phrases of the above type. It is very rarely encountered in *sentences*, since formal passives with an explicit agent are as a rule avoided in Latvian, cf. section on voice, p. 140. Note also the obligatory word order (1. agent, 2. attributive participle, 3. head noun) in the noun phrase just quoted, in contrast with **parakstīta direktora vēstule,** which would mean "a/the written letter belonging to the director" (with **direktora** in the function of a possessive genitive, cf. p. 166 above and chapter 14 on word order, p. 227 below).

2. Partitive Genitive
(Dalāmais ģenitīvs)

The partitive adnominal genitive can be governed by a noun, an adjective, a numeral and certain other quantifiers.

With non-countable objects the genitive singular is used, with countable the plural.

A. The governing Word is a Noun

Unlike the non-partitive genitive after a noun, the partitive is *postposited*.

Contrast the partitive **tasīte tējas** *a cup of tea* with the non-partitive **tējas tasīte** *tea-cup* (cf. 1 A g above).

Other examples with the partitive genitive after a noun:
litrs piena *a liter of milk*, **metrs zīda** *a meter of silk*, **gabals maizes** *a piece of bread*, **vairākums studentu** *the majority of students*. As illustrated through these examples the *singular* is used with *non-countable nouns, the plural with countable*.

B. The governing Word is an Adjective

The adjectives **pilns** *full* and **bagāts** *rich in / abundantly supplied with* require a partitive genitive: **sniega pilna iela** *a street full of snow*, **bagāts zivju ezers** *a lake rich in fish*.

Contrast these adjectives with the genitive requiring adjectives in non-partitive function on p. 168 above.

Besides the genitive construction, the construction with **ar** (+ the accusative/dative) is also possible: **pilna ar sniegu iela, bagāts ar zivīm ezers**. With **bagāts** the alternative **ar**-construction seems to be preferable.

C. The governing Word is a Numeral

The following cardinal numbers require the genitive (plural): 1) the numerals 11-19, 2) all "decades", i. e. **desmit, divpadsmit** etc., 3) the "centades", i. e. **simt(s), divi simti** etc., 4) the thousands ("millades"): **tūkstoš / tūkstotis, divtūkstoš** etc., 5) **miljons, divi miljoni, miljards / triljons** etc.

Examples: **desmit / deviņpadsmit / simts/pieci simti / tūkstoš / miljons / miljards latu** *ten / nineteen / hundred / five hundred / thousand / one million / one billion lats.*

Note: all remaining (cardinal) numbers (as well as all ordinal numbers) show *agreement* (cf. p. 215 ff.) between the numeral and the counted entity, i. e. the noun. See also chapter on numerals, syntax section.

In the case of *compound numbers,* the syntax is determined by the last unit, as illustrated by the following contrasting example:
pieci simti deviņdesmit latu vs. **pieci simti deviņdesmit divi lati**
five hundred and ninety lats : five hundred ninety two lats
See also chapter 5: "Numerals", p. 74 ff.

D. The governing Word is a Quantifier other than a Numeral

The partitive genitive is also mandatory after quantifiers (occasionally also referred to as "undetermined numerals") like **daudz** *much*, **pār daudz** *too much*, **tik daudz** *so much*, **vairāk** *more*, **maz** *little, few*, **pār maz** *too little / few*, **tik maz** *so little / few*, **mazāk** *less*, **cik?** *how much / how many?*

Examples:
cik Jums ir gadu? *how old are you?* **daudz/maz/vairāk vīna** *much/little/ more wine;* **daudz/maz/vairāk draugu** *many/much/ more friends.*

The above examples illustrate that the *singular* is used with *non-countable nouns,* the *plural with countable.*

II Adverbal Function

As pointed out above (p. 166), the adverbal genitive can be either partitive or non-partitive.

1. Non-Partitive

A. Genitive-governing Verbs

A considerable number of Latvian verbs (reflexive and non-reflexive) govern or can govern the genitive. They belong mainly to such semantic fields as a) "striving for/towards" and b) "avoidance of":

Genitive-governing verbs with similar meanings are also found in a number of other Indo-European languages.

Under a) should be mentioned: **alkt** *thirst/crave for*, **ilgoties** *long for*, **slāpt** *thirst for*; **gaidīt** *wait for*, **gribēt** *wish*, **lūgt** *ask for*, **meklēt** *search / look for*, **prasīt** *ask for/demand*.

With the verbs appearing before the semi-colon an alternative construction with **pēc** (after) + the genitive is admissible, e.g. **alkt laimes : alkt pēc laimes** *thirst for fortune,* whereas with the remainder a construction with the accusative is possible (and in modern Latvian even preferable): e.g. **gaidīt vilcienu (vilciena)** *wait for the train*, **lūgt padomu (padoma)** *ask for advice*, **prasīt palīdzību (palīdzības)** *ask for help*.

Under b) are to be mentioned: **baidīties** *fear/be afraid (of)*, **bēgt** *run away / flee (from)*, **bīties** *fear/be afraid (of)*, **kaunēties** *be ashamed (of)*, **kautrēties** *feel shy (for)*, **sargāties** *protect oneself (from)*, **vairīties** *avoid*, e.g. **baidīties suņa** *be afraid of a/the dog*, **vairīties briesmu** (plural noun) *avoid danger*.

Besides the non-prepositional genitive construction, an alternative construction with the preposition **no** + the genitive is possible with these verbs.

Note the *transitive : intransitive* opposition in a case like **baidīt ko** (+ acc.) *frighten sby* : **baidīties** (+ gen.) *be frightened = fear / be afraid*.

For genitive-governing verbs with meanings 'to be lacking' and 'to be sufficient', see next paragraph.

B. Negative Constructions

a) Whereas in positive statements the direct object of transitive verbs is in the accusative case, in the corresponding negated sentences the object can be in the genitive, especially in the case of a *double negation* (**ne + ne**), e.g. **neredzēt neviena mākoņa** *not see a single cloud*, **nelasīt avīžu** *not read papers*.

In today's Latvian there is a tendency to use the accusative rather than the genitive in such cases, e.g. **nelasīt avīzes** rather than **nelasīt avīžu**.

> The origin of this genitive of negation, which is also found in Slavic, with parallels in Balto-Finnic languages, remains obscure. Some scholars hold it to be of an ablative (deprivative) nature (cf. the b-verb sphere in the preceding paragraph), while others tend to connect it with the partitive.

b) The (logical) subject (= grammatical object) of negated existential and related constructions is always in the genitive in Latvian, for example: **zooloģiskajā darzā nebija lauvu** *in the zoo there were no lions*, **tēva pašlaik nav mājās** *father is not at home at present*.

In the corresponding positive statements, the genitive must be replaced by the nominative (in the role of a grammatical subject): **zooloģiskajā darzā bija lauvas; tēvs pašlaik ir mājās**.

The genitive is further used with the verbs **netrūkt** *not be lacking (be sufficient)*, **nepietikt** *not be sufficient (be lacking)*, e.g. **nepietiek spēka** *there is not sufficient strength/force*.

Note: The genitive is mandatory with these two verbs, even when they are not accompanied by a negation: **trūkst līdzekļu** *there is a lack of means*, **pietiek līdzekļu** *there is enough/sufficient means*. With these verbs a nuance of partitiveness is felt, cf. next section.

2. Partitive

a) A partitive function is encountered after some otherwise *transitive* verbs (i. e. verbs requiring a direct object in the accusative case), such as **(no)pirkt** in **(no)pirkt piena/puķu** *buy (some) milk/flowers*.

The genitive is here contrasted with the accusative, cf. **(no)pirkt pienu/puķes** *buy (all) the milk/the flowers*. Other examples: **ēst siera** *eat cheese*, **gribēties augļu** *want fruit*.

Thus, an important opposition is apparent between the *genitive* – expressing a *part* (hence the notion partitive) of the object encompassed by the verbal action, and the *accusative* – implying command of the *whole object*. However, in contemporary Latvian it seems possible also to use the accusative instead of the genitive without any real difference in meaning: **ēst sieru, gribēties augļus**.

The genitive:accusative case opposition often corresponds to the *indefinite:definite* opposition in languages which have developed a system of articles, such as English, German and the Nordic languages.

In Standard Russian the partitive function is restricted roughly to verbs in the perfective aspect (compare for example *kupiť* (pf.) *xleba* (gen.) 'to buy (some) bread' : *kupiť xleb* (acc.) 'to buy (all) the bread', but always *pokupať* (ipf.) *xleb* (acc.) 'buy (the) bread'. This principle is not observed in Latvian, cf. the imperfective **pirkt** *buy* above.

III Adverbial Function

The adverbial function of the Latvian genitive is very marginal. One can even question if it exists at all. The only possible candidate seems to be the *genitive of time,* in cases like **ik (pār)dienas** *every (second) day*, **ik (pār)nedēļas** *every (second) week*, **ik (pār)naktis** *every (second) night*, **ik reizes** *every time*. The endings *-as* / *-es* / *-is* are (at least in a diachronic perspective) most probably to be analyzed as genitive singular forms, and not as accusatives plural (irrespective of cases like **ik gadus**, on which see below). The question arises as to whether the genitive is not ultimately determined by **ik,** in which case we could be dealing with a partitive genitive after a quantifier of the **cik**-type, cf. p. 162. The etymology and grammatical status of **ik**, however, remains obscure. Equally puzzling is the fact that in a number of cases, the accusative (not the genitive) is used after **ik**, e.g. **ik brīdi** *every moment (minute)*, **ik minūti** *every minute*, **ik stundu** *every hour*, **ik vakaru** (beside the accusative plural **vakarus**) *every evening*, **ik mēnesi** *every month*, **ik gadu** (beside the accusative plural **gadus**) *every year*. From a synchronic point of view, both the genitive-like forms and the accusative forms have been adverbialized. Instead of the **ik**-construction, one can use the pronoun **katr-** *every*: **katru dienu, katru gadu** etc. (i. e. with an adverbial accusative, cf. p. 174).

The Genitive in Exclamations

An example of this is the locution: **tava muļka prāta** *you fool*.

THE ACCUSATIVE

The accusative in Latvian may to some extent be said to be in a state of complementary distribution with the genitive, as far as its adverbal functions are concerned (cf. the non-partitive direct object in positive statements, in contrast to the partitive genitive object and to the genitive object after transitive verbs in negative constructions). Furthermore, the adverbial function is the only one which the accusative and the genitive have in common, since the accusative lacks the adnominal function and the genitive the adverbial, which – alongside the adverbial – is of such vital importance with the accusative.

The accusative falls into two categories, the *adverbal* and the *adverbial,* whereas the adnominal is lacking (for the possibility of speaking of an adnominal type in connection with certain adjectives of quantity, see under the adverbial accusative below).

I Adverbal Accusative

Latvian verbs can govern different oblique cases, the genitive, the accusative, the dative and the locative. The absolute majority of the verbs, however, require the accusative (as a direct object) and are called *transitive*, e.g. **lasīt vēstuli** *to read a letter*, **uzbuvēt māju** *to build a house*.

A basic feature of verbs with the accusative is that they can be transferred from active to passive forms, cf. **lasīt vēstuli / uzbuvēt māju** *to read a letter / to build a house* : **lasāma vēstule / uzbuvēta māja**, cf. p. 157.

A special type of accusative object, so-called "inner object" is encountered in cases like **domāt domu** lit. *to think a thought*, **dziedāt dziesmu** *to sing a song*, **dejot deju** *to dance a dance*.

In opposition to the Slavic languages, where *reflexive* verbs are more or less incapable of governing the accusative case, this restriction is not observed to the same extent in Baltic, where an accusative object can also be governed by a reflexive verb: for example, **nopirkties jaunu velosipēdu** *to buy a new bicycle*, **mācīties matemātiku** *to learn (study) mathematics*, **izgaidīties vilcienu** *to wait for the train*, **atcerēties pasaku** *to recall a fairy-tale*. The meaning of the reflexive is here "in one's own interest" (cf. p. 143 under reflexive and non-reflexive verbs).

Since the number of verbs governing other cases than the accusative is rather limited, it is customary to to present lists of verbs governing the other oblique cases, not the accusative, because such a list would be very long and therefore impossible in a grammar. It belongs naturally in the dictionary.

Also more than one object may occur. Thus, the combination *dative + accusative* is frequent (see also under the dative case p. 177), with the indirect object (denoting a person) in the dative, and the direct (denoting a thing) in the accusative, e.g. **dot/sutīt kādam** (dative) **ko** (accusative) *to give/send sby sth*.

Finally, the accusative in the function of an *object predicative* in cases like the following should be mentioned:

mēs viņu pazīstam kā labu ārsti *we know her as a good physician*.

II Adverbial Accusative

As in a number of other Indo-European case languages, the accusative covers the adverbial functions of:
1. *time*
2. *measure, price and weight*

Common to both a) and b) is the feature [+ *quantity*].

1. can be divided into two subdivisons:

A. *duration* (answering the question *how long?*): **viņi bija nedēļu / divus gadus Rīgā** *they spent a week / two years in Rīgā*,

B. *frequency* (answering the question *how often?*): **viņi dejoja katru dienu** *they danced every day*.

2. answers the questions *how much/far?* **mēs jau gājām divas stundas** *we have already walked (for) two hours*, **šis žurnāls maksā (vienu) latu** *this journal costs one lat*, **grāmata sver (vienu) kilogrammu** *the book weighs one kilogram*.

Certain cases of the accusative of quantity can be accompanied by adjectives of quantity, like **vecs** *old* (e. g. **bērns ir divus gadus vecs** *the child is two years old*), **augsts** *high* (e. g. **divus stāvus augsta māja** *a house two stories high*), **plats** *wide* (e. g. **laukums ir kilometru plats** *the square is one kilometer wide*), **dziļš** *deep* (**upe ir tikai divus metrus dziļa** *the river is only two meters deep*), **garš** *long* (e. g. **divus kilometrus gara iela** *a street two kilometers long*), **biežs** *thick* (e. g. **vienu metru biežs ledus** *one meter thick ice*). It would have been possible here to speak of an *adnominative* accusative, but because of the constraint to certain adjectives alone we have – for matters of economy – abstained from establishing an adnominative section in connection with the accusative.

The Accusative in Exclamations

Finally and separately, mention should be made of the accusative in exclamations, e.g. **tavu muļķi!** *you fool!*

For the use of the possessive pronoun, cf. also Nordic *din idiot* 'you fool' which may represent a genitive form of the personal pronoun reinterpreted as a possessive. If this interpretation is correct, we would in a historical perspective be dealing with a *genitivus definitivus*, cf. p. 167f. Could the Latvian construction with an unambiguous possessive pronoun be explained through Swedish intermediary? Besides this construction, Latvian also has at its disposal an alternative construction with the personal pronoun which is known from a number of European languages: **tu muļķi**.

A Contrastive View of the Genitive and the Accusative

As pointed out (p. 173) these two cases are (to a considerable extent) in a state of *complementary distribution*. This relationship can be summarized in the following chart:

	Genitive	Accusative
Adnominal	+	-
Adverbal	+	+
Adverbial	-	+

THE INSTRUMENTAL

As pointed out (p. 41), we do not recognize the existence of the instrumental as an independent case in contemporary Latvian. From a diachronic perspective, however, certain adverbialized forms are likely to be identified, e.g. **vietām/vietumis** (function of place), **laikiem/reizēm** (function of time), **iet/nākt bariem, iet soļiem, iet/braukt riksiem/aulekšiem, visiem spēkiem** (function of manner). Note also the locution **būt vienis pratīs (ar kādu)** *be of the same opinion as sby*.

For expression of the meaning of instrument, see chapter on prepositions (s. v. **ar**).

THE DATIVE

The dative is most frequently used with persons, to a lesser degree with things. It often has the meaning of a logical subject. In a number of cases the dative is not necessary to obtain a correct grammatical construction, but its absence would modify the meaning.

I Adnominal Dative

1. The governing Word is a Noun

The dative case may be accompanied by certain nouns derived from adjectives and verbs which require the dative case (see below), e.g. **pateicība kam** *gratefulness to sby* (: **pateicīgs kam** *grateful to sby*), **kaitīgums veselībai** *harm (destructiveness) to health* (: **kaitīgs kam** *harmful to sby/sth.*, **kaitēt kam** *harm sby/sth.*) **atbilde kam** *answer to sby* (: **atbildēt kam** *answer sby*), **palīdzība kam** *help to sby* (: **palīdzēt kam** *help sby*), **pārmetums kam** *reproach to sby* (: **pārmest kam** *sby reproach sby*).

2. The governing Word is an Adjective

The adjective **līdzīgs** *alike, similar* is construed with the dative, e.g. **viņš ir līdzīgs tēvam** *he is like his father,* **šis trijstūris ir līdzīgs otram trijstūrim** *this triangle is similar to another/the other triangle.* Another dative governing adjective is **derīgs** *useful*, e.g. **gramatika ir**

derīga studentiem *grammar is useful to the students.* In this case, the use of the dative is easy to grasp, in opposition to **līdzīgs**. Adjectives with the meaning of similarity are, however, often construed with the dative case in Indo-European languages: for example, German *gleich (mir)*, Lithuanian *lygus kam* 'alike sby/sth.', Russian *ravno (čemu)* '(a)like (sth.)'.

Note that the adjectives **vienlīdzīgs** *equal* and **proporcionāls** *proportional* are not construed with the dative case, but with the preposition **ar** (+ the accusative).

For the dative with numerous adjective-like predicatives, see p. 179 below.

3. The Dative of Age

Finally, mention should be made of the dative of age: **Cik Jums gadu? Man ir piecdesmit gadu.** *How old are you? I am fifty years old.*

II Adverbal Dative

1. Dative + Nominative

See the *have-* and debitive-constructions under points 4 and 6 below.

2. Dative + Accusative

The dative is used in the function of an indirect object, referring to the person or addressee, with transitive verbs also accompanied by a direct accusative object, for example: **dot/rakstīt/teikt/sūtīt** etc. **kam** (dative) **ko** (accusative) *to give/write/say/send sby. sth.*, cf. also the well known German formula *einem etwas geben* etc. Reference should also be made to the accusative above.

3. Dative as the only Object

A group of *intransitive* verbs known in grammatical terminology as *verba commodi et incommodi*, i. e. verbs denoting 'to somebody's benefit or disadvantage', require a dative object as the *only* object. The following list of verbs can be given:

A. Verba commodi:

aplaudēt *to applaud*, **atbilst** *to satisfy*, **derēt** *to suit, fit*, **glaimot** *to flatter*, **imponēt** *to impress*, **kalpot** *to serve*, **palīdzēt** *to help*, **pateikties** *to thank*, **simpatizēt** *to sympathize with*, **uzticēties** *to trust*.
Examples:

atbilst visām prasībām *to satisfy all demands*, **viņš neuzticas draugiem** *he dosn't trust his friends.*

B. Verba incommodi:
apnikt, atriebt kādam ko/par ko, draudēt *to threaten,* **kaitēt** to *hurt,* **pretoties, traucēt** *disturb.*

Examples:
zēnam neapnika skatīties *the boy didn't get bored by looking,* **mitrais gaiss kaitēja veselībai** *the moisty air did harm to the health*

Further mention should be made of some additional dative-governing verbs which are not so easy to incorporate in the framework of the *verba commodi et incommodi*. Here belong verbs like **atbildēt kam** *answer sby,* **piederēt kam** *belong to sby,* **pārmest sby** *reproach sby,* **gatavoties kam** *prepare for sth.*

Under this heading, one should also mention *dative + nominative*-constructions (with the latter in the role of grammatical subject), e.g. **man (ne)garšo gaļa** *I (don't) like meat,* **man (ne)patīk šita filma** *I (don't) like this film,* cf. point 5 below.

4. Dative + *ir/bija/būs* etc. as Equivalents to *have*-Constructions in English

In opposition to *have*-languages, such as English, German, the Nordic languages and Romance, Latvian (like Russian, Balto-Finnic languages and many others) is a *be*-language, e.g. **man ir (bija, būs, ir bijis, bija bijis, būs bijis) velosipēds** *I have (had, shall have, have had, had had, will have had) a bicycle* (lit. *for me is/was etc. bicycle*). The grammatical subject, which understandably must be in the form of the nominative, is **velosipēds**. See also under the nominative case on p. 181 below. The corresponding question would be **kas man ir/bija (etc.)?** *what do/did I have (etc.)?*

The *negated* counterpart to the sentence just quoted is **man nav (nebija, nebūs, nav bijis, nebija bijis, nebūs bijis) velosipēda** *I don't have (didn't have, shall not have, have not had, had not had, shall not have had)* with a *logical* subject (= **velosipēda**) in the genitive case, cf. p. 171f.

Here one may also mention the *verb of belonging* **piederēt** which is construed in a similar way, e.g. **man pieder velosipēds** *I have a bicycle* (lit. *to me belongs bicycle*), again with **velosipēds** in the function of a grammatical subject, whence the nominative is required. When 'belong to' has the meaning of 'belonging to a category / class' and not 'as property', the prepositional construction **piederēt pie** must be used, e.g. **lauva pieder pie zvēriem** *the lion belongs to the wild animals,* cf.

a parallel distinction for instance in German and Russian between *gehören/prinadležať* + the dative and *gehören zu / prinadležať k*.

5. Dative in Impersonal Constructions
A. Verbal:
Also mportant is the dative with certain verbs in a number of *impersonal* constructions (for definition, see p. 198 below), e.g. **man liekas (, ka)** (inf. **likties**) *I think (it seems to me /that/),* **man šķiet (, ka)** (inf. **šķist**) *I think (it seems to me (that)),* **man slāpst** (inf. **slāpt**) *I am thirsty / I want to drink,* **man nākas** (inf. **nākties**) *I have to,* **man salst** (inf. **salt**) *I feel cold,* **man trūkst kā** (inf. **trūkt**) *I am lacking sth.,* **man vajag ko** (inf. **vajadzēt**) *I need sth.*

Constructionss like **man ir velosipēds** *I have a bicycle* (cf. preceding paragraph) are per definition not considered impersonal, since they have a grammatical (nominative-case) subject. For the same reason, constructions like **man garšo šokolāde** *I like chocolate,* **man patīk filma** *I like the film* (cf. German: *der Film gefällt mir*) or **man sāp galva** *I have headache* should not treated under this point, but rather under point 3 above.

B. Nominal:
Equally important is the dative with numerous *predicatives* (cf. also p. 169), e.g. **man ir labi/patīkami/bēdīgi/slikti/auksti/karsti/žēl** *I feel well/bad/cold/warm/sorry* (lit. *to me it is...*).

6. Dative in the Debitive Construction
For the function of the dative as *logical subject* in the debitive construction, see p. 130.

For the dative as *part of the nominal predicative* in debitive constructions, cf. p. 130.

7. Dative with the Infinitive Passive
Example:
Nav labi tikt ievainotam *it is not good to be accused*
For explanation of the dative **ievainotam**, see p. 146.

8. Dative + Infinitive Constructions
For this function, see p. 145.

Dative with Gerunds (The Absolute Dative)

For this so-called *absolute dative*, see p. 150f.

III Adverbial Function

The only possible candidate for this function is the dative of purpose (dativus finalis): **vilna cimdiem** *wool for gloves*, **papīrs rakstīšanai** *paper for writing*, **āda kožokam** *a pelt for a fur coat*.

Other adverbially used datives in Latvian have been fully adverbialized, e.g. **apmēram** *approximately*, **piemēram** *for example*.

THE LOCATIVE

As stated on p. 184, the Latvian locative can never be governed by a preposition. The historical reason for this is that the locative marker reflects the merger of a regular case ending with a postposition (cf. p. 41).

The locative in Latvian has adnominal, adverbal and adverbial functions, with the latter as the overwhelmingly dominant one.

As examples of the *adnominal* and *adverbal* functions respectively may serve: **piedalīšanās** (refl. verbal noun) **kā** *participation in sth.* and **piedalīties kā** *participate in sth.* (e. g. **konferencē** *a conference*), **klausīties kā** *listen to sth.* (e. g. **koncertā** *a concert*).

Note especially the transitional case between the adverbial and adverbal functions. As adverbal function may be regarded the *locative after verbs expressing motion with the prefix* **ie-** *in(to)*, e.g. **ieiet istabā** *go into / enter the room*. This use of the locative is surprising to students familiar with German or Slavic case languages, where this is a typical accusative sphere. The situation is parallel to that after verbs expressing motion, in cases like **vilkt mugurā** *take on* (about clothes), lit. *pull on the back*, **likt galvā mici** *put the cap on one's head*, **aut kājās** lit. *take / put on the feet* (about shoes and similar). Note finally **sasalt ledū** *freeze (in)to ice*, as well as the adnominal type **kalnā kāpējs** *"alpinist"* (lit. *climber onto the hill*).

Typical *adverbial functions* of the Latvian locative are:

1. the *locative of place* (answering the question *where / in which place?*): **strādāt lasītavā** *work in the reading-room*, **sēdēt istabā** *sit in the room*,

2. the *locative of time* (answering the question *when?* about time units such as *hour, day, night, days of the week, week, month, year and similar*): **atbraukt divos vakarā / naktī / sestdienā(s) / šajā nedēļā / jūlijā / pagājušajā gadā / jaunībā** *arrive at two o'clock / in the evening / at night / on Saturday(s) / this week / in July / last year / in one's youth*.

3. the *locative of manner*: **runāt skaļā balsī** *speak in / with a loud voice*. (A construction with the preposition **ar** + the accusative is

also possible, but is ambiguous in meaning: with the help of one's own voice *or* with another voice.)

4. the *locative of reason*: **samelot bailēs** *to lie out of fear*, **apstāties izbrīnā** *to stop of / by / in surprise*.

5. the locative of *reference*: **spēcīgs matemātikā** *strong / clever in (with respect to) mathematics*

6. the *locative of purpose*: **iet ogās / sēnēs** *go for / collect berries / mushrooms*, **iet viesos** (< **viesis** *guest*) *go for a visit*, **braukt medībās** *go hunting*.

THE NOMINATIVE

The nominative case has four main functions in Latvian:
1) as *grammatical subject* in *two part sentences* (see p. 205) which can be in the *active* or *passive* voice (p. 135 ff.), e.g. **bērns zīmē (suni)** *the child is drawing (a dog)* and **māja tiek celta** *the house is buing built*. Observe also the type **man ir velosipēds** (p. 178).

2) as the *only principal member (galvenais loceklis)* in so-called *nominative one part sentences* (p. 207), e.g. **vakars** *(it is) evening*, and

3) as part of the *nominal predicate* (p. 198), i. e. in the form of a *nominal word class* (i. e. a noun, adjective or pronoun) after a *copulative verb* (i. e. verbs with the meaning of *be* in a non-existential sense and *become,* cf. also p. 198), e.g. **viņš (ir) bērns** *he is a child*, **vinš (ir) jauns** *he is young*. Note the use of the nominative, not the genitive case in the corresponding negative statement **viņš nav** (copulative verb) **bērns/jauns** *he is not a child/ young* in opposition to, for example, **te nav bērnu** *there are no children here* with an automatic genitive after the existential verb **nav**.

Observe also formula *saukt ko kas*: **viņu sauc Jānis** *his name is Janis* (lit. 'they call him John') as well as the construction **kļūt par** (+ the accusative) *to become* in the sense of German *werden zu*: **kļūt par ārstu** *to become a physician*.

In connection with 3) one may also mention the nominative after **kā** *as* in constructions of the type **viņa ir zināma kā ļoti interesanta dzejniece** *she is known as a very interesting poet*.

4) as *object* in *debitive* constructions (cf. p. 130), e.g. **man jāraksta vēstule** *I have to write a letter*. If the debitive predicate consists of a phasal auxiliary plus an infinitive, either the nominative or the case required by the infinitive can be used: **man jasāk rakstīt vēstule** (nom.)/**vēstuli** (acc.) *I must begin writing the letter*. The nominative object is avoided with pronouns of the 1st and 2nd person: **man tevi** (not ***tu**) **jāredz** *I have to see you* (but: **man viņš jāredz** *I have to see*

him). Observe that the *logical subject* of the debitive construction is always in the *dative* case (cf. p. 130).

5) A last, but marginal function of the nominative is encountered in certain *appositions* (see p. 219), e.g. **romānā "Mērnieku laiki"** *in the novel "The Times of the Landsurveyors"*.

THE VOCATIVE

The vocative is the case of *address*.

For examples, see chapter on adjective (p. 62), where information about the form of both an attributive adjective and the noun is given.

Chapter 9
PREPOSITIONS
(Prievārds)

This is a natural continuation of the immediately preceding chapter on *Case,* which we found convenient to reserve almost exclusively for non-prepositional use, even though a full description of case should include prepositions as well. The purpose of this chapter on prepositions is to give a brief survey of the prepositions most commonly encountered in modern Standard Latvian and information on the case(s) required after them, their meanings presented in simple, illustrative examples. A less practically oriented grammar should in addition have paid attention to a number of theoretical, semantic and grammatical aspects concerning prepositions and case grammar.

Preposition vs. Prefix
In a number of cases *prepositions* and *prefixes* (see 159 ff.) show the same form, namely **aiz, ap, no, pa, par, pār, pie** and **uz** .

Preposition vs. Adverb. Semi-Prepositions
There is also a formal overlapping between certain *prepositions* and *adverbs*, e.g. **priekš/ā** *in front (of)*.
Moreover, Latvian has a set of prepositions which may be said to be primarily adverbs. They can be referred to as *semi-prepositions* or *prepositional adverbs*. Some examples: **cauri** *right through* (cf. the preposition **caur** below), **garām** (cf. the preposition **gar**) *along*, **pāri** *across* (cf. the preposition **pār**), **pretī** (cf. preposition **pret**) *against*. Illustration of use: **mēs gājām garām** *we went past* (function as adverb) : **mēs gājam garām upei** *we went (were going) along the river* (function as preposition). Contrast further cases like **pāriet pār ielu : iet pāri ielai** *to cross the street* where the preposition **pār** is used with the perfective verb, whereas the imperfective partner is accompanied by the semi-preposition/adverb **pāri**. For oppositions of this type, section on aspect in chapter 6 should be consulted. These adverb-prepositions posit a problem, in that they can be either preposited or postposited to the

noun, according to somewhat obscure rules. Thus, for example, **iet pāri** + *noun* seems to be preferred to (the equally possible) sequence **iet** + *noun* + **pāri**. With **cauri**, however, the tendency seems to be the opposite, i. e. *noun* + **cauri** rather than **cauri** + *noun* (cf. for example **šķēršļiem cauri** *through obstacles*). However, as a rule of thumb preposition/postposition is optional.

As pointed out on several occasions in this grammar, Latvian is very interesting in a *typological* perspective, i. e. in a transitional stage between Indo-European and Finno-Ugric. With respect to prepositions Latvian can be said to offer a compromise between the two groups of languages in that it has developed a set of adverbs (Finno-Ugric type) alongside prepositions (Indo-European type). The former have partly adopted prepositional (or rather postpositional) properties.

Preposition vs. Noun

Prepositions ending in **-pus** (e. g. **ārpus** *outside*, **otrpus** *on the other side*) represent *petrified nouns* (cf. **puse** *side*), which explains why these prepositions govern the genitive (from a historical point of view this is an adnominal genitive, see the preceding chapter). In the case of **laikā** (< **laiks** *time*) *during* (with the genitive, e.g. **kara laikā** *during the war*) the "preposition" has the appearance of a petrified case (locative), cf. pp. 188 and 193 (point 14 D). A similar case is that of **vidū** (< **vidus** *middle*) *in the middle of*.

Preposition vs. Postposition

Except for the ambiguous (i. e. in terms of linear order) semi-prepositions, the majority of Latvian prepositions really are *preposited*; only two (**dēļ** *because of, for the sake of* and **labad** *on behalf of, for the sake of*) are *postposited*, and hence strictly speaking *postpositions*, even though they are treated under the same heading as the prepositions.

Case Government

The genitive, accusative and marginally the dative can be governed by prepositions in Latvian, whereas the locative – and, of course, the nominative and the vocative – cannot. Genetically speaking, the locative has an "imbedded" postposition. As mentioned (p. 41 above) we do not see the necessity of working with an instrumental case in Latvian because of the merger of this case with the accusative in the singular, the dative in the plural.

Only two prepositions govern *more than one case*, namely **pa** (accusative and dative) and **uz** (accusative and genitive). When governed by the accusative, **pa** has the following meanings: *along, on; through; during/in; by;* with the dative it has a "distributive" meaning, cf. below.

The preposition **uz** takes the accusative in the sense of *to*. When combined with the genitive it corresponds to English *on* (and rarely *in*).

One preposition (**līdz** *until*) governs the dative case. *It should, however, be emphasized that all semi-prepositions/adverbs* (cf. above) *also require the dative case.* Notice also that accusative- and genitive-governing prepositions in certain idiomatic expressions combine with the dative when followed by the demonstrative pronoun **tas**: **bez tam** *besides;* **pie tam** *moreover* (but **bez tā** *without that,* **pie tam** *at (near) that*). Observe also the conjunction **pēc tam kad** *after (when)*.

Eight prepositions govern the accusative case. They will be mentioned in alphabetical order and should be learned by heart by the student: **ap** *around,* **ar** *with,* **caur** *through,* **gar** *along,* **par** *about (concerning),* **pār** *across,* **pret** *against, towards* and **starp** *between, among*.

All remaining prepositions govern the genitive which consequently is the case most frequently encountered after prepositions in Latvian. The two postpositions **dēļ** and **labad** (together with **laikā**) also require the genitive case (adnominal genitive, cf. p. 166 ff.), since they originally represent petrified noun forms. The genitive governing prepositions are the following (in alphabetical order):

aiz *behind; across; after; because of (for),* **ārpus** *outside,* **bez** *without; except (but),* **dēļ** *because of; for (the sake of);* **kopš** *since,* **labad** *for the sake of,* **no** *from; out of,* **otrpus** *on the other side,* **pēc** *after; for,* **pie** *at; with; to,* **pirms** *before; ago,* **priekš** *before,* **virs** *over; above,* **zem** *under; beneath*.

Finally, under this point a peculiarity of Latvian (which has also attracted the interest of linguists in general) and an extremely important feature in the grammar of Latvian prepositions should be noticed: *in the plural all Latvian prepositions govern the dative – irrespective of the case (or cases) they require in the singular,* e.g. **pa ielu** (acc.sg.) *along the street* : **pa ielām** (dat.pl.) *along the streets,* **bez drauga** (gen.sg.) *without a friend* : **bez draugiem** (dat.pl.) *without friends.* The two postpositions, **dēļ** and **labad,** however, retain their genitive government also in the plural, e.g. **grūtību dēļ** *due to difficulties,* **bērnu labad** *to the benefit of the children*.

Note: all prepositional adverbs (cf. p. 183) govern the dative case in both numbers.

Subsequent Disposition

There are several ways of presenting prepositions in a grammar of Latvian. One strategy would be to group them according to the case they govern in the singular. Another possibility would simply be to deal with each one of them in alphabetical order. Here, however, a third strategy will be followed, namely grouping according to their functions (meanings). Thus, prepositions 1) of *place*, 2) of *time*, 3) of *instrument*, 4) *purpose*, 5) *comparison*, 6) *cause* whereas subgroup 7) is reserved for remaining cases.

1. Prepositions of Place

A distinction can be drawn between *directional* and *non-directional* (locational) prepositions. Here, however, it should be borne in mind that one preposition, e.g. **uz**, can have both functions (provided that one is willing to accept that it is one preposition and not two homonyms). Further, a preposition like **virs** *above, over* can refer to *position*, but also *movement above (over)* a place. A similar duality is also seen with other prepositions, for example, in **starp** *between* which can express *location*, but also *passage between two objects*. In addition we are faced with the fact that in Latvian, unlike Lithuanian, Slavic, German and many other case languages *movement into* is expressed not by a preposition + the accusative, *but usually with the locative*, which in Slavic (and its substitute, the dative, in German) is reserved for *location in*, not movement into.

A. Accusative-governing Prepositions

ap *around*: **sēdēt ap galdu** *sit around the table* (location in the vicinity of sby/sth.); **apiet ap māju** (notice the repetition of the preposition in the verbal prefix) *walk around the house (movement around)*;

caur *through; via*: **jāt caur mežu** *ride through the forest*, **saule iespīdēja caur logu** *the sun shone through the window*; **smaidīt caur asarām** *smile through tears* (movement through sth.); **braukt caur Kopenhāgenu** *go via Copenhagen*.

Note: the preposition **caur** in the meaning *through* is used when some kind of physical obstacle is involved. Otherwise the preposition **pa** is used, see below.

Observe also the semi-preposition **cauri** (with the dative) mentioned above. Illustration: **cauri sienai** *right through the wall*.

gar *along*: **staigāt gar krastu** *walk along the bank*. Here again a parallel semi-preposition, viz. **garām** (with the dative) should be noticed: **garām upei** *along the river*.

pa *along (about, in); through*: **staigāt pa istabu/ielu/mežu/sniegu** *walk about (in) the room/in (along) the street/in the forest/in the snow* (movement along a surface); **skatīties pa logu** *look through the window* (cf. under **caur** above); **iziet pa vārtiem** *go out through the gate*; **pa labi/pa kreisi** *on (to) the right/left;*

pār *across, over*: **(pār)peldēt pār upi** *to swim across the river* (movement to a place across sth; note the repetition of the preposition in the verbal prefix); **Pār laukiem spīd saule** *the sun is shining over the fields* (location);

Note also the parallel semi-preposition **pāri** (with the dative) mentioned above. Example: **braukt pāri upei** *go across the river*. For absence of verbal prefix, see chapter on aspect (p. 115 ff.);

pret *against, towards*: **peldēt pret straumi** *swim against the stream*, **jāt pret kalnu** *ride uphill*;

starp *between; among*: **ceļš ir vidū starp mežu un ezeru** *the road is in the middle between the wood and the lake;* **starp visiem kandidātiem viņš ir vispiemērotākais** *among (of) all candidates he is the most suitable one*;

B. *Genitive-governing Prepositions*

aiz *behind*: **māja ir aiz ezera** *the house is behind the lake* (location); **ūdens aiztecēja aiz apkakles** (observe the repetition of the preposition in the verbal prefix) *the water flowed behind the collar* (movement to a place behind sby/sth.); **viņi gāja cits aiz cita** *they were marching one after another* (sequence);

no *from; out of*: **atbraukt no Rīgas** *to arrive from Riga*, **jāt no kalna** *ride (down) from the hill*; **krist no jumta** *fall from the roof*, **saņemt vēstuli no drauga** *get a letter from a friend*, **aizņemties no ko** *borrow from sby*, **izkāpt no vagona** *get out of the carriage*; **izņemt no kabatas** *take out from/of the pocket*. In all these examples the sense of *movement* is felt, in opposition to the following two, which denote *location* and *origin*: **tas ir netālu no šejienes** *that is not far from here;* **viņa ir no Piebalgas** *she is from Piebalga*.

The combination *from – to* is rendered by **no** (+ genitive) – **līdz** (+ dative), e.g. **no Rīgas līdz Kopenhāgenai** *from Riga to Copenhagen*.

pie *at; near; with (at the house of); to*: **sēdēt pie galda** *sit at the table*, **pie mājas ir puķu dobe** *at (near) the house there is a flower bed;* **dzīvot pie tēva** *live (stay) with the father* (location in the vicinity of); **braukt/iet pie tēva/zobārsta** *go to one's father/the dentist* (movement to animate beings); **iet pie skapja** *go to the cupboard/ wardrobe* (with inanimate objects the preposition **pie** denotes limited movement as opposed to **uz**, on which see below);

virs *above, over*: **bilde karājas virs gultas** *the picture is hanging abover the bed;* **putns lidoja virs koku galotnēm** *the bird was flying over the tops of the trees*;

zem *under*: **sēdēt zem koka** *sit under a tree;* **būt zem spiediena** *be under pressure* (figurative sense);

vidū (+ genitive) *in the middle of*: **istabas vidū** *in the middle of the room*. Observe the *postposition* of **vidū**.

priekšā (+ genitive) *before, in front of*: **garāžas priekšā** *in front of the garage*. Note the *postposition* of **priekšā**.

C. *Dative-governing Prepositions*
There is only one, namely
līdz *to* (the terminal point for the movement): **līdz jūrai** *to the sea*

D. *Prepositions governing more than one Case*

uz (+ accusative) *to, towards*: **braukt uz Rīgu** *go to Riga*, **steigties uz staciju** *hurry to the station* (movement / direction towards);

Note: movement *into* is expressed in Latvian by the prefix **ie-** + verb of motion + the *locative*, cf. pp. 180 above.

uz (+ genitive) *on, on to*: **uz galda guļ grāmata** *on the table there is a book* (location on a surface); **likt cepuri uz plaukta** *put the hat on(to) the shelf*, **uzlēkt / uzkāpt uz jumta** *jump onto the roof* (limited movement);

2. Prepositions of Time

A. *Accusative-governing:*
ap *around:* **ap pulksten vienu** *around one o'clock*
uz *for*: **uz brīdi** *for a moment*

B. *Dative- governing:*
līdz *till, until, to; by:* **līdz rītam** *till the morning;* **līdz rītdienai** *by to-morrow*

C. *Genitive- governing:*
kopš *since:* **Viņi ir draugi kopš bērnības** *they have been friends since childhood;*
no *from:* **no bērnības** *from childhood*
Note the combination **no – līdz** *from – till*: **no rīta līdz vakaram** *from morning till night (evening)*, **no pieciem līdz septiņiem** *from five to seven (o'clock)*

pēc *after; in:* **pēc kara** *after the war;* **viņš atgriezīsies pēc nedēļas** *he will be back (return) in a week*. Observe the construction **pēc tam** *after that, afterwards, thereupon* with the dative.

pirms *before; ago:* **pirms kara** *before the war,* **pirms gada** *a/one year ago;*

laikā *during:* **brīvdienas laikā** *during the holiday* (notice the mandatory postposition of **laikā**).

3. Prepositions designating the Instrument
There is one preposition in this function, namely:
ar (+ accusative): **rakstīt ar zīmuli** *write with a pencil*, **braukt ar vilcienu** *go by train*

This function corresponds to the non-prepositional instrumental case in Slavic case languages (and Lithuanian).

4. Prepositions of Purpose
par (+ accusative) *for*: **mirt par brīvību** *die for freedom*, **maksāt par kaut ko** *pay for sth. (as repayment for)*, **nopirkt grāmatu par latu** *buy the book for a/one lats;*

pēc (+ genitive) *for/after*: **iet pēc ūdens** *go for (to fetch/bring) water*

5. Prepositions of Comparison
par (+ accusative): **viņš ir jaunāks par mani** *he is younger than me*. An alternative construction is that with the *conjunction* **nekā** + the nominative (cf. also p. 57): **viņš ir jaunāks nekā es** (i. e. **es esmu**) *he is younger than I (am)*.

6. Prepositions of Cause
aiz *(+genitive) from, by:* **aiz pārsteiguma** *from / by surprise*, **aiz bailēm** *from fear;*

ar (+ accusative) *of*: **mirt ar vēzi** *die of cancer;*

no (+ genitive) *of, from* : **smaidīt no prieka** *smile from joy;*

Finally, mention should be made of the postposition

dēļ (+ genitive) *because of*: **slimības dēļ** *due to illness*.

7. Prepositions of other Meanings
The prepositions in question are listed in alphabetical order:

ar (+ accusative) *with, in the company of*: **runāt ar kolēģi** *speak with a colleague*; *manner*: **gaidīt ar nepacietību** *wait with impatience*

bez (+ genitive) *without; except*: **bez izņēmuma** *without exception*; **bez manis, arī mani draugi bija klāt** *besides me, also my friends were present.*

Observe the construction **bez tam** *in addition* with the dative.

pa (+ dative) in distributive function: **Jums jāpaņemt pa tabletei trīs reizes dienā** *you have to take a pill three times a (per) day*

par (+ accusative) *about; as / in the capacity of*: **sarunāties par kaut ko** *to speak about sth.;* **strādāt par skolotāju** *work as a teacher.* Observe further: **kļūt par** *become*, e. g. **kļūt par skolotāju** *become a teacher*

pēc (+ genitive) *according to:* **pēc likuma/ziņām** *according to the law/the news;*

pie (+ genitive) *by:* **paņemt pie rokas** *take by the hand;*

pret (+ accusative) *against*: **pret manu gribu** *against my will*, **cīnīties pret ienaidnieku** *struggle against the enemy,* **zāles pret gripu** *medicine against influenza*. Observe the parallel semi-preposition preti(m) (with the dative) mentioned above: **viņa sēdēja pretī man** *she was sitting just opposite me.*

Finally, *combinations of adverb + preposition* should be observed, e.g. **kopā ar** *together with*, **prom no** *away from*.

Chapter 10

TIME EXPRESSIONS

Some expressions of time have been included in the two preceding chapters. Some relevant expressions are mentioned also in the chapter on numerals. It seems, however, practical to concentrate such expressions in one place with the advantage of allowing a more detailed and lucid presentation.

1. The 24 Hours Cycle

in the morning/in the evening	**no rīta/vakarā**
in the morning/evenings	**rītos/vakaros**
during the day	**dienā**
during the night	**naktī**
during (in) the nights	**naktīs**
yesterday morning	**vakar no rīta**
this morning/evening	**šorīt/šovakar**
today/tonight	**šodien/šovakar**
tomorrow	**rīt**
tomorrow morning/night	**rīt no rīta (rītnorīt)/rītvakar**
the day before yesterday	**aizvakar**
two days before yesterday	**aizaizvakar**
the day after to-morrow	**parīt**
in (after) two days	**aizparīt**
early in the morning	**agri no rīta**
late in the evening	**vēlu vakarā**
in (during) the night from–to	**naktī no – uz pirmdienu**

2. Hours

what time is it?	**cik pulksten(i)s?**
it is 1 (2, 5) o'clock	**pulksten(i)s ir viens (divi, pieci)**
it is ten to two	**pulksten(i)s ir bez desmit divi (desmit pirms diviem)**
it is ten past eight	**pulksten(i)s ir desmit pāri (pēc) astoņiem**

it is a quarter past eight	**pulksten(i)s ir ceturksnis pāri (pēc) astoņiem**
it is half past eight	**pulksten(i)s ir pusdeviņi**
at what time?	***cikos?***
(arrive) at 1 (2, 5) o'clock	**(atbraukt) vienos (divos, piecos)**
(arrive) at half past eight	**(atbraukt) pusdeviņos (pusē de viņos)**

3. The Days of the Week

on Monday etc.	**pirmdien(ā)**
on Mondays	**pirmdienās**
in (during) this week	**šonedēļ**
next week	**nākamnedēļ; jaunnedēļ**
last week	**pagājušajā nedēļā**

4. The Month(s)

in January etc.	**janvārī**

5. The Seasons of the Year

during (in) the spring	**pavasarī**
this/last/next spring	**šopavasar/pagājušajā pavasarī/ nākamajā pavasarī**
during (in) the summer	**vasarā**
during (in) the winter	**ziemā**

6. The Year

in this year/last year/next year	**šogad/pagājušajā gadā** (*or:* **pērn)/nākamgad**
in the twenties	**divdesmitajos gados**

7. The Century

in this century	**šai gadsimtā**

8. Dates

today is August 18, 1996   **šodien ir tūkstoš deviņsimt deviņdesmit sestā gada astoņpadsmitais augusts**

Note the nominative case of the date/month combination (because of the function as grammatical subject of the sentence).

on August 18, 1996   **tūkstoš deviņdesmit sestā gada astoņpadsmitajā augustā**

Notice the locative case of the date/month combination in the adverbial function.

9. Undetermined Time Expressions
locative:
in childhood/ youth/old age **bērnībā/jaunībā/vecumā**
(**vecumdienās**)

10. How long? How often?
Accusative without preposition:
twice a week **divreiz nedēļā**

11. For how long?
for how long? **uz cik ilgi? / uz cik ilgu laiku?**

12. Before/after
A. *before*: **pirms** (+ genitive):
before the war **pirms kara**
B. *after*: **pēc** (+ genitive)
after the war **pēc kara**
after (in) two days **pēc divām dienām**

13. From - to (till):
from spring till winter **no pavasara līdz ziemai**
from morning till night **no rīta līdz naktij (vakaram)**

14. During
A. see under 1 above
B. *during the early hours of Sunday morning* **svētdien(ā) agri**
C. *during (in) the years 1945-1991* **no tūkstoš deviņsimt četrdesmit piektā līdz tūkstoš deviņsimt deviņdesmit pirmjam gadam**
D. *during* (= in the period/reign of):
under Ulmanis **Ulmaņa laikā**

15. In (after):
in five days **pēc piecām dienām**

16. Towards
towards the evening **pret vakaru**

17. Ago:
many years ago **pirms daudziem gadiem**

Chapter 11

CONJUNCTIONS
(Saiklis)

In this chapter we will just list the most important conjunctions of Standard Latvian and their English equivalents. Some of the (coordinate) conjunctions are capable only of uniting words (or word groups), not sentences, whereas others can do both.

For the *use* of conjunctions, see chapter 12 on compound sentences (p. 208 ff.).

It is customary to distinguish between *coordinating* and *subordinating* conjunctions.

1. Coordinate

Coordinate conjunctions are divided into the following groups: A. copulative, B. adversative and C. disjunctive:

A. Copulative:
un *and* (plus others, see p. 208)

B. Adversative:
bet *but*

C. Disjunctive:
vai *or*
jeb *or* (= "alias", or in other words)
vai nu - vai (arī) *either - or*

2. Subordinate

Subordinate conjunctions can be classified according to the following two main groups:

A. Explicative:
ka *that*
vai *if*

B. Adverbial
This group has numerous subclasses. The most important are: conjunctions of time, of purpose, of result, of reason, and conditional, concessive and comparative conjunctions:

a) Conjunctions of time
kad *when*
kamēr *while*
tikmēr *as long as*
tikko / līdzko / kolīdz / tiklīdz *as soon as*
kopš *since*
līdz *until*
pēc tam ka(d) *after (when)*

b) Conjunctions of purpose
lai (+ the subjunctive) *in order to, in order that*

c) Conjunctions of result
tā ka *so that*

d) Conjunctions of reason
tāpēc ka / tādēļ ka *because, since*
tā - ka *so - that*

e) Conditional
ja *if*

f) Concessive
kaut gan / kaut lai / kaut arī / lai gan / lai arī *although*

g) Comparative
kā *as; like*
it(in) kā *as if*
nekā *than*
tāpat kā / kā kad / tā - kā / tā - it(in) kā / tāpat ka / tikpat kā *(similarly) as, like*

jo - jo *the - the*

Chapter 12

THE SENTENCE
(Teikums)

Definition

A sentence can be defined as a *prosodically complete speech unit of a specific structure, expressing a relatively complete thought*. This is only one of many possible definitions of the notion "sentence". It is binary, in the de Saussurian sense that it focuses both on the *formal* side and that of the *content*.

THE MEMBERS OF THE SENTENCE

The Latvian sentence can have the following members: the *subject* (priekšmets), the *only principal member* (galvenais loceklis) and the *predicate* (izteicējs), which are labeled the *principal* members of the sentence, in contrast to the *object* (papildinātājs) and the *adverbial* (apstāklis), which constitute the *dependent* members of the sentence. Latvian (and other) grammarians also often include the *attribute* (apzīmētājs) and the *apposition* (pielikums) in the class of (dependent) sentence members.

Furthermore, in Latvian tradition *dubultloceklis* (lit. "double member") and *ierobežājs* (lit. "limitator") are encountered. The former refers to the subject or the object and at the same time to the predicate, and may be regarded as a special kind of attribute ("predicative attribute"), whereas the latter is functionally close to the object or the adverbial and can be attributed to one of them.

The Principal Members

The Subject
(Priekšmets)

Here we have in mind the grammatical subject, which is most frequently expressed by a noun or a pronoun in the *nominative* case. It can also be expressed by a nominal form of the verb, i. e. the infinitive. For examples, see under predicate below. In one-part sentences (for definition, see next chapter / section) there is no grammatical subject.

Omission of Subject Pronoun
In Latvian deletion (omission) of a personal pronoun in the function of a subject may take place in compound sentences, p. 208 ff. (including participle constructions) in instances of the following kind:
Mēs apgājām tam apkārt, un tas nozīmē, ka esam kļuvuši drusku svētaki
We went around it (i. e. the hill), and that means that we have become more sacred;
Kad iepazinos ar Plasido, viņš teica, ka gribot man palīdzēt
When I had become acquainted with Placido (Domingo), he said that he wanted to help me.
Viņa teica, ka nevarot *She said that she couldn't*
Note also the following example from a dialogue:
Un jums roks nepatīk? - Patīk - tad, kad vadu mašīnu vai mazgāju traukus *And you don't like rock music? Oh, yes, I like it when I am driving (my car) or am doing the dishes.*

The Only Principal Member
(Galvenais loceklis)
The *galvenais loceklis* is the name of the only principal member in *one-part sentences* (for the term, see p. 205 ff.). Although (often) identical in form with either the subject or the predicate, it cannot be functionally identified with either of these.
Examples: **Vakars** *(it is) evening*; **tumst** *(it) is growing dark (darkens)*; **klusu** *(it is) quiet/silent.*

The Predicate
(Izteicējs)

The predicate may be of two kinds: *verbal* or *nominal*. This holds true both for *two-part* and *one-part sentences* (on which terms, see p. 205).

1) a *verbal predicate* is expressed by a *finite* form (definition on p. 82) of a non-copulative verb (see below). It can be *simple* (e. g. **studenti raksta** *the students are writing*; **satumst** *it is getting dark*) or *compound* (e. g. **viņš sāka rakstīt** *he began writing*, **viņš grib rakstīt** *he wants to write;* **sāka satumst** *it began getting dark*). As illustrated through these examples, a compound predicate consists of a verb auxiliary (phasal or modal) in a finite form plus an infinitive.

2) a *nominal predicate* consists of a *copulative* verb (i. e. verbs with the meaning of *be* (in a non-existential sense) or *become*) + a *nominal part* which may be either a noun, an adjective or a pronoun: **es esmu skolotājs** *I am a teacher*, **viņš ir skolotājs** *he is a teacher*, **viņa ir jauna** *she is young*, **viņi bija vieni** *they were alone*, **vakars** *(it is) evening*.

Omission of Copulative Verb

The form **ir** *is; are* can be omitted where an adjective constitutes the nominal part of the predicate as, for example, in **Anda jauna** *Anda is young*, but as a rule it is not omitted in this environment.

Note: if both the subject and the nominal part of the predicate are expressed by nouns, **ir** cannot be omitted: **Jānis ir skolotājs** *John is a teacher*.

Moreover, **ir** is frequently omitted in constructions with a logical subject in the dative case, e.g. **cik tev gadu?** *how old are you?* along with **cik tev ir gadu?**

The form **ir** is usually omitted in the present tense of the debitive mood (p. 130 f.), e.g. **man jāstrādā** *I have to work* (instead of the less frequent construction **man ir jāstrādā**).

The negative **nav** can never be omitted.

Copulative verb forms others than **ir** (i. e. **esmu, esi, esam, esat**) are very rarely omitted. Furthermore, omissions are restricted to the present tense.

Where the copulative verb is omitted before a past participle, we are more likely to have a form of the relative mood (p. 131 ff.) rather than a compound past form of the indicative. Thus, the form **dzimis** in the sentence **Rudolfs Blaumanis dzimis Vidzemē** *Rudolf Blaumanis is (was) born in Vidzeme* represents the relative mood (and can be encountered in an encyclopaedic entry) while the construction **ir dzimis** is a plain indicative.

The Syntactic Relationship between Subject and Predicate

The *syntactic relationship between the subject and the predicate* as main members of the sentence, is one not of dependency, but of *interdependency*.

The predicate may be conceived as the central member of the sentence 1) since in one-part sentences (see p. 205 ff.) the principal sentence member may (often) be identified as a predicate, and 2) since the dependent sentence members (objects and adverbials) are immediately dependent on the predicate (and not on the subject).

The Dependent Members

As demonstrated through examples under the principal members of the sentence above (as well as in the table on basic sentence patterns, p. 204), complete sentences can consist only of a subject and a predicate in two-part sentences (p. 205) and in one-part sentences (p. 205 ff.) of a predicate alone. However, both two-part and one-part sentences can be *extended* by dependent members, namely the *object* and the *adverbial*.

The Object
(Papildinātājs)

Like the subject, the object is usually expressed through one of the nominal word classes, noun or pronoun, but – unlike the subject – it must be in a dependent, i. e. non-nominative case (except for the nominative object in debitive constructions, see p. 130 above). Like the subject, the object can also be in the form of an infinitive. Examples: **Aina lasa grāmatu** *Aina is reading a book*; **Aina to lasa** *Aina is reading it* (i. e. the book); **bērns iemācās lasīt** *the child is learning to read*.

A distinction is made between the *direct* object in the accusative case after *transitive* verbs and the *indirect* with intransitive verbs, i. e. verbs requiring dependent cases other than the accusative. Example of an indirect object: **palīdzēt mammai** *to help (the) mother*.

The question as to whether the genitive of negation or the partitive genitive in connection with transitive verbs should be labeled a direct or indirect object seems to be a kind of grammatical grey zone. For examples, see chapter 8 on case.

Depending on the case, one can speak of *accusative, genitive, dative* and *locative objects, e.g.* **lasīt grāmatu** *to read a book;* **kaunēties dēla** *to be ashamed of the son;* **palīdzēt mātei** *to help the mother;* **piedalīties sacīkstēs** *to participate in the competetion*.

An object (in the accusative, genitive or dative) expressed through a prepositional phrase is called a *prepositional object*. An example illustrating a prepositional object: **Šī grāmata pieder pie autora labākajiem darbiem** *this book belongs to the best works of the author*.

Finally, it should be emphasized that some predicates can or must be combined with more than one object, whereby a frequent combination is that of an indirect (dative) object denoting a person and a direct (accusative) object for the thing: **Viņš nopirka viņai dārgu gredzenu** *he bought her an expensive ring*.

The type of subordination with objects is *government*.

Government (Latvian *pārvaldījums*) is (together with agreement (cf. p. 215) and adjunction (cf. under adverbial below)) one of the three *ways* of expressing *subordination* in Latvian. The formal *means* for expressing subordination are inflection and inflection combined with preposition. Government implies that one morpheme x presupposes another y in the utterance (sentence), but not the other way round (i. e. y does not presuppose x). Thus, *books* in *read books / they read books* offers an example of government. The governing word (head) is most frequently a verb, but can also be a preposition, a noun, an adjective, a numeral or another quantifier.

The Adverbial
(Apstāklis)

The adverbial can be expressed by an adverb or – like the object – by a noun phrase or a prepositional phrase. Examples: **Viņi *ilgi/ilgu laiku* dzīvoja ārzemēs** *they lived abroad for (a) long (time)*, **viņa uzrakstīja vēstuli *vienas stundas* laikā** *she wrote the letter in one hour*.

As in the case of adverbs (p. 163), several types of adverbials are distinguished: *temporal* (cf. examples just quoted), *local* (e. g. **atgriezties no pilsētas** *return from the city*), of *manner* (**viņš iet ātri** *he walks fast*), of *purpose* (**iet senēs un ogās** *go to gather mushrooms and berries*), of *reason* (**drebēt no aukstuma** *tremble from cold*) and others.

Forms of subordination here are *government* and *adjunction*.

For *government*, cf. above. *Adjunction* (or "juxtaposition", Latvian *pieklāvums*) may be defined negatively as the way of subordination which cannot adequately be described as agreement or government. Typical cases of adjunction are encountered with indeclinable words like adverbs, gerunds or infinitives. Some examples: **ātri** (adverb) in **iet ātri** *walk fast*, **ļoti** (adverb) in **ļoti ātri** *very fast*, **steigdamies** (gerund) in **iet steigdamies** *walk hastily (hurrying)* and **vēlēšanās atpūsties** *wish (desire) to rest*. When adverbials are expressed by a noun phrase as, for example, **ilgu laiku** (instead of the adverb **ilgi**) in **dzīvot ilgu laiku ārzemēs** (cf. example quoted above) one can equally speak of adjunction (or by way of alternative 'weak government').

Latvian grammatical tradition also makes use of a term *ierobežotājs*, lit. "limitator", cf., for example, **viņš ir spēcīgs *matemātikā*** *he is strong in math*. The *ierobežotājs*, which is most frequently expressed by a noun in the locative case, has the limiting sense of 'with respect to'. In chapter 8 on case we held this to be an adverbial function of the locative.

Difficulties in distinguishing Objects from Adverbials

It is often difficult to distinguish between an object and an adverbial. In the case of prepositional phrases it is crucial whether there is only one possible and obligatory preposition required by the verb or whether more (non-verb) determined prepositions can be applied. The former situation is an indication of an object: **piederēt pie grupas** *belong to a group*, the latter of an adverbial, e.g. **braukt no Rīgas** *go from Riga*, **braukt uz Rīgu** *go to Riga*.

A practical test often used is that *adverbials* answer questions with an *adverb*, in contrast to the object, which is determined by a question with a *pronoun*. Thus, in the sentence **laukos viņa man katru dienu atnes no dārza ābolu** *in the countryside she brings me an apple from the garden every day* the dependent members **man** and **ābolu** answer the pronominal questions **kam?** *for whom?* and **ko?** *what?* whereas **katru dienu** and **laukos** answer questions with the adverbs **kad? / cik bieži?** *when? / how often?* and **kur?** *where?* respectively. For determining the character of **no dārza**, however, both the question with an adverb (**no kurienes?** *from where?*) and that with a pronoun (**no kā?** *from what?*) seems possible. The conclusion is that the test is not applicable in every case. This means that additional criteria must be used. By comparing **no dārza** in the above sentence with, for example, **no dārza** in **muiža sastāv no dārza un lielas mājas** *the estate consists of a garden and a big house* one feels the much closer connection with the verb in the latter case which allows us to speak of a prepositional object as opposed to an adverbial in the former, i. e. in [...] **atnes no dārza ābolu**).

The Attribute
(Apzīmētājs)

The attribute is expressed by an adjective, an adjectival pronoun, a participle or a numeral. It can be *congruent* (i. e. subordinated to a noun through agreement, cf. p. 215 below) or *incongruent* (in which case it is subordinated through government, cf. p.200). As examples of congruent attributes may serve **jauna** in the noun phrase **jauna māja** *a new house*, **mana māja** *my house*, **cita** in **cita māja** *another house*, **pieminētā māja** *the house mentioned*, **trešā** in **trešā māja** *the third house*, **piecas** in **piecas mājas** *five houses* and of incongruent **mūsu** in **mūsu māja** *our house*, **tēva** in **tēva māja** *father's house* (and from a logical point of view **desmit** in **desmit māju** *ten houses*).

As indicated in the introduction to this chapter, it is dubious as to whether the attribute should strictly speaking be regarded as a member of the sentence, since it is subordinate either to the subject, the object or the adverbial and – to the extent that it is a sentence member at all – can therefore count only as an indirect one of low (tertial) rank in the sentence hierarchy.

A special case of *apzīmētājs* is the so-called *dubultloceklis* (lit. 'double member'). The ratio for this term is the double reference, namely both to the subject / object and the verb, e.g. **viņa nāca viena** *she came alone*; **mēs atradām viņu vienu** *we found her alone* where **viena** and **vienu** are labeled *dubultlocekļi* in Latvian grammatical tradition.

The Apposition
(Pielikums)

Attributes in the form of nouns which are subordinated to other nouns by means of agreement (p. 215) or adjunction (p. 200) are regarded as appositions. Examples: the title in the noun phrase **profesore Rudzīte**, Gen. **profesores Rudzītes** etc. *Professor Rudzīte* and the proper noun in **netālu no rūpnīcas "Rīga"** *not far from the factory "Riga"*.

That which was said about the status of the attribute as a member of the sentence also holds true for appositions.

Classification of the Sentence

There are many ways of classifying a sentence:
1. From the point of view of modality it can be classified either as A. *declarative*, B. *hortatory (imperative)* or C. *interrogative*.

Examples of types A-C:
A. **Pēteris lasa grāmatu** *Peter is reading a/the book*,
B. **Lasi grāmatu, Pēteri!** *read a/the book, Peter!*
C. **Vai Pēteris lasa grāmatu?** *is Peter reading a/the book?*

Moreover, a sentence can be *affirmative* (**Pēteris lasa grāmatu** *Peter is reading a/the book* / **viņš ir liels** *he is big*) or *negated* (**Pēteris nelasa grāmatu** *Peter is not reading a/the book* / **viņš nav liels** *he is not big*).

Point 1 will not be further elaborated in this chapter, but types A-C will be described in detail in chapter 14 on word order.

2. Departing from the structure the sentence can be classified either as A. *two-part* (divkopu teikums) or B. *one-part* (vienkopas teikums). An obligatory requirement of the former is the presence of the two principal members of the sentence, i. e. a grammatical subject *(priekšmets)* in the nominative case + a predicate *(izteicējs)*, which agrees with the subject, as opposed to one-part sentences, which are in the possession of only one principal member, in Latvian labeled *(galvenais loceklis*, lit. *the (only) principal member* (p. 197), a term unmistakably inspired by Russian grammatical tradition).

Examples of A. two-part sentences are: **Pēteris lasa** *Peter is reading* / **Pēteris ir jauns** *Peter is young*

and of
B. one-part: **satumst** *it is getting dark* / (**ir**) **auksts** *it is cold.*

One-part sentences should not be confused with *incomplete* sentences since one-part sentences are considered to be structurally complete. An example of an incomplete sentence is: **Pēteris** (instead of the complete **lasa Pēteris**) as an answer to the question **kas lasa?** *who is reading?*

Point 2 will be dealt with in more detail below.

3. Sentences containing other sentence members than the principal members, i. e. dependendent members, are called *extended* (or *expanded*) sentences (p. 199). Both two-part and one-part sentences can be extended.

4. Finally, a distinction must be made between *simple* (vienkārši) and *compound* (salikti) *sentences* (teikumi). The simple sentence will be defined and described in the immediately following passage. For the compound sentence, see p. 208 ff.

Subsequent Disposition

The distinction between the simple and the compound sentence will have the highest hierarchical rank in the subsequent disposition. The simple sentence will be divided into two main sections, according to the two parameters two-part and one-part sentences respectively, presented in point 2 above. This bifurcation will not be implemented in the case of the compound sentence, since it cannot be applied to the compound sentence as a whole, only to its constituents, which are in fact identical in structure with simple sentences. For the same reason, the term *basic sentence patterns,* which will be introduced in the following, is reserved for the simple sentence.

THE SIMPLE SENTENCE
(Vienkāršs teikums)

The simple sentence may be defined as *a sentence containing one single predicative center.* A simple sentence is classified as either two-part or one-part, cf. p. 205 f. The *basic sentence patterns* valid for Latvian are:

Two-part sentences		*One-part sentences*	
I: Nom$_{subst/pron}$ + V$_{fin}$	**viņi strāda / ceļ** *they are working / building*	I: V$_{fin3pers}$	**salst** *it is cold* **strādā** *one is / they are building*
II a) Nom$_{subst/pron}$ + Cop$_{fin}$ + Adj	**viņi ir jauni** *they are young*	II a): Cop$_{fin3pers}$ + Adj	**(ir) auksts** *it is cold*
IIb) Nom$_{pron}$ + Cop$_{fin}$ + Adv	**tas ir interesanti** *that is interesting*	II b): Cop$_{fin3pers}$ + Adv	**(ir) klusi** *it is silent*
III: Nom$_{subst/pron}$ + Cop$_{fin}$ + Nom	**viņa ir studente** *she is a student*	III: Nom$_{subst}$	**vasara** *it is summer*
IV: Dat$_{subst/pron}$ + V$_{fin/esse}$ + Nom$_{subst/pron}$	**viņam ir grāmata** *he has a book*	IV: Dat + infinitive	**tev sēdēt!** *you will have to sit!*

The symbols used in the diagram should be almost self-explanatory. V$_{esse}$ stands for finite (fin) form of the verb **būt** in non-cop(ulative) function (cf. p. 198). The scheme has a certain resemblance with that presented in Valdmanis 1987, 76-77, but does not contain all his types. Further, our concepts deviate in some respects because our theoretical basis is somewhat different.

The basic sentence types given in the diagram can be *extended* by dependent members (for the term, cf. p. 191). Thus, an object or an adverbial (as well as attributes etc.) can be added: for example, **viņi ceļ māju** *they are building a house*, **ir klusi mežā** *it is silent in the wood*, **viņi strādā dārzā** *they are working in the garden*, **salst ārā** *it is cold ouside*, **viņa ir (jauna) studente Rīgā** *she is a (new) student in Riga*.

A problem arises in connection with the *valence* of verbs. It seems unnatural or impossible to say, for example, **es devu** *I gave* without adding a direct and even an indirect object as well: **es (ie)devu viņai rozi** *I gave her a rose*. The inclusion of objects appears to be obligatory with the verb **dot** *give*. From such considerations one may ask whether sentences containing objects (and possibly also adverbials - other than the predicative ones found in the above diagram) should also be regarded as basic, but their inclusion is also problematic since not every object (or adverbial) is an obligatory member of the sentence. Thus, for example, in **es nopirku viņai rozi** *I bought her a rose* the indirect object **viņai** is optional (in the sense that a grammatically correct sentence can be construed without it), whereas the inclusion of the direct object (**rozi**) in this case seems obligatory, in contrast to **māju** in e.g. **viņi ceļ**. It is, however, possible to work with structures of the type Nom $_{subst/pron}$ + V$_{fin}$ + Obj$_{dir}$ and Nom$_{subst/pron}$ + V$_{fin}$ + Obj$_{indir}$ + Obj$_{dir}$ among basic sentences. One the other hand, the above diagram is attractive in terms of linguistic economy.

Two-Part Sentences
(Divkopu teikumi)

Two-part sentences must *contain a grammatical (i. e. nominative) subject + a predicate which agrees* (p. 215) *with the subject*, cf. the table of sentence patterns quoted above. In addition, they can have dependent sentence members (object, adverbial), see comments to table just referred to.

Two-part sentences in Latvian do not deviate considerably from those known from Germanic and other languages, and will therefore not be described in detail here.

The main types are given in the survey of sentence patterns above. For further examples, see chapter 14 on word order which also gives an overview of the different positions which can be occupied by the members of the sentence.

One-Part Sentences
(Vienkopas teikumi)

One-part sentences should be examined in more detail than two-part, since they show structures which are either absent or very rarely encountered in many other languages. Students with knowledge of a Slavic language will be familiar with such structures, whereas many others will have to study them very carefully.

In contrast to two-part sentences, *one-part sentences can never contain a grammatical (i. e. nominative) subject in agreement with a predicate*. The obligatory component of a one-part sentence is the *galvenais loceklis* (the only principal member), cf. p. 197.

Depending on the form of this member, a distinction is drawn between *verbal one-part sentences* (with the subgroup infinitival sentences) and *nominal one-part sentences*.

The term *impersonal sentence* is often encountered in grammatical expositions. As far as Latvian is concerned, it can in most cases be said to be identical with one-part sentences.

Verbal One-Part Sentences

Verbal one-part sentences can be defined as one-part sentences with a *verbal principal member* (for the term, see p. 198). This member is usually in the 3rd person.

1) The simplest structure is represented by sentences consisting of the principal member only. Here belongs a group of verbs incapable of taking an object, for instance, the "meteorological" **aust** *become light / dawn*, **tumst** *become dark*, **līt** *rain*, **smidzināt** *drizzle*, **snigt** *snow*, **zibeņot** *flash (of lightning)*, **salt** *freeze*.

Examples: **tumsa** *it was becoming dark*, **salst** *it is freezing*, **sniga** *it was snowing*. With some of the verbs a tautological noun in the nominative case may be added, thus changing the structure into a personal (automatically two-part) sentence: **līst** or **līst lietus** *it is raining* (lit. 'the rain is raining').

After *phasal auxiliaries* the above verbs will be in the form of an infinitive, e.g. **beidza līt** *it stopped raining*. The combination **sāka līt** can be referred to as a compound verbal principal member (p. 198).

In this place mention should also be made of the Latvian equivalents of the *man*-sentences of German and the Nordic languages: **raksta** *one writes/is writing (man schreibt)*, **meklē** *one searches/is searching (man sucht)*, **runā / teic / saka (ka ...)** *one says/it is said (that ...), man sagt, (dass ...)* etc. Such sentences are one-part, but personal. Also here the infinitive must be used after phasal auxiliaries, e.g. **sāka rakstīt** *one began writing (man fing an zu schreiben)*.

2) *Adverbial extensions* (on extension, see p. 199) are possible, e.g. **vakar visu dienu nepārtraukti lija** *yesterday it was raining uninterruptedly all day long*; **par to rakstīja avīzēs** *one writes about that in the papers / it is being written about that in the newspapers*. The adverbials used here are optional, in the sense that they are not required by the valence of the verb.

3) One part-sentences with a verbal principal member can have an *obligatory object* in the *accusative, genitive* or *dative*.

A. An accusative object is found in cases like **kuģi šūpo** *the ship is rocking* (lit. 'it is rocking the ship').

B. The genitive object is typical of *negative existential constructions*: **nav sniega** *there is no snow*. Grammatically **sniega** has to be classified as an object, even though from a logical point of view it can be conceived as a subject. Here belong also constructions with **trūkt** *be* *lacking*, e.g. **trūkst sniega** *snow is lacking* (and, of course, **netrūkt** *not be lacking*: **sniega netrūkst**).

C. The function of a grammatical object, but logical subject is also observed in the dative in sentences of the type **viņai veicas** (infintive **veikties**) *she is lucky*.

Here on may also mention *debitive* constructions: **man jāstrādā** *I have to work*, cf. p. 129 ff.

Infinitive Sentences

Infinitive sentences can be regarded as a special kind of verbal one-part sentences, with an *infinitive in the function of the* "galvenais loceklis" (cf. p. 197) *alone*, e.g. **ko mums darīt?** *what shall we do?* Here the infinitive is grammatically independent (with **ko** and **mums** as sentence members dependent on the infinitive), as opposed to cases like, **sāka līst** *it began raining* or **viņš sāka strādāt** *he began working*, where the infinitives are dependent on the phasal verb auxiliary. Thus, the latter type are not infinitive sentences according to the definition just given.

Infinitive sentences in Latvian express different *modal shades of meaning* (thus, besides questions like those in the above example also *wish, command* and others): **koku nocirst!** *the tree must be cut down!*

Here one can also mention constructions of the type **man nav ar ko runāt** *I have nobody to speak with;* **man nav kur sēdēt** *I have nowhere to sit* (cf. pp. 72 and 155 above).

Nominal One-Part Sentences

A nominal one-part sentence is a one part sentence with a nominal *galvenais loceklis* (for the term, see p. 198).

Two different types should be distinguished, cf. table of basic sentence patterns above, namely

1) sentences in which the *galvenais loceklis* is expressed by a passive participle or adjective / adverb + a copulative verb,
 and
2) sentences in which the *galvenais loceklis* is in the form of a noun in the nominative case.

The latter type is often referred to as a *nominative* sentence.

Examples of 1): **ir auksts** *it is cold*, **būs saulains** *it will be sunny*, **bija kluss** *it was quiet,,* **kļuva siltāks** *it became warmer*.

In *extended* constructions (see p. 199), the above adjectives, which are in the unmarked masculine gender (cf. p. 40), adopt the form of an adverb-adjective ending in -*i* (cf. p. 162), e.g. **man ir auksti** *I feel cold*, **vakar šeit bija klusi** *yesterday it was quiet here*.

The following examples may serve as illustrations of 2): **zibens** *(it /there is) lightning*, **putenis** *(it / there is) snow-storm*.

In cases like **bija zibens** *there was a lightning*, **būs putenis** *there will be a snow-storm*, **ir bijis zibens** *there has been a lightning*, it can be argued that we are dealing with two-part constructions, since there is a subject noun in the nominative accompanied by/in agreement with a predicate verb. It would also be possible to regard cases like **zibens** and **putenis** as sentences with a deleted (omitted) verb in the (unmarked) present tense and thus as a potential candidate for a two-part construction.

THE COMPOUND SENTENCE
(Salikts teikums)

A compound sentence *contains more than one predicative centre*. The predicative centers can be linked together through *syndetism* or *asyndetism*. The former device involves the implementation of conjunctions (see chapter 11) or conjunctive words (= relative pronouns and adverbs, see chapters 4 and 7).

Conjunctions are either coordinating or subordinating, whence also the distinction between *coordinate* and *subordinate* clauses. In the following exposition syndetism will have our main attention, but a note on asyndetism will be given at the end of the chapter.

Coordination
(Teikuma sakārtojums)

The most important coordinating conjunctions were listed in above chapter 11 on conjunctions. In addition, there are a good number of others which may be said to have the functions of coordinate conjunctions, for which more comprehensive grammars of Latvian and dictionaries should be consulted.

Examples:
un:
Es rakstu un tu raksti
I am writing and you are writing
ir ... ir:
Nāca jaunie, ir vecie
Both young and old came
kā ... tā (arī):
Kā es rakstu, tā tu arī (raksti)
Both I (am writing) and you are writing

gan ... gan:
Bērni gan spēlēja bumbu, gan peldējās
The children now/ both played ball, now /and took a bath
bet:
Es rakstu, bet tu lasi
I am writing, but (whereas) you are reading
vai:
(Vai) man vai tev būs jādara šis darbs
(Either) I or you have to do this work
ne ... ne; ne ... nedz; nedz ... nedz:
Ne vilnītis šalc, ne lapa kokā kust (Rainis)
Not (neither) a wave is roaring, not (nor) a leaf is moving in the tree;
To nezina nedz viņš, nedz tu
Neither he nor you know that
Ne viņš var, nedz grib ko darīt
He is neither able nor willing to do anything

Subordination
(Teikuma pakārtojums)

As the heading implies, this classification is made on the basis of the subordinate clause. There are different kinds of subordinate clauses and several ways of classifying them. Here the following scheme will be followed:
1) explicative
2) determinative
3) adverbial clauses

The most important subordinate conjunctions are listed in the chapter on conjunctions.

1. Explicative Clauses

The verb in the main clause belongs to the semantic sphere of *saying, asking, seeing, feeling* and the like, and the subordinate conjunction will correspond to English *that* (Latvian **ka** or **lai**, for distribution, see below) or *if* (Latvian **vai**). These conjunctions are typical of indirect discourse (in a broad sense). The **vai**/*if*-clause is used in indirect questions. Indirect questions not introduced by **vai**/*if*, but by an interrogative pronoun or adverb, will also be treated in this section.
Examples:

A. *Non-interrogative:*
a) **Viņa teica, ka šodien (ir) skaists laiks**
She said that today the weather was fine
b) **Viņa teica, lai es tulīt atnākot**
She said that I should come at once

In b) **lai** has to be used to the exclusion of **ka,** since **teica** here has the meaning of a *command* or *request (she demanded that).* The conjunction **lai** requires the relative mood (or the subjunctive), cf. pp. 127 f. and 132. Also in a) the relative mood could have been used (instead of the indicative), but with a somewhat different shade of meaning, see p. 132.

B. *Interrogative:*
a) *yes/no*-questions: **Viņa jautāja, vai laiks (ir) skaists / vai es atnākšu**
She asked if the weather was fine / whether/if I would come
b) *wh*-questions: **Viņa jautāja, kas atnāca / kā un kad viņš atnāca**
She asked who had come / how and when he came;
Viņa jautāja, cik grāmatu jāpirkt
She asked how many books it was necessary to / she should buy

In examples of the above type, a discrepancy in the use of tenses will often be observed between Latvian and English etc. This is because in indirect speech Baltic (as well as Slavic) *retains the tense of the direct speech, whereas English (and the Nordic languages) has developed a mechanism called* "consecutio temporum", which means that the tense of the verb of the dependent clause repeats that of the verb in the main clause, cf. **Viņa teica: "Šodien (ir) skaists laiks** → **Viņa teica, ka šodien (ir) skaists laiks** and *she said: "Today the weather is nice"* → *She said that today the weather was nice.*

2. Determinative Clauses

There are two kinds of determinative clauses:
A. *noun determinative* and B. *pronoun determinative.*
Type A is illustrated in: **Tie studenti, kas vakar atnāca uz Rīgu, bija** [...] *those students who yesterday arrived in Riga, were* [...], where the noun **studenti** is said to be determined by the clause introduced with **kas**. In the following sentence: **Rīga, kur viņi atnāca vakar, ir** [...] *Riga, where they arrived yesterday, is* [...] the noun **Rīga** is determined by a clause starting with **kur**.

Type B is exemplified in: **Visi, kas vakar atnāca uz Rīgu, bija** [...] *all who arrived in Riga, were* [...]. Here the pronoun **visi** is determined by **kas**.

As demonstrated through the examples in both types, the conjunctive word is either a relative pronoun or an adverb. For further examples, see under relative pronouns and adverbs (pp. and above).

As a subtype of B one might mention cases such as **kas nestrādā, tas neēd** *the one who doesn't work, doesn't eat*.

3. Adverbial Clauses

Adverbial clauses form a large group with many subdivisions, such as adverbial clauses of time, purpose, reason and others. They are labeled adverbial because the subordinate clause may be said to be syntactically equivalent to an adverbial extension of the main clause, just like an adverb or adverbial: for example, ***kad es atnāca*, viņas tur nebija** *when I came, she was not there* and ***tai laikā* viņas tur nebija** *then/at that time she was not there*.

For "semi-clauses" expressed by gerunds, see p. ff. 150 ff.

The examples quoted under 1) the explicative type could have been labeled object clauses (p. 209 f.) since the dependent clause here functions as an object, cf. **viņa teica to** (object) *she said that* : **viņa teica, kad** [...] (object) *she said that* [...].

A. Clauses of Time

The conjunction most commonly used here is **kad** *when*. Other important conjunctions of time are **kamēr** *while; till, until*, **pirms** *before*, **pēc tam kad** *after (when)*, **kopš** *since*, **tiklīdz / līdzko / tikko** *as soon as*.

Examples:
Zēns ienāca, kad stunda jau bija sākusies *the boy came in when the lesson had already begun*; **iešu tad, kad mani sauks** (note the correspondence **tad – kad**), *I'll go (then) when they will call for me*; **viņš lasīja grāmatu, kamēr bērni rotaļājās** *he was reading a book while the children were playing*; **gaidīšu, kamēr atnāks tēvs** *I'll wait until father comes*; **neatdošu grāmatu, pirms to nebūšu izlasījis** *I'll not give the book back until I have read it through* (observe the use of the compound future in the dependent clause (lit. *until I shall have* ...) and compare with the simple future in the same sense in the preceding example); **pagājis jau mēnesis, kopš viņš aizbrauca** *a month has already passed since he left*; **tiklīdz viņu ieraudzīju, tūlīt pazinu** *as soon as I caught sight of him/her, I recognized him/her*.

Note the lack of symmetry between **pēc tam kad** and **pirms (tam kad)** in that the latter can be used without the addition of **tam kad**: **izdari to tagad, pirms (tam kad) neesi aizmirsis** *do it now before you forget* (lit. *have forgotten*) *it*.

B. Clauses of Purpose

Clauses of purpose and intent have the conjunction **lai** *in order that, (in order) to*. It is followed by the subjunctive mood (cf. p. 127):
Viņš aizbrauca, lai viņa sieva atpūstos *he went away in order that his wife should have a rest*; **viņš aizbrauca, lai atpūstos** *he went away (in order) to rest*. Observe that when the subjects of the main and the subordinate clause of purpose are identical (as in the second example), many languages (among them English) choose a construction with the infinitive rather than using a subordinate clause. This, however, is not possible in Latvian, where a subordinate clause with the subjunctive is obligatory, regardless of the reference indicated by the subject.

The same strategy is found in cases with a *general*, not explicitly expressed subject: **lai varētu labāk pārredzēt apkārtni, bija jāuzkāpj tornī** *in order that one (they) might better see across the surroundings, one (they) had to climb onto the tower*; **lai labāk pārredzētu apkārtni**, [...] *in order to see better across the surroundings* [...].

C. Clauses of Result

Such clauses are characterized by the conjunctions **tā, ka** *so that* plus the indicative: **Viņš runāja tā, kā visi viņu saprata** *he spoke so (in such a way) that everybody understood him*, which can be contrasted with the adverbial clause of purpose with the subjunctive (cf. B): **Viņš runāja tā, lai visi viņu saprastu** *he spoke so (in such a way) in order that everybody (should) understand him*.

D. Clauses of Reason

For this function Latvian has at its disposal **tāpēc ka / tādēļ ka** (cf. Swedish *därför att*) *because, since*: **Durvis bija ciet tāpēc, ka visi bija aizgājuši** *the door was locked because everybody had gone away/out*.

E. Clauses of Condition

Such clauses are introduced with **ja** *if* (in the event that), which should not be confused with the explicative conjunction *if* = **vai**, see p. 209 above: **Ja laiks būs labs, iešu uz mājām kājām** *if the weather will be nice, I'll walk home on foot*. The verb of the **ja**-clause is in the indicative mood if the condition is not an unreal, hypothetical one, in which case it would appear in the subjunctive mood, both in the main and the subordinate clause (for examples, see section on mood, p. 127).

F. Clauses of Concession

The conjunctions in question are **kaut (gan/arī), lai (gan/arī)** *although, even though*.
Examples:
Kaut gan lija, laiks bija silts *although it was raining, it was warm*; **lai arī ziema bija auksta, augļu koki nebija nosaluši** *even though the winter was cold, the fruit trees did not freeze*.

G. Clauses of Comparison

Adverbial clauses of comparison are formed with the help of the conjunctions **kā** *as, like*, **it kā** *as if*: **Viņš izturas, kā neviens pirms tam nebija izturējies** *he behaves in such a way as nobody had behaved before that;* **mežā bija tik klusu, it kā vēja nemaz nebūtu** *it was so quiet in the forest as if there were no wind at all*.

As can be concluded from the examples, **kā** implies a real comparison or one imagined to be real and is therefore followed by the indicative, as opposed to **it kā** which is used in connection with assumptions or hypothetical comparisons, and consequently combines with the subjunctive. In many cases the clause introduced by a comparison is incomplete (with the verb deleted), cf. **viņš ēd kā vilks** *he eats like a wolf*.

Equivalents of English "than" and "the – the"
Under point G constructions with **nekā** *than* (cf. p. 60 f. and 195) and **jo – jo** *the - the* (p. 195) can also be mentioned.
Examples:
Šogad mēs dzīvojam labāk, nekā (mums bija) pagājušajā gadā *this year we are having a better life than (we were having) last year*, **jo ātrāk, jo labāk** *the sooner, the better*; **jo tuvāk pavasarim, jo gaišākas dienas** *the closer to spring, the lighter the days*.

H. Clauses of Manner

Here one finds among others, the correlative type with gradual meaning: **viņa bija tik skaista, ka man apžilba acis** *she was so beautiful that my eyes were dazzled.*

Final Remarks

It should be mentioned that most descriptions of adverbial clauses also include clauses of place, but they can easily be formed with the help of *adverbs of place* (**kur**), e.g. **kur esat/ejat?** *where are you/are you going?*

In the above exposition combinations of two clauses have only been commented upon, but, of course, sentences of a more complex, structure are also encountered. Such sentences can be labeled *complex* in contrast to the compound ones demonstrated above.

Asyndetism

Asyndetism (for definition, see p. 208) can have the functions of both coordination and subordination. Which of these two main functions is present in each concrete case, becomes evident through the context. Thus, a sentence like **dod man to smirdošo ābolu – es viņu apēdīšu** can be interpreted either as *give that stinking apple to me, and I will eat it* or *if you give [...], I [...].*

Chapter 13
AGREEMENT
(Saskaņojums)

Agreement is one of the three ways of expressing subordination in Latvian (cf. p. 200) and can be defined as a *morphological repetition (through desinences) of one and the same grammatical category within certain syntactic relations*.

Relevant *grammatical* categories are: 1. *gender*, 2. *number*, 3. *person* and 4. *case,* and the relevant *syntactic* relations are:

A. that between *attribute* and *governing* word, cf., for example, **jauna māja : jaunas mājas : jaunu māju** *a new house : of a new house : of new houses* where the attributive adjective agrees in gender, number and case with the head noun,

B. that between the *subject* and *predicate*, e.g. **māja ir jauna : mājas ir jaunas** *the house is new : the houses are new* (agreement in gender, number (and case) between the subject and the nominal part of the nominal predicate), and

C. that between the *antecedent* and the *anaphoric* pronoun (including the relative) as, for instance, in: **kādā parkā sēdēja vīrietis. Ar viņu runāja sieviete** *there was a man sitting in a park. A woman was speaking with him*; [...] **vīrietis, ar ko runāja sieviete** [...] *a man with whom a woman was speaking.*

For convenience, relation A. is generally referred to as attributive agreement and B. as predicate agreement. Relation C. will only be marginally commented upon.

There are two kinds of agreement: *formal* (or *grammatical*), and *logical* (*semantic*). The explanation above relates only to the former type. To cover logical agreement, the definition should be modified as follows: *systematic covariation between a formal or semantic property of one element and a formal property of another*. An example of logical agreement would be: **jau ir atnākuši liels daudzums gāju putnu** *a large number of birds of passage have already arrived,* whereas formal agreement would be **jau ir atnācis liels daudzums gāju putnu** *a large number of birds of passage has arrived* with the participle **atnācis** in agreement with **(liels) daudzums** in gender, number and case (nominative). The English translation illustrates logical vs.

formal agreement with respect to number. From a normative point of view, the use of formal agreement seems to be preferable for the case in question, as far as Latvian is concerned.

Agreement can be regarded from two different angles:
I that of the grammatical categories (i. e. 1-4)
II that of the syntactic relations (i. e. A-C).
The exposition below will follow I. It should also be pointed out that emphasis will be put on *special cases* which may cause trouble for the student, rather than uncomplicated ones like those alraedy quoted in the above illustrations.

1. Special Cases of Agreement in Gender
For generalities on gender, see p. 40 f. above.

A. Common Gender Nouns in -a and -e
Latvian has a quite limited group of nouns ending in *-a* and *-e* denoting human beings (so-called hybrids or *kopdzimtes lietvārdi* in Latvian), which are masc. when they refer to males, but fem. if females are referred to, cf., for example, **pļāpa** *chatterbox*, **slepkava** *murderer*, **bende** *hangman*, and also some family names like **Liepa** and **Priede**.

Examples:
Relation 1):
bīstams (male) / **bīstama** (female) **slepkava** *a dangerous murderer*
Relation 2):
Slepkava ir bīstams (male) / **bīstama** (female) *The murderer is dangerous*
Relation 3):
Atnāca slepkava *a murderer came.* **Viņš bija bīstams** *He was dangerous* / **Viņa bija bīstama** *She was dangerous*

Nouns denoting *professions* do not show the same ambiguity with respect to gender in Latvian as the above cases, since they obligatorily form pairs of the type **pedagogs** (male) : **pedagoģe** (female) *pedagogue,* **profesors** (male) : **profesore** (female) *professor,* **skolotājs** (male) : **skolotāja** (female) *teacher,* **ārsts** (male) : **ārste** (female) *physician.* Consequently, they do not entail complications with respect to agreement. It should, however, be emphasized that masc. is the unmarked gender (cf. p. 40). Thus, a general introductory statement like **mūsu ciemā ir jauns ārsts** *in our village there is a new physician* does not exclude the possibility that the new doctor is a woman.

B. Personal Pronouns of the 1st and 2nd Person

The personal pronouns of the 1st and 2nd persons (**es** *I*, **mēs** *we*, **tu** *you (thou)*, **jūs** *you*) are also gender differentiating: for example, **es esmu dzirdējis** (male) vs. **dzirdējusi** (female) *I have heard*, **jūs esat dzirdējuši** (male) vs. **dziredējušas** (female) *you have heard*. If **mēs** and **jūs** refer to a group including both males and females, the unmarked masc. gender has to be used.

For **kas** *who*, see section B, point g).

C. Indeclinable Nouns

This point is devoted to *indeclinable* nouns. When the gender rules given on p. 51 are observed, these nouns do not cause much trouble in terms of agreement, e.g. **jauns auto** a new car (agreement with the unmarked masc. gender). Observe, however, the case of *proper names* (geographical designations), e.g. **garā Misisipi** *the long Mississippi (river)* where the noun is feminine through association with the feminine common noun **upe** *river*. If the *state* of Mississipi is meant, masc. agreement is encountered (due to the association with **štāts** *state*). Cities show feminine agreement, e.g. **Oslo ir skaista (pilsēta)** *Oslo is a beautiful city*.

D. Abbreviations

For *abbreviations* the guiding principle is agreement with the grammatical head noun of the abbreviation, cf., for example: **MLLVV** (= **Mūsdienu Latviešu Literārās Valodas *Gramatika***) **ir diezgan liela** *the MLLVG-grammar is rather big*.

In some cases *associative* (or near to associative) agreement (cf. point c) is also found. Thus, for instance, the name of the British Broadcasting Corporation, **BBC**, can be associated with **korporācija** and take feminine agreement.

E. Noun Combinations

Noun combinations of the type frequently found in Slavic (Russian etc.) are rare in Latvian. One example would be **izstāde-pardošana** *sales exhibition*, but this particular case would not cause any trouble in terms of agreement.

F. Interjections

This point is reserved for *interjections*. Such words, deprived of gender attributing indications, – like the bulk of indeclinable nouns – show masculine agreement, since masc. is the unmarked gender in Latvian (cf. p. 40): **skaļš br-br-br** *a loud br-br-br*.

2. Special Cases of Agreement in Number

A. Plural Nouns
Such nouns (cf. 51 f.) require modifiers in the plural:
Sacīkstes bija interesantas *the competition was / the competitions were interesting*; **interesantas sacīkstes** *an interesting competition / interesting competitions;* **Cēsis ir lielas** *C. is big* (but also the alternative **Cēsis ir liela** – through association with **pilsēta** *city* – was accepted by my informant).

B. Collective Nouns
For nouns of this type (see p. 53), the norm requires modifiers in the singular: **modernā jaunatne** *modern youth*, **Latviešu jaunatne – kur tā** (not *tās/tie) **iet?** *the Latvian youth - where is it going?*

C. Indeclinable Nouns
Indeclinable nouns (p. 50 f.) require singular or plural agreement dependent on the reference to the extra-linguistic situation. Thus, **jauns auto** means *new car* whereas **jauni auto** must be translated as *new cars,* cf. point c under agreement in gender above

D. Abbreviations
This point pertains to *abbreviations*. Under 1 D above it was stated that agreement in this case basically follows the form of the head noun. This rule also holds with respect to agreement in number, e.g. **ASV (= Amerikas Savienotās Valstis) tika dibinātas 1776. gadā** *The USA was founded in 1776.*

E. Two (or More) Coordinate Nouns Qualified by One and the Same Adjective
When two (or more) coordinate nouns are qualified by one and the same adjective(s), the adjective(s) can be put in the plural to avoid ambiguity: **lieli brālis un māsa/ lieli māsa un brālis** *the little sister and brother* (i. e. both of them are small), but such solutions are found to be somewhat strange and are usually avoided (by repeating the adjective).

F. The Polite Form of the 2nd P. Pl. Pronoun
Further, the polite form of the personal pronoun **Jūs** *you* requires singular agreement with adjectives and participles when one person is referred to; a finite form of the verb, however, must be in the plural: **Vai Jūs esat** (pl.) **vesels/vesela / noguris/nogurusi?** *are you healthy / tired?*

G. The interrogative Pronoun **kas**

The pronoun **kas?** *who?* is used with singular agreement, irrespective of the number of persons or objects referred to: **Kas ir atnācis – Jānis un Pēteris, vai tikai Jānis?** *who has come – John and Peter or just (only) John?* (It should further be noted that in the Standard language **kas** shows only masculine agreement, not feminine.)

H. Group Subjects

Finally, mention should be made of group subjects with quantifiers in the role of grammatical head, accompanied by a noun or pronoun in the genitive plural: **jau ir atnācis daudz ļaužu** lit. *much people has already arrived.* In such cases – according to the norm – agreement should be used.

3. Special Cases of Agreement in Person

Generally it can be stated that the 1st person dominates the 2nd, and the 2nd takes precedence over the 3rd person, e.g. **tu un es (= mēs) ejam** *you and I (we) go*; **tu un viņš/viņa (= jūs) ejat** *you and he/she go*; **mēs un viņi/viņas ejam** *we and they go*; **jūs un viņi/viņas ejat** *you and they go.*

The relative pronoun **kas** or **kurš/kura** in the function of subject is expected to show agreement with the 3rd person. However, when the relative pronoun points to another person than the 3rd person, the verb of the relative clause will usually be in the 1st or 2nd person: **es, kas/kurš/kura te dzīvoju** *I who am living here,* **tu, kas/kurš/kura dzīvo te** *you who are living here.*

4. Special Cases of Agreement in Case

Here mention should be made of *combinations of common noun + proper name* where the latter appears in quotation marks as, for example, in book titles etc. In such cases the proper name will remain undeclined independent of the case of the common noun, e.g. **romānā "Karš un miers"** *in the novel "War and Peace".* However, if the common noun is deleted, the title must be declined (provided that it is declinable): **"Karā un mierā"** *in "War and Peace".*

With *titles of professions + personal names,* however, the title and the proper name harmonize with respect to case, e.g. **attiekties uz profesori Rudzīti** *to apply to Professor Rudzīte,* cf. also p. 168 and 202.

*Constructions with **kā** 'as' and similar*

The item appearing after **kā** *as* may be regarded as an apposition in a broader sense. The corresponding items on either side of **kā** must appear in the same case. When the apposition refers to the grammatical subject (which, by definition, is in the nominative case), the second member may be characterized as a kind of subject predicative, e.g.:

viņš ēd kā vilks *he eats as (like) a wolf*; **suns kauc kā vilks** *the dog is howling like a wolf*.

With transitive verbs, the direct object is in the accusative, as is its reference, which may be labeled *object predicative* (or so-called double accusative): **viņš raksturoja to** (accusative object) **kā skandālu** (object predicative) *he characterized it as a scandal*.

Note: contrast the following two examples: **es viņu pazīstu kā draugu : es viņu pazīstu kā draugs**, both meaning *I know him as a friend*. The former utterance expresses that he is a friend (of somebody, also of me), whereas in the latter, **draugs** refers to the subject, i. e. **es, būdams viņa draugs, [...]** *I, being a friend of his [...]*.

The same-case-on-either-side of **kā** principle also holds true for intransitive verbs, e.g. **viņš balstījās uz generatīvas gramatikas** (genitive) **kā labas teorijas** (genitive) *he based himself upon generative grammar as a good theory*. Exceptions to the rule are found in instances such as **tādās pilsētās kā Rīga, Viļņa un Tallina** *in such cities as Riga, Vilnius and Tallinn*. Neither in Latvian nor English is it natural to say *****tādās pilsētās kā Rīgā, Viļņā un Tallina** **in such cities as in Riga, Vilnius and Tallinn*. Observe also the following example: **nekad neatradīsi tādu meiteni kā Sarma** (i. e. [...] **kā ir Sarma**) *you will never find such a girl as Sarma (is)*.

Finally, a reference should be made to pp. 60, 130, 137 and 146 for the dative of the predicative adjective or participle (when it is co-referential with a logical (either overtly expressed or implicit) subject in the dative case).

Chapter 14

WORD ORDER
(Vārdu secība)

Introductory Remarks

The introduction of a bipartite *communicative analysis* of the utterance, in *theme* (i. e. given or known information) and *rheme* (= new information), by Czech linguists (Mathesius, and further elaborated by Daneš and others) signified no less than a revolution with respect to our knowledge about the mechanisms and principles that govern word order.

In prosodically neutral declarative sentences, the position of the theme is *initial,* while the rheme occupies sentence *final* position. The theme-rheme segmentation seems to be important in all languages, but is of special importance in a non-article language like Latvian. In Germanic and Romance languages the articles are of great help in identifying the theme and the rheme, since the former usually adopts a definite form in opposition to the latter, which normally shows either indefinite or zero article, cf. the following example from English: – Yesterday I met *an old man* (rheme). *The man/he* (theme) was sitting outside *a little, red house* (rheme). *The house/it* (theme) had *small windows* (rheme). The notions theme and rheme make sense only within a *context* which is built up by theme-rheme chains as illustrated in the above example.

A context must necessarily start at some point, whence the introductory part will usually be context non-dependent and consequently themeless. For examples, see p. 223.

Languages without a case system, such as English and the Nordic languages, do not offer the same possibilities for variations in word order as do case languages. In the former type of languages word order has a grammatical function. Thus, in sentences containing the three constituents subject (S), verb (V) and object (O), the subject must occupy the initial position in caseless languages whereas this is not obligatory in a language like Latvian where the subject can be distinguished from the object through the case ending, whereby their place in the sentence is not so vital. Thus, in Latvian it is possible to say **Pēteris sita Povilu** (SVO) or **Povilu sita Pēteris** (OVS). The former sentence is translated into English as *Peter hit Paul* while for the second we have to choose a *passive* construction *Paul was hit by Peter* to satisfy both the grammatical need for reserving the initial position for the subject and the communicative need of preserving the theme-rheme structure of the Latvian sentence. From the two sentence variants in Latvian it can be concluded 1) that they are not identical from a *communicative* point of view since their theme-rheme structures are different and 2) that an active OVS sentence in Latvian often corresponds to a passive construction in English (see also section on voice, p. 140 ff.).

Generally, it should be emphasized that the variations in word order are fewer in non-fictional prose than in fiction and above all in colloquial speech (as well as in poetry). The presentation below is more or less restricted to the sphere of non-fictional prose. Further, our description concentrates on simple sentences (p. 203) since very little has been done in the field of word order in compound sentences (p. 208), especially large text units. A further complication is that there are few works on word order in Latvian (Ceplīte and Ceplītis 1991 contains a short section devoted to this subject as does Rūķe-Draviņa 1977).

Finally, one must distinguish between *changeable and non-changeable word order*. The latter category includes the structurally determined obligatory sentence initial position of the interrogative particle **vai** (**vai Jūs esat Kalniņa kungs?** *are you Mr. Kalnins?*), as well as the position of the negation immediately before the word which is negated: for example, **viņš neraksta** *he doesn't write* : **viņš raksta ne tikai stāstus, bet arī dzeju** *he writes not only short stories, but also poetry*. Moreover, among constructions with unchangeable word order could probably be included a good number with a dative in the function of a logical subject (debitive constructions with synonyms and others, see p. 130 f.

It should be observed that changeable word order is not synonymous with *free* word order. Even though word order in Latvian is changeable to a considerable degree, it is not free in the sense that variation in word order is of no importance. This is because a change in word order will normally imply another communicative structure and thus alter the content of the utterance. A change in word order can also alter the style.

The disposition below will be proceed according to the following scheme:

I The position of the members of the sentence
II The position of the members of the noun phrase

I THE POSITION OF THE MEMBERS OF THE SENTENCE

The analysis will start with sentences containing the sentence members subject (S) and verb (V) only. From such structures we will proceed to *extended* structures (p. 199) including an object (O), i. e. SVO-, OVS-structures etc. and also the somewhat looser structures with adverbials (SVAdv/AdvVS etc.).

Many grammarians would prefer the opposite approach by starting from and regarding the SVO-structure as basic and deduce other structures, including the simpler SV/VS-structures from it.

Our analysis will concentrate on sentences with a *verbal predicate* (see p. 198), almost to the exclusion of sentences containing a nominal predicate (p. 198). This is because the latter has to a considerable degree been dealt with elsewhere (in connection with the adjective p. 60 f. and the participles p. 156 ff.), and also because sentences of this type show less variation in word order.

Here declarative sentences will be dealt with first. A description of word order in interrogative sentences of different types follows.

1. Declarative Sentences

Let us start our short survey of word order in Latvian by commenting on:

A. Non-Extended Sentences

Such sentences consist of subject and verb only, whereby the usual (and unmarked) word order is SV: **Jānis lasa** *John is reading*.

In *themeless* sentences, i. e. introductory, existential and similar ones, however, the unmarked word order is VS: **[reiz sensenos laikos] dzīvoja tēvs [...]** *[once upon a time] there was/lived a father [...]*; **bija vakars** it was evening; **atnāca skolotājs** *a/the teacher came*. In such cases the verb typically belongs to the spheres of *existence* and *appearance*.

According to V. Rūķe-Draviņa (1977, 121) the word order VS is more frequently used in recent years. She quotes the example **iet strādnieks un domā: [...]** *there goes a worker and thinks: [...]*. It is not clear to me whether this tendency – if Rūķe-Draviņa's observation is correct – is due to influence from Russian or not.

In sentences after direct speech, both the SV and VS are found in more or less free variation: **- Nē, - atbildēja zēns.** / **- Nē, - zēns atbildēja** *"No", the boy answered*. If in such cases the subject is expressed by a pronoun, the order SV seems to be preferred: **- Nē, - viņš atbildēja** *"No", he answered*.

B. Extended Sentences

a) Adverbial Extensions

Adverbial modifiers can simply be placed before the V in VS type sentences: **istabā iegāja meitene** *into the room a girl entered*; **uz sienas karājas glezna** *on the wall a painting is hanging*. These AdvVS structures with thematic adverbial + rhematic subject are in contrast to SVAdv-constructions with thematic subject + rhematic adverbial: **meitene iegāja istabā** *the girl entered the room*, **glezna karājas uz sienas** *the painting is hanging on the wall*.

The structure AdvSV is also encountered, e.g. **svētdienās avīzes neiznāca** *on Sundays newspapers were not published*.

b) Object Extensions

One Object

Such sentences have to some extent already been commented upon, in the examples quoted above, namely SVO (**Pēteris sita Povilu**) vs. OVS (**Povilu sita Pēteris**), under introductory remarks (p. 221 f.). For that illustration a transitive verb (**sist**) was chosen. The definition of transitivity in caseless languages, however, differs from that which is valid for case languages. In the former group, a verb can be defined as transitive without any constraint as to the nature of the object by which it is accompanied, whereas in the latter (as a rule), only verbs which govern the accusative (without involvement of prepositions) can be transitive, i. e. can be "transformed" from active to passive or vice versa. Thus, a sentence like *the boy was helped* should be rendered in Latvian by **zēnam palīdzēja** and not **zēns tika palīdzēts* since the verb **palīdzēt** *to help* requires the dative case and is consequently intransitive.

The *unmarked* (or *neutral*) word order of Latvian is probably SVO. This order is obligatory in cases where the object cannot formally be distinguished from the subject, e.g.: **mātes mīl meitas** *mothers love daughters*.

Two Objects

As in the case of adverbial modifiers, there may be more than one object in the sentence. A frequent case is that with an indirect (dative) object denoting a person + a direct accusative object referring to a thing, e.g. **meitene deva zēnam grāmatu** *the girl gave the boy a book.* A neutral reading of this sentence with no particular emphasis on any sentence member implies that the dative object is thematic, the accusative object rhematic. This $SVO_{ind}O_{dir}$ order will probably be the commonest (and consequently "neutral") word order pattern for sentences containing both a dative and an accusative object. If the order of the dative and the accusative object is reversed, the latter will take over the thematic role whereas the former will turn into a rhematic object: **meitene deva grāmatu zēnam** *the girl gave the book to a/the boy.* In both cases the objects both occur in postverbal position.

In the case of *pronominalization* the pronoun (be it the indirect or direct object) will usually precede the noun object, e.g. **meitene deva viņam grāmatu** (or, may be, even more commonly: **meitene viņam deva grāmatu**), **meitene deva to zēnam** *the girl gave it, i. e. the apple, to a (the) boy.*

If both the indirect and the direct object are pronominalized, the normal word order will be preverbal position for both, with the indirect object preceding the direct one: **meitene viņam viņu deva** *the girl gave it to him.* Pronominalization of this kind naturally signalizes thematization. If the situation is clear, one of the pronominal objects can be deleted, e.g. **meitene izņēma grāmatu no somas un viņam deva** *the girl took a book out of the bag and gave (it) to him.*

2. Interrogative Sentences

So far some basic patterns of word order in simple declarative sentences have been examined. For the sake of economy, our treatment of interrogative sentences will be quite restricted. Two types of interrogative sentences should be distinguished:

1) those containing an interrogative pronoun or adverb (so-called *wh*-questions in English, *k*-questions in Latvian)

and

2) those not possessing an interrogative pronoun or adverb, but possibly the particle **vai** (*yes/no*-questions).

Illustrations of type 1) questions:

SV: **Kas spēlē?** *Who is playing?* Answer (V)S: **Spēlē Anda** *Anda (is playing)*;

AdvVS: **Kur spēlē Anda / Kur viņa spēlē?** *Where is Anda/she playing?* Answer: (SV)Adv: (**Anda/viņa spēlē**) **restorānā** *(Anda/she is playing) in a restaurant,* AdvVS: **Kur spēlē Anda?** *Where is Anda playing?* Answer: **restorānā** *in a restaurant*;

OVS: **Ko darīja Anda?** (or OSV: **Ko Anda darīja?**) *What did Anda do?* Answer: (S)V/(S)VO: **(Viņa) spēlēja / (Viņa) spēlēja klavieres** *She played / She played piano*;

AdvSVAdv: **Kad Anda/viņa griezās no restorāna?** *When did Anda/she return from the restaurant?*

Type 2) questions can be with or without the interrogative particle **vai**. It was also emphasized that this particle is only encountered in sentence initial position: **Vai studenti/viņi lasa grāmatas?** *Do (the) students/tehy read books?* If the **vai** particle is omitted, the remaining word order can be preserved: **Studenti/viņi lasa grāmatas?** In speech, however, this variant must be pronounced with a specific interrogative intonation, in order to separate it from a declarative sentence with the same word order: **studenti/viņi lasa grāmatas** *students read books*.

The variants **vai lasa studenti grāmatas?** (VSO) and **vai lasa grāmatas studenti?** (VOS) are stylistically marked and were felt to be strange by my informant.

II THE POSITION OF THE MEMBERS OF THE NOUN PHRASE

A noun phrase can be defined as a word group (*vārdkopa*) consisting of a combination of two or more words of a nominal class, constituting a semantic unit. One word (a noun) in the group occupies the role of grammatical head, under which the other constituent/s is/are subordinated (through agreement, government or juxtaposition, see pp. 200 and 215).

Non-Participle Attributes
Examples: **jauna māja** *(a) new house* (agreement), **tēva māja** *father's house* (government). These are *simple* word groups in opposition to *complex*: **jaunā tēva māja** *father's new house*.

A typical example of "juxtaposition" (p. 200) could be the combination of a verb and an adverb (e. g. **iet ātri** *to walk fast*), but verbal word groups of this kind have practically already been dealt with under I above.

The *neutral* position of attributes, both congruent (expressed by adjectives, adjectival pronouns and numerals) and non-congruent (expressed by nouns and certain pronouns), is before the governing noun, i. e. **jauna māja** (**māja jauna** would be understood as *the house is new*), **tēva māja** (but: **viņa jaunā māja** *his new house*), **alus pudele** *a new house, father' house, a beer bottle*. Exceptions to this rule are rare, but can be found in poetry (e. g. **no mālāja smagā** *from the heavy* *clayey soil*, **no kātiņa trauslā** *from the fragile shaft* (of a leaf) (V. Belševica)).

Note the opposition between **piecas stundas / desmit kilometru** *five hours / ten kilometers* and **stundas piecas / kilometru desmit** *some/around five hours / some/around ten kilometers*. The order noun + numeral (inversion) implies *approximate* number.

With the adnominal *partitive* genitive postposition is the normal (and mandatory) order: **pudele alus** *a bottle of beer*.

Further, the congruent attributive is normally placed before the non-congruent, i. e. **jauna tēva māja** *father's new house,* rather than *tēva jauna māja.

In sequences of the type *all these my beautiful flowers* the order of words is determinative pronoun + demonstrative + possessive + adjective: **visas šitas manas skaistas puķes**.

Observe finally the order of words in "genitive strings", e.g. **Latvijas Universitātes Filoloģijas Fakultātes Angļu valodas nodaļas pirma kursa studenti** *students of the first year (course) of (at) the Department of English language of (at) the Faculty of Philology of (at) the University of Latvia:* Contrary to English, German, the Nordic languages etc., in Latvian the broadest concept occupies the leftmost position, the narrowest the rightmost.

Participle Attributes

Such attributes, as a rule precede, the word governed by them: for example, **gulēdama uz galda grāmata** *a/the book lying on the table, das auf dem Tisch liegende Buch* rather than **uz galda gulēdama grāmata**, but both types are found. Observe that the *genitive agentive* (p. 168 f.) must follow the participle, not precede it (to distinguish it from the possessive function), e.g. **parakstīta profesora vēstule** *the letter signed by the professor* (vs. **profesora parakstīta vēstule** *the professor's signed letter*).

Reference Literature

A. Monographs and Articles

Baldunčiks, J. 1989, *Anglicismi latviešu valodā*, Rīga.
Bergmane, A., Blinkena A. 1986, *Latviešu rakstības attīstība*, Rīga.
Budiņa-Lazdiņa, T. 1966, *Teach yourself Latvian*, London (2nd ed. Michigan 1979).
Butkus, A. 1995, *Latviai*, Kaunas 1995.
Ceplīte, B., Ceplītis 1991, *Latviešu valodas praktiskā gramatika*, Rīga.
Ceplītis, L., Rozenbergs, J., Valdmanis, J. 1989, *Latviešu valodas sintakse*, Riga.
Dini, P. 1993, *Le lingue baltiche*, La Nuova Italia.
Eckert, R., Bukevičiūtė, E.J., Hinze, F. 1994, *Die baltischen Sprachen. Eine Einführung*, Leipzig etc. (Langenscheidt).
Eiche, A. 1983, *Latvian declinable and indeclinable participles. Their syntactic function, frequency and modality*, Stockholm.
Endzelin, J. 1922, *Lettische Grammatik*, Rīga.
Endzelīns, J. 1971-81, *Darbu izlase* I-IV, Riga.
Endzelīns, J. 1971, *Comparative Phonology and Morphology of the Baltic Languages*, The Hague-Paris (= English translation of the original from 1948 (Riga)).
Erhart, A. 1984, *Baltské jazyky*, Praha.
Fennell, T.G. 1980, Gelsen, H., *A Grammar of Modern Latvian* I-III, The Hague (Mouton).
Fennel, T.G. 1975,, "Is there an Instrumental Case in Latvian?", *Journal of Baltic Studies* 6/1, 41-48.
Fraenkel, E. 1950, *Die baltischen Sprachen*, Heidelberg.
Gāters, A. 1977, *Die lettische Sprache und ihre Dialekte* (in: *Trends in Linguistics. State-of-the-Art-Reports* 9), Mouton.
Hauzenberga-Šturma, E. 1979, "Zur Frage des Verbalaspekts im Lettischen", *Zeitschrift für vgl. Sprachforschung* 93, 279-316.
Kabelka, J. 1975, *Latvių kalba*, Vilnius.
Blinkena, A. (ed.) 1977, *Kontakty latyšskogo jazyka*, Riga (Zinātne).
Lasmane, V. 1985 (1st ed.), 1988 (2nd ed.), *A Course in Modern Latvian*, American Latvian Association .
Laua, A. 1969, *Latviešu literārās valodas fonētika*, Riga.
Laua, A. 1981, *Latviešu leksikoloģija*, Rīga.
Liepa, E., *Vokālisma un zilbju kvantitāte latviešu literārajā valodā*, Rīga 1979.
MLLVG 1959-62 = *Mūsdienu latviešu literārās valodas gramatika* I-II (ed. by A. Bergmane et al.), Riga.
Lötzsch, R. 1978, "Zur Frage des sog. Instrumentals im Lettischen", *Zeitschrift für Slawistik* 23, 667-671.
Nītiņa, D. 1978, *Prievārdu sistēma latviešu rakstu valodā*, Rīga.
Priedīte, A., Ludden A. 1992, A., *Lettisch intensiv!*, Hamburg.
Rudzīte, M. 1964, *Latviešu dialektoloģija*, Riga (Russian edition 1989, Riga).
Rudzīte, M. 1993 A, *Latviešu valodas vēsturiskā fonētika*, Rīga.
Rudzīte, M. 1993 B, *Ievads baltu valodniecībā*, Riga.
Rūķe-Draviņa 1974, *Vārds īstā vietā. Frazeoloģismu krājums*, Stockholm.
Rūķe-Draviņa, V. 1977, *The Standardization Process in Latvian (= Acta Universitatis Stockholmensis. Stockholm Slavic Studies 11)*, Stockholm.
Sehwers, J. 1915, *Die deutschen Lehnwörter im Lettischen*, Zürich.

Smoczyński, W. 1988, *Języki bałtyckie* in: *Języki indoeuropejskie* II, pp. 817-905, Warsaw.
Stang, Chr. S. 1942, *Das slavische und baltische Verbum*, Oslo.
Stang, Chr. S. 1966, *Vergleichende Grammatik der baltischen Sprachen*, Oslo-Bergen-Tromsø.
Steinberg, A. 1977, *The Phonology of Latvian*, Illinois .
Stelle, A., Straume, A., Liepinš, P. 1989, *Izučaem latyšskij jazyk*, Riga.
Stolz, Th. 1991, *Sprachbund im Baltikum? Estnisch und Lettisch im Zentrum einer sprachlichen Konvergenzlandschaft*, Bochum.
Valdmanis, J. 1987, "Vienkāršā teikuma formālās uzbūves modelis", *Latvijas PSR Zinātņu akadēmijas vēstis*, 4, 73-82.
Veksler, B. Kh., Yurik, V. A. 1978 (3rd ed.), *Latyšskij jazyk*, Rīga.
Zeps, V. 1962, *Latvian ans Finnic Linguistic Convergences, Uralic and Altic series 9*, Bloomington-The Hague (Indiana University).

B. Dictionaries

1. General:
Birzvalka, I., Sosāre, M. 1989, *Angļu-latviešu un latviešu-angļu dictionary*, Riga.
Birzvalka, I. 1995, *English-Latvian dictioanry*, Riga (Jāņa sēta).
Grambe, K., Pampe, E. 1990, *Vācu-latviešu vārdnīca*, Riga.
Latviešu-krievu vārdnīca (autoru kolektīvs) 1979, Riga.
Latviešu-vācu vārdnīca (autoru kolektīvs) 1980, Rīga.
Latviešu valodas vārdnīca (ed. by D. Guļevska) 1987, Riga.
Mühlenbach, K. (& Endzelin, J.) 1923-32, *Latviešu valodas vārdnīca* I-IV, Riga.
LLVV 1972- = *Latviešu literārās valodas vārdnīca* I-VIII, Riga .
Turkina, E. 1982, *Latviešu-angļu vārdnīca*, Riga.
LVV 1987 = *Latviešu valodas vārdnīca, A-Z*, Riga.

2. Special:
Metuzāle-Kangere, B. 1985, *A Derivational Dictionary of Latvian*, Hamburg (Buske).
Karulis, K. 1992, *Latviešu etimoloģijas vārdnīca* I-II, Riga 1992.
Soida, E., Kļaviņa 1970, S., *Latviešu valodas inversā vārdnīca*, Riga 1970 (rotaprint edition from the University).

C. Some relevant periodicals
Acta Baltico-Slavica (1963-), Poznań.
Baltistica (1965-), Vilnius.
Balto-slavjanskie issledovanija (1972-), Moscow.
*Baltu filoloğija (*1991-), Riga (Latvijas Universitāte, Baltu valodu katedra).
Ceļi 1931-39: Riga; 1961-1979: Lund; 1989: USA; 1991: Stockholm.
Filologu biedrības raksti / FBR 1921-1940, Riga.
Journal of Baltic Studies (1970-), USA (AABS).
Latviešu valodas kultūras jautājumi (1965-1993), Riga.
Latvijas Universitātes raksti (1921-29), Riga.
Linguistica Baltica (1992-), Warsaw.
Ponto-Baltica (1981), Firenze.
Res Balticae (1995-), Pisa.

Rīgas Latviešu biedrības zinātņu komitejas rakstu krājums. A. Humanitāri raksti (1876-1940), Riga.
Studi Baltici (1931-38), Firenze.
Valodas aktualitātes (1983/1984-1991/1992), Riga (Zinātne).
Valodas un literatūras institūts. Raksti (1952-64), Riga.
Vēstis / Latvijas (PSR) Zinātņu akadēmijas vēstis (1947-), Riga.

Indexes

The alphabetical order is that of the English alphabet. Diacritics are ignored in the sense that *č* is found under *c*, *š* under *s*, *ē* under *e* etc.

ablaut 35
abbreviations 217, 218
absolute function 150
abi/abas 72, 76
accentuation (see also stress)
accusative 173 ff.; 173 f. (adverbal), 174 f. (adverbial), 175 (in exclamations)
active 81, 135
adjective 57 ff., 149, 150
adhortative 125
adjunction 200
address 62, 181
adnominal 165
-ads/-ada 63
adverb 162 ff.
adverbial 165
adverbial clauses 211 ff.
adversative conjunctions 194
affricates 22
after 193
agent(ive) 135, 140, 141, 168, 227
agent deletion 140
"agent hiding" 140
agentless passive constructions 141
ago 193
agreement 215 ff., 215 (formal), 215 (grammatical), 216 f. (gender), 218 f. (number), 219 f. (person), 219 (case)
-ains/-aina 63
aiz 187, 189
aiz- 159 f.
-āj- 52
akmens 45
aktionsarten 118
alternations 24, 35
alveolar 22
antecedent 215
any 70
anybody 70
anything 70
ap 186
ap- 159, 160
apical 22
apkārt 160

appositive 60, 156, 157
apposition 196, 202
approximate number 227
apstākļa vārds 162
apstāklis 196, 200
apzīmētājs 196, 201
ar 41, 183, 189
arā 160
articulator 22, lower a. 22, upper a. 22
asmens 45.
aspect 81, 115 ff.
assimilation 26 f., 29
associative gender 51, 217
asyndetism 208, 214
at- 159, 160
atgriezeniskie darbības vārdi 143
Atis 45
-atn-e 53
atpakaļ 160
atstāstījuma izteiksme 123, 121 ff.
attributive 60, 156, 157
augšā 161
auxiliary 112, 136
before 193
bet 194
bez 189
bez- 64
bij-, see *būt* 103
binary 115
birzs 48
both 72, 76
braukt 90
broken tone, see tone 39
būt 103
cardinal numbers, see numerals
case 41, 165 ff., 219 f.
caur 185, 186
causative 159
celt 98
ciest 97
cieti 160
cik 170
cits 72
cits/cita cit- 67

close vs. open *e/ē* 29 ff.
collective nouns 53, 218
communicative analysis 221
comparative 59, 61, 162
comparison 59, 61, 189, 213
compensatory lengthening 32
compound sentence 203, 208
compound tenses (see also mood and voice) 112 ff. (formation), 120 ff. (meaning and use)
conjugation, see verb
conjunctions 194 ff.
consecutio temporum 210
consonants 22 ff.
continuos 116
coordination 208 f.
copulative conjunctions 194
copulative verbs 198
co-referential 150, 151
coronal 22
dabūt 99
dam-gerund/-participle 82, 148, 151
darbības vārda kārta 135
darbības vārds 82 ff.
dates 79, 191 f.
dative (use of) 176 ff.
dative + infinitive 179, 207
daudz 78, 163, 170, 219
dažs 71
dažs labs 71
debitive (see also mood) 81, 129 ff.
decimal fractions 80
declarative 202
declension 40-73; 152 ff.
definite form (adj.) 58 f., 61 f., 221
degrees of comparison 59 f., 162
dēļ 184, 189
deletion 197, 198
dental 22
determinative clauses 210 f.
dev-, see *dot*
devoicing 26
diez(in) kāds 70
diezin kas 70
diphthongs 33 f.
direct object 174, 177
direct speech 224
disjunctive conjunctions 194
distributive function 189
divdabji 146

divkopu teikumi 205
dod-, see *dot*
dorsal 22
dot 103, 104
double accusative 220
double negation 164
dubultloceklis 196
during 193
dzimte 40 f.
dzirnavas 52
dzirnus 48, 52
dzīvot 104
each 72; 189 (distributive)
each other 67
-ēj- 52 (noun)
-ējs/-ēja 64
-ens/-ensa 63
es 65
esmu, see *būt*
even tone, see tone
every 72
everybody 73
everything 73
existential constructions 171 f., 207
explicative clauses 209 f.
factitive
falling tone, see tone
finite forms 82
fractions 79 f.
fricatives 22
from - to 193
FSP, see functional sentence perspective
functional sentence perspective (FSP) 139
future tense 109 ff., 120
future perfect 81, 113, 122
gāj-, see *iet*
galvenais loceklis 196, 197
gandrīz 36
-gans/-gana 63
gender 40 f.; 216 f. (gender)
genitive (form, see declension); 166 ff. (use of)
gerund 81, 145, 147 ff.
government 206
grammatical category 40 f., 81, 115, 215
gribēt 105
griezt 96 f.

gulēt 106
half 80
"Handlungspassiv" 136
'hard' 44, 46
have-constructions 178
have to 129 ff.
historically palatalized 25
how long? 193
how often? 193
-ība 53
ie- 159, 160
iekšā 160
ierobežājs 196
iet 103
-iet-is 53
ievērojāmi 163
-īgs/-īga 63
ikdiena 36
ikkatrs 36
ikreiz 36
ikviens 35
imperative (see also mood) 81, 123 ff.
imperfective (see also aspect) 81, 115
imperfectivization 118
impersonal 131, 206
in (after) 193
in (about time) 193
in (spatial) 180
-iņ- 54
indeclinable nouns 50 f., 217, 218
indefinite form 57 f., 60 f.
independent (grammatically) 207, 145
indexes 231 ff.
indicative (see also mood) 81, 123
indirect object 177, 224
indirect questions 210
indirect speech 210
infinitive 82, 145 f.
infinitive sentences 207
interjections 217
intonation, see tone 39
interrogative 69; 163; 225 f.
intransitive 142
īpašības vārds 57
ir, see *būt*
-isks/-iska 63
istenības izteiksme 123
-īt 54 (noun suffix); 159 (verb suffix)
it (in) kā 195, 213
iz- 159, 160

izteicējs 198
izteiksme 123
ja 195, 213
j-affix 86, 98 and passim
jeb 194
jebkad 36
jebkāds 36, 70
jebkas 70
jebkur 36
jebkurš 36
jo - jo 195, 213
jūs 65
Jūs 66, 113 f., 213
just 96
juxtaposition, see adjunction
ka 195, 209 f.
kā 195, 213
kad 195, 211
kāds 69
kamēr 195, 211
kas 69 f., 70, 219
kas par 69
katrs 72 f.
kaut 129, 195
kaut arī 195, 213
kaut gan 174, 189
kaut kāds 70
kaut kas 70
klāt 161
kļūt 102
kolīdz 195
kondicionālis (see *vēlējuma izteiksme*)
kopā 190
kopā ar 169
kopdzimtes lietvārds 40, 216
kopš 188 (prep.), 195 (conj.), 211
kost 97
krist 95
krītošā intonācija 39
krogs 48
kur 163, 210
kura/kuras/kuru 70 (rel.)
kurš 69
labdien 36
labial 22
labrīt 36
lai 127, 195, 212
lai gan 195
laikā 184, 188, 193
laiks 115

lasīt 105 f.
laterals 22
lauztā intonācija 39
lengthening 32, 37 f.
līdz 188 (prep.), 195 (conj.)
līdzko 195
lietvārds 40 ff.
likt 92 f.
limitative aktionsart 118
literature, see reference literature
locative 180 f.
locījums 41 f.
logical subject 130, 145, 178, 179
lokamie divdabji, see *divdabji*
long form (adj.)58 f., 61 f.
ļoti 61, 163
mans/mana 66
marked 115
maz 163
mazgāt(ies) 104 f.
mēness 45
mēs 65
minimal pairs 38
mīt 88, 90
mixed diphthongs, see semi-diphthongs
modality
mood 123 ff.
morphophonemic rules
mophophonemically palatalized 25
much + comparative 61, 163
must, equivalent of 129 ff., 131
mūsu 65, 66
n-affix 86, 93, 100 f.
nākt 96
nasals 22
nav 103, 164
ne 164
negation 164
nekā (gen. of nekas) 36, 72
nekā (conj.) 36, 195, 213
nekad 36, 163
nekāds 36, 72
nekas 36, 72
nekur 36, 163
nelokamie divdabji, see *divdabji*
nemaz 36
ņemt 94
nenoteiksme 145
nesen 36
nez(in) kāds 70

nez(in) kas 70
neviens 36, 72
-nieks/-niece 53
-nīc-a 54
no 187, 188
nobody 72
nominal predicate 198
non-continuous 116
nost 142
non-finite forms 82
nothing
noun 40 ff.
noun combinations 217
noun phrase 222, 226 f.
number 41, 218 f.
numerals 74 ff.
nupat 36
object 199 f.
object predicative 220
object vs. adverbial 201
omission, se deletion
one another 67
one of 73
one-part sentences 205 ff.
open *e/ē,* see close vs. open *e/ē*
ordinal numbers, see numerals
orthographic representation 24, 29
otrs 72
OV 140
OVS 140, 224, 226
ought to
pa 184, 186
pa- 160
palatal 22
palatalization 23, 25
palatalized 23
papildinātājs 196, 199
par 189
pār 186
pār- 186 f.
pāri 186
passive 136 ff.
past, see preterite
past perfect 81, 113
patient 135
pats 73
pavēles izteiksme 123 ff.
pēc 188, 189, 193
pēc tam kad 195
pelus 48, 52

perfect, see present perfect, past perfect, future perfect
perfective (see also aspect) 81, 115
perfectivization 217
person 81, 219
phonology 22 ff.
pielikums 196, 202
pirms 168 (prep.), 174 (conj.), 187
pie 187, 190
pie- 161
pirkt 92
plosives 22
plural nouns 51 f., 218
polite address 112 ff.
positive degree 59 (adj.), 162 (adv.)
praesens dramaticum 117
praesens historicum 117
predicate 198
predicative 57
prefixation 159 ff.
prepositions 183 ff.
present (simple) 81, 82, 85-112, 119 f.
present perfect 81, 112 f.
pret 183, 187
preterite (simple) 81, 82, 85-112, 120
priekšā 188
priekšmets 196, 197
prievārds 183
principal forms 83
productive 84
pro(jā)m 160
prom no 169
pronominalization 225
pronoun 65 ff.
proper names (see also surnames) 219
pusotra 36, 80
quantity 37 ff.
quantifiers 170
questions 145, 202, 225 f.
ragus 48, 52
reference literature 228 ff.
reflexiva tantum 143
reflexive nouns 49 f.
reflexive pronouns 66
reflexive verbs 143 f.
relative (see pronoun and mood)
rheme 139 f., 221
rudens 45
runāt 104
sa- 161

šāds 68
saiklis 194
salikts teikums 208
sāls 45
-šana 53
saskaņojums 215
savs/sava 66 f.
sēdēt 106
semantics 147
semi-diphthongs 34
sentence 196 ff.
sentence patterns 203 f.
sēsties 97 f.
sev- 66
sex 40
shall, should 207
short form (adj.) 57 f., 60 f.
simple tenses (see also mood and voice) 112 ff. (formation), 120 ff. (meaning and use)
singular nouns 51
šis/šī 68
skaitlis 41
skaitļa vārds 74
"soft" 44, 46 (see also palatalized)
some 70 f.
somebody 70 f.
something 70 f.
starp 187
st-affix 86, 101 ff.
stieptā intonācija 39
stress, see also accentuation
strīds 48
subject 197
subjunctive (see also mood) 125 ff.
subordinate (conjunctions) 194
subordination 200
substantivization 62
suffixation 159
suns 45
superlative 60 (adj.), 162 (adv.)
suprasegmentals 36 ff.
surnames 41
šurp 160
SV 223 f.
SVO 224 f.
syntax 58, 74, 77, 128, 143, 147, 154, 161, 163-191, 194-225
tad - kad 211
tādēļ ka 212

tāds 68
-tāj- 52
tā kā 195, 212
tāpat kā 195
tāpēc ka 195, 212
tas/tā 68
tas pats 73
tapt 93
-tav-a 54
tavs/tava 66
teikums 196
tense 81, 118 ff.
than 60 f., 213
theme 139 f., 221
tiesie darbības vārdi 143
tikko 195
tiklīdz 195, 211 f.
tikmēr 195
time expressions 191 ff.
tone 39
towards 193
transitive 142, 174
transitivity 224
tu 65, 66
turklāt 36
turpretīm 36
-tuv-e 54
two-part sentences 205
ūdens 45
-um-s 53
un 194
unaspirated 23
unmarked 40, 115
uz 184, 188
uz- 161
vai 194, 209 f.
vairāk 163
vajadzības izteiksme 123, 129 ff.
vaļā 160
Valdis 45
varbūt 36
vārdu secība 221
veids 115
velar 22
vēlējuma izteiksme 123, 125 ff.
verb 81 ff.
verb stems 82
verba commodi 177
verba incommodi 178
verbal noun 158
verbal predicate 198
very + positive degree 61
vibrants 22
vidū 187
vienkāršs teikums 203
vienkopas teikumi 205
vienmēr 36
viens/viena- otr- 64
viens no 73
viesis 45
vietniekvārds 65
viņa/viņas/viņu 66
viņš/viņa 65, 68
virs 187
vis- 36
vismaz 35
viss/vissa 73
visvairāk 163
Visvaldis 45
vocalization 35
vocative 41, 44, 45, 46, 47, 48, 62
voice 81, 135
voicing 26
VOS 226
vowels 27 ff.
VSO 226
wh-questions 210, 225
what 69
which 69
who 69 f., 210, 217
whose 70
word final position 35 f.
word formation 52 ff. (nouns), 63 f. (adjectives), 159 ff. (verb)
word order 221 ff.
yes/no-questions 210, 225
zem 187
zibens 45
zīmēt 104